"SHOCKING THE WEB reveals many of

— **Rodney Alan Greenblat,**
Creative Director, The Center for Advanced Whimsy

"Creating rich interactive media is complicated. This book provides the design and technical insights required to create compelling online content."

— **Clement Mok,**
Chairman, Studio Archetype, founder and CEO, CMCD, Inc., founder and Chief Creative Officer, NetObjects

"DXM understands the importance of designing content to suit the delivery medium. If you are planning to add Shockwave to your site, read this book first."

— **David Siegel,**
founder of Studio Verso, author of Creating Killer Web Sites

"Using Shockwave, multimedia developers can now publish their work to a huge new audience on the Web—and this book shows you how to do it right!"

— **Joe Sparks,**
founder of Pop Rocket

"The authors have done a fantastic job of looking at Director as a whole and pulling out all the features, Lingo, and real-world production techniques that are relevant to Shockwave development. This makes the book a great resource for anyone interested in developing multimedia in a networked environment."

— **John "JT" Thompson,**
Senior Software Designer and inventor of Lingo, Macromedia

Macintosh Edition

Cathy Clarke

Lee Swearingen

David K. Anderson

MACROMEDIA
PRESS

Shocking the Web
Macintosh Edition

Cathy Clarke, Lee Swearingen, David K. Anderson

Macromedia Press
2414 Sixth Street
Berkeley, CA 94710

510/548-4393
510/548-5991 (fax)

Find us on the World Wide Web at: **http://www.peachpit.com**
http://www.macromedia.com

Published by Macromedia Press,
in association with Peachpit Press, a division of Addison Wesley Longman.

Editor: Nancy Davis
Copyeditor: Karen Whitehouse
Contributor and Technical Editor: Eric Fixler
Interior Design and Production: Meggan Jones
Production: David Van Ness
Cover Design: TMA Ted Mader Associates
Third Party Review & Management: Tim Morgan and Dana De Puy Morgan
Contributor: Dan Kwak
Proofreader: Heidi Anderson
Index: Steve Rath
Inhouse Production: Mimi Heft

ISBN 0-201-88663-4

9 8 7 6 5 4 3 2 1

Printed and bound in the United States of America

Is Shocking the Web for You?

Shocking the Web is intended for people who fall into one of two broad categories: Web developers who want to create and publish multimedia content and multimedia developers who want to create and publish Web content.

More specifically, this book is written for anyone who creates, or wants to create, compelling interactive content for the Web using Shockwave for Director.

You will get the most value from *Shocking the Web* if you are familiar with Macromedia Director and its built-in authoring language, Lingo. In the event that you are a new Director user, we suggest you read Appendix A, "Director Basics," and explore the Director source files on the *Shocking the Web* CD-ROM bundled with this book. (A save-disabled version of Director 5 is provided on the CD-ROM.)

Ideally, you also should be connected to the World Wide Web. If, however, you are new to the Web and require basic information about getting connected, refer to Appendix B, "Internet Basics," before getting started.

Finally, any experience with HTML and Web authoring tools is helpful—but definitely not required.

A Book, a CD-ROM, and a Web site

In writing a book about Internet technologies and applications, we gathered and distilled information that is in a constant state of flux and revision. We have taken measures to extend the functionality of the book and to provide you with the most current information about Shockwave by providing a companion CD-ROM and corresponding Web site.

The techniques and principles of design and production shared by developers throughout this book apply to your current and future Shockwave projects. We have tried to ensure that any example material included in *Shocking the Web* is *upward-compatible*—that is, all example movies that were created using Director 4 have been tested for compatibility with Director 5 and the Shockwave plug-in for Director 5.

We have built a companion Web site at **http://www.shockingtheweb.com** to keep you updated and informed, and to gather your comments and feedback. New examples will be posted regularly, as will links to cool Shockwave projects. Don't forget to visit the site—bookmarks are provided on the CD-ROM.

We hope you benefit from this shocking experience, and we promise that the remainder of the book contains no other shocking puns.

Feel free to contact the authors through the Web site or by sending email to feedback@shockingtheweb.com.

Book Content Overview

Part I, Shockwave Reference

The first part of this book provides an overview of the World Wide Web and the recent evolution of the Web to include multimedia content. Chapters 3 through 7 introduce Shockwave for Director—the premiere tool for creating dynamic Web content—and detail the Shockwave development process. Chapter 8 defines network Lingo for Shockwave. The section concludes with a look at where Shockwave and multimedia Web technologies are heading.

Part II, Case Studies

The second part of this book examines a collection of in-depth case studies for projects completed by the authors. A wide variety of technical and design techniques are discussed. The *Shocking the Web* CD-ROM provides source files for each of the Shockwave case studies discussed.

Part III, Shocking Developments

Part three of this book is a gallery of Shockwave developer examples that features useful tips and techniques. HTML and Shockwave files are included on the *Shocking the Web* CD-ROM for all example movies, and the majority of developers have generously contributed their source files for exploration.

Appendices

The appendices offer contextual and supplemental information about the Internet and what you need to know about Director to use it as a tool for creating multimedia content for the Web. The JavaScript Reference appendix examines JavaScript code elements that are relevant to Shockwave movies, and emphasizes differences and similarities between Lingo and the JavaScript language. The section includes useful JavaScript functions that you can implement during Shockwave authoring.

Resources

Be sure to check out the enclosed *Shocking the Web* CD-ROM, and visit the Web site that we have created to keep this book a dynamic source of information— http://www.shockingtheweb.com.

Acknowledgments

The authors wish to extend special thanks to our editor, Nancy Davis, and to our co-worker, Eric Fixler, for their friendship and extensive contributions to the content and quality of this book. Additional thanks to the contributing developers who provided text and source code for the gallery section of the book; David Rogelberg of Studio B Literary Agency for his representation and support; Meggan Jones for her excellent design skills and patience; David Van Ness for his competence and diligence; Karen Whitehouse for encouragement and copyediting; Dana DePuy Morgan and Tim Morgan of Digital Dreams Talk Media for developer contact and management; Buzz Kettles of Macromedia for his Shockwave audio expertise and willingness to help; and Terry Schussler of g/matter for his ongoing cooperation.

We also would like to acknowledge some of the great people at Peachpit Press and Macromedia Press with whom we interacted throughout this project, including Ted Nace, Nancy Ruenzel, Roslyn Bullas, and Victor Gavenda of Peachpit, and Suzanne Porta, Tim Bigoness, and David Mendels of Macromedia Press.

Lastly, a word of thanks to clients, co-workers, and friends James Harris, Jeff Jones, Paul Fehrnstrom, Geoff Katz, Cary Savas, Mitch Solomon, Kate Wesley, Cynthia Hulton, Mary Castellone, Dan Kwak, Erik Bryan Slavin, Terbo Ted, Jean-Francois Boisvert, Bill Rollinson, Yoshi Asai, Toshimitsu Takagi, Mie Ishii, John Thompson, Victoria Dawson, Carrie Meyers, James Khazar, Karyn Scott, Heidi Anderson, Rodney Alan Greenblat, David Siegel, Jeff Essex, Peter Fierlinger, Sasha Magee, Noel Rabinowitz, Betsey Biggs, Granted Savage, Christoph Diermann, Warren Croce, and Jackie Browne.

Table of Contents

Part 1:
Shockwave Reference

The Birth of an Industry
An Introduction to the World Wide Web

From a historical point of view, it can be said that we are all new to the World Wide Web. While the conceptual groundwork for the Web was laid more than 50 years ago—and Ted Nelson coined the term hypertext more than 30 years ago—the World Wide Web as we know it today was first proposed by Tim Berners-Lee at CERN in 1989. The Web was prototyped in 1990, and not widely acknowledged until 1993. If the Web itself is young, then interactive multimedia on the Web is still in its infancy. But new technologies such as VRML, Java, RealAudio, and Shockwave, combined with the promise of increased bandwidth through faster modems and networks, are paving the way for the creation of rich, interactive online experiences.

The Web is growing up fast; and it is growing exponentially. The growth rate has outpaced that of telephone, radio, television, fax and computer technologies, with only a few years representing multiple generations of technology. Even experienced Web developers must stay on their toes to keep up with changing standards and new technology.

The popularity of the Web over other Internet services can be linked to a number of interrelated events, either directly or indirectly. The Web is capable of displaying graphics, animation, sound, and other media types in addition to text, thereby making its point-and-click graphical user interface (GUI) much easier to use than other Internet services. The emergence of the Web coincides with the shift to GUIs seen in all areas of computing.

As the prices of computer hardware continue to drop and the number of personal computers in homes, schools, and businesses increases, more and more people around the world are getting wired each day. In line with the growth of the consumer computer market, consumer multimedia appeared and rapidly gained acceptance in the 1990s, as the Web was being prototyped. As multimedia became a household word, the Web continued to grow and support multiple media types. Traffic on early Web sites featuring multimedia content surged. Simple animated GIFs attracted crowds when they first appeared on the Web in 1994. It is now common knowledge that crowds equal dollars on the Web (in the form of advertising, sponsors, self-promotion, and commerce opportunities). The business sector has contributed greatly to the validation of the Web as a viable multimedia distribution platform.

In parallel, 1995 saw a decline in CD-ROM sales for many developers as more and more people scrambled to connect to the Internet. CD-ROMs and other local storage media provide random access, relatively high data rates, and the ability to browse and interact with digital content. The Web goes a step beyond CD-ROM interactivity by allowing the end user to view and edit shared media, and to create and contribute proprietary content across various platforms. Although the notion has been somewhat romanticized, the Web provides everyone with a tool for self-publishing and a forum to communicate with others. Individuals, as well as businesses, governments, organizations, and educational institutions, benefit from increased communication and shared access to information resources. This fundamental difference between the "closed," read-only CD-ROM experience of the past and the open-ended Web experience is one of the most exciting aspects of developing online multimedia content.

As a starting point, the next section provides an overview of the Web within the larger framework of the Internet by describing what happens behind the scenes when you view a Web page. This background information serves as a foundation for developing Web content—whether you are creating still images, Java applets, or Shockwave movies.

How the Web Works

The World Wide Web is not a tangible thing or a specific location; it's a network of linked data (or hypermedia) that conforms to a set of standards established for the Internet. The Internet, in turn, is a globally distributed network of computers that interface with each other using a common protocol—TCP/IP (Transmission Control Protocol/Internet Protocol). You can think of the Web as a "hyper-network" which can be visualized as a space on top of—or within—the Internet that uses Internet tools and standards for exchanging data.

When you view a Web page using a Web browser, there are three related components at work, the Internet, a Web server, and Web browser. These components operate under the client-server network computing model. A Web browser is referred to as "client" software because it runs on a client computer, and it accesses a host server in order to communicate and transport information.

A networked web does not necessarily require the Internet in order to exist. Webs can exist in conjunction with intranets, or any local or wide-area network. Corporations and other groups can create webs of data within proprietary intranet networks. Or, proprietary webs also can be created within the larger, public Internet framework. There are many different network configuration options. The World Wide Web, however, links global Internet data. Throughout this book, the term Web (with an uppercase "W") refers to the World Wide Web in conjunction with the global, public Internet. However, keep in mind that Shockwave can be implemented within any web environment.

The Transaction Model

HTTP, HyperText Transport Protocol, is the protocol that governs all Web transactions. HTTP enables a Web client to request and retrieve specified hyper-media items (known as HTTP items) from a remote Web server across the net-work. The process is a simple one. A client computer connects to a server via a Web browser and requests an HTTP item. The request is sent by the browser in the form of a URI (Uniform Resource Indicator), more commonly referred to as a URL (Uniform Resource Locator). The URL is the Web address of the requested item.

The browser first determines whether the requested item exists in the local disk cache, which means the requested item has been previously downloaded and has not been flushed. If it exists, the item is retrieved from memory. If not, the browser connects to the server to issue the client request. The server responds by sending the requested item—if it exists—and the connection is then closed. (Both Netscape Navigator and Microsoft Internet Explorer display the status of each Web transaction in the lower left corner of the browser window.) If the browser is unable to connect to the server or a requested item is not located, an error message is returned.

HTML Basics

The HTTP item most often requested by the Web client is the HTML document.
HTML (HyperText Markup Language) is the standard language used to create
Web pages. The browser interprets the HTML code and displays a formatted
Web page within the browser window. HTML documents are the building blocks
of the Web.

HTML documents are ASCII files that contain the text to be displayed on a Web
page, along with formatting codes or tags that define attributes of the page elements. Any simple text editor can be used to generate HTML files (.htm or .html
is the appropriate filename suffix). A growing number of more sophisticated
WYSIWYG editors and Web page creation tools are now available. HTML tags,
which are surrounded by symbols (< and >) are interpreted by the browser but are
invisible to the end user. The following is an example of a simple page containing
four basic tags. These standard tags should be included in all HTML pages.

```
<HTML>


<HEAD>
<TITLE>Most Basic Web Page</TITLE>
</HEAD>


<BODY>
Display text belongs here, along with formatting information,
hyperlinks, embedded objects and other elements for display.
</BODY>


</HTML>
```

Here is the resulting Web page when
it is displayed by the browser.

Each of the HTML tags displayed in the example requires an end tag, such as </TITLE>, which specifies where formatting ends. End tags are prefixed by a forward slash.

The standard <HTML> tag defines the MIME (Multimedia Internet Mail Extension) type, or data type, for the browser. The <HEAD> tag is placed before and after elements that define the properties of the Web page. These elements, such as title and search keywords, provide the browser with information about the page display. The <TITLE> tag, within the <HEAD> tag, designates the title that appears in the title bar of the display window and is used in the browser's history list. The <BODY> tag includes the items to be displayed (such as text, images, and Shockwave movies) within the browser window, together with their associated attributes and parameters.

HTML tags provide Web developers with control over formatting attributes such as general document formatting (e.g., headers, paragraphs, block quotes, and tables), text styles (e.g., bold, underlining, and italics), and text formatting such as code, emphasis and list formatting. HTML tags also provide the mechanism for hyperlinking and the display of inline graphics, Java applets, Shockwave movies, and other MIME types supported by Web browsers and their plug-ins.

Note

Web browsers allow you to view the source HTML document for any Web page by choosing the View Source option from the browser menu. You also can choose File...Save to save the Web page in source format to a local hard disk. This technique enables you to use the entire Web as an HTML reference. If you find a Web page you admire, view the document source to learn how the page was created.

About MIME Types

In order for a Web browser to display various MIME types, translation code must be available to the server and client. The translation of certain MIME types is built into the browser, so those file formats are automatically recognized. For example, Navigator 3 and Internet Explorer 3 added built-in support for inline display of Java applets. This means that Java applets launch and display seamlessly within the browser window, without requiring external software installation.

Other MIME types require external software in order to display inline (seamlessly integrated) within the browser window. These external software modules are called plug-ins (for Netscape and other plug-in compatible browsers), or controls (for Microsoft's ActiveX architecture). Shockwave for Director is currently a plug-in for Navigator, and an ActiveX control for Internet Explorer, which must be installed by the end user in order to add multimedia capabilities to their browser. Plug-ins and controls often require minor configuration of server software to ensure that the server also recognizes the MIME type.

If a retrieved MIME type is not recognized by the Web browser or its plug-ins or controls, the browser searches the client system for an external helper application that will display the file. If a helper application is found, it is launched by the browser and it displays the file within its own application interface. The file does not display inline. If a helper application is not found, the unrecognized file can be saved to a local disk for manual processing in lieu of being displayed.

Each client may be configured with a different selection of plug-ins, controls, and helper applications. It is important to remember that visitors to your Web site may have very different experiences based on the configurations of their browsers. Chapter 5, "Designing for Shockwave," raises some issues that should be considered when designing Web content for a wide range of browsers and system configurations.

The Web Industry: Under Construction

In the early 1990s, the group that was building and using the Web was comprised largely of programmers and scientists. Today, the information providers on the Web are as diverse as the general population. New Web sites are launched each day by individuals as well as corporations, businesses, organizations, and government and educational institutions. In some cases, sites are developed by individuals with little Web development experience. However, as bandwidth increases and sites evolve from text-based pages to multimedia experiences, the skills of various disciplines become necessary. Multimedia creation combines the skills of the computer industry with those of art, design, publishing, broadcasting, education, and other disciplines.

In order to capture the attention of potential viewers, sites must be designed and programmed to communicate effectively and meet the needs of the target audience within the constraints imposed by the medium. This is not an easy task, and it usually requires a set of skills beyond the capabilities of a single individual. As more and more sites compete for attention, quality and production values become differentiating factors. Increasingly, Web site development teams include writers, editors, graphic designers, interface designers, artists, animators, programmers, HTML experts, and project managers. As greater bandwidth and support for multimedia become widely available, teams also can include audio and video production professionals.

The people required to fill these roles are moving (in what seems like hordes) to the Web from all other areas of computing. Many individuals, from print designers to CD-ROM title developers, are transitioning their skills to the networked environment. For the multimedia developer, it is a time of great opportunity. Little time has passed since the first attempts at serving multiple media types on the Web, such as GIF animation and server push/server pull, were made. These early attempts can be improved upon to provide end users with a greater degree of interactivity. As the Web infrastructure evolves to support multimedia content, every message from the sublime to the trivial can be viewed as a potential multimedia application.

Chapter 2

Introduction to WEB multimedia

Beyond the Static Page
An Introduction to Web Multimedia

Shockwave enables developers to publish multimedia content on the Web. It is a multi-purpose technology that supports multiple media types and formats. Unlike Shockwave, many emerging Web technologies support the display of a single media type on the Web. These technologies usually fall into one of the following categories: text-based, graphics, animation, audio, video, and virtual reality. This chapter introduces you to some of these technologies before you move ahead to create Shockwave movies in Chapter 3.

Netscape pioneered the Web plug-in architecture, which makes the Navigator Web browser extensible. With the release of Microsoft's Internet Explorer 3.0 and Microsoft's ActiveX architecture, ActiveX controls were introduced. ActiveX controls are OLE (Object Linking and Embedding) controls that have been introduced by Microsoft for extending the Internet environment. Like plug-ins for Navigator and other plug-in compatible browsers, ActiveX controls add functionality and support for various file formats and media types. Many developers are now creating ActiveX controls for existing plug-ins in an attempt to be compatible with the widest range of installed Web browsers. For the sake of brevity and convenience, throughout this section we refer to "plug-in" technologies, but it is important to note that many of these plug-ins may be, or soon may be, ActiveX controls as well.

Through the use of plug-ins, controls, and helper applications, Web browsers such as Netscape Navigator and Microsoft Internet Explorer are making multimedia widely and instantly available to a worldwide audience.

Text-Based Media

Multimedia has been described as some combination of text, animation, audio, and video, usually within an interactive framework. Heretofore, the only way to access these media was via CD-ROM or some other "hard" form of delivery. The advent of the World Wide Web has changed that distribution model profoundly and within a very short period of time. The Web has become the most dynamic medium of information delivery in history and is evolving on a daily basis. Let's examine the data types that are now being distributed over the Web, beginning with the first and most universal, text.

Text was the original communication medium of the Web and is arguably still the most important. The original Web was conceived as a medium for the delivery of text-based documents between researchers and scientists. Today, all Web documents are still composed in the HyperText MarkUp Language or HTML and transferred across the Internet as ASCII text. Text is an extremely efficient way to transmit ideas and information and requires very little bandwidth. Consequently, almost all sites use text to convey information.

Plain ASCII text, while still ubiquitous on the Web, is being replaced in certain circumstances by more upscale varieties of text documents. These new forms of text transmission incorporate sophisticated formatting and inlining of vector graphics. Today, Web browsers are utilizing plug-in technology to make these documents available within Web pages.

Here are a few of the more notable examples:

> **Acrobat** (Macintosh and Windows) by Adobe Systems Incorporated
> http://www.adobe.com
>> Adobe has brought their Portable Document Format (PDF) to the Web via a plug-in for Netscape Navigator that enables PDF documents to be viewed inline within the browser window. Documents saved in the PDF format maintain the look of the original document's typefaces and retain formatting, as well as any embedded vector graphics. PDF files viewed within a Web browser via the plug-in can be printed to any PostScript printer in a resolution-independent manner. The text can be hyperlinked and will appear anti-aliased for clear on-screen viewing. Adobe's push onto the Web is a component of their overall strategy to make PDF a standard for document storage and retrieval.

Envoy (Macintosh and Windows) by Tumbleweed Software
http://www.twcorp.com

> Tumbleweed Software is positioning their Envoy technology and Tumbleweed Publishing Essentials' (TPE) format as a rival to Adobe's PDF format. Envoy is based on Bitstream Corporation's TrueDoc font-embedding technology. Although TPE was not designed around a printing metaphor—as PDF was, the Envoy plug-in works in much the same way as Acrobat. The documents, however, must be composed in, or converted to, TPE using Envoy tools, which are much less common in the graphic arts world than are Adobe's PostScript tools.

Word Viewer Plug-In (Macintosh and Windows) by INSO Corporation
http://www.inso.com/plug.htm

> Another plug-in that uses a proprietary text format is the Word Viewer plug-in from INSO Corporation. Word Viewer is based on the company's Quick View Plus application. Word Viewer enables a user to view Microsoft Word 6.0 or 7.0 documents embedded in a Web page. One caveat, however, is that the document will print as white space if the HTML within the embedded Word document is printed from Netscape.

Netscape Chat (Macintosh and Windows) by Netscape Corporation
http://home.netscape.com

> A completely different multimedia use for text is in a chat application. Netscape has released Netscape Chat, which when used in conjunction with Netscape Navigator, allows users from anywhere on the Internet to hold real time "conversations" via typed lines of text. Although technically this cannot be considered "multi" media (as only text is used), chat software is a unique vehicle for information transmission and can be used to trigger other media, such as in the context of an online game.

Graphic Images

Although several of the previous multimedia examples included inlined graphics within a Web page, those were within a larger context of portable documents. Most Web browsers today have the capability to display inlined JPEG and GIF images without plug-ins. However, to view other graphic formats a plug-in or a helper application is necessary. These graphic formats fall into one of two categories: bitmap graphics or vector graphics.

Bitmap Graphics

As mentioned above, most browsers today support the JPEG and GIF bitmap graphics formats. JPEG is the acronym for Joint Photographic Experts Group and is a open standard for the compression of photographic-quality bitmap images. JPEG compression is a lossy process—that is, degradation of the original image occurs. However, JPEG provides the best method for compressing photographic images and maintaining image quality.

GIF is the acronym for Graphics Interchange Format. It is a proprietary image format established by CompuServe that uses a patented compression algorithm held by the Unisys Corporation. GIF is a hardware-independent file format that is 100 percent lossless—that is, an image that is decompressed on the user's drive is the same as the original uncompressed image. GIF images can contain up to 256 colors, and any single color within an image's palette can be made transparent. GIF files may be saved as interlaced, which means that as a GIF is downloaded, a low resolution image appears and gradually improves as more of the file downloads.

The world of image compression extends beyond JPEG and GIF. Most of the following plug-ins were written by companies eager to disseminate their own image compression formats. This is also true of the vector graphics formats discussed below.

Lightning Strike (Macintosh and Windows) by Infinet Op
http://www.infinop.com
> The Lightning Strike Plug-In for Netscape Navigator uses wavelet compression to minimize images for transmission over the Internet. Wavelet compression works similarly to JPEG compression using a mathematical process known as a transform.

Wavelet Image Viewer (Windows) by Summus

http://www.summus.com

> The Wavelet Image Viewer plug-in also uses wavelet compression for image transmission and is also proprietary. The Summus Web site provides a very good explanation of wavelet technology for those who are interested in exploring compression technologies further.

Shockwave Imaging: xRes (Macintosh and Windows) by Macromedia

http://www.macromedia.com/shockwave

> Shockwave Imaging for xRes allows users to view and interact with dynamic xRes images over the Web without having to download an entire image file. Using server-side CGI technology, compressed high-resolution images are streamed to the client at appropriate zoom levels. Features include zooming (up to 26,500%), panning, and an optional Shockwave toolbar.

Figleaf Inline (Macintosh and Windows) by Carberry Technology/EBT

http://www.ct.ebt.com

> According to Carberry Technology, the Figleaf Inline plug-in enables Netscape Navigator to display a variety of common graphic formats that include the following: Computer Graphics Metafile (CGM), Tagged Image File Format (TIFF), Encapsulated PostScript (EPSI/EPSF), Microsoft Windows Bitmap (BMP), Microsoft Windows Metafile (WMF), Portable Network Graphics (PNG), Portable Pixmap (PPM), Portable Greymap (PGM), Portable Bitmap (PBM), Graphics Interchange Format (GIF), and Joint Photographic Experts Group (JPEG).

PNG Live (Macintosh and Windows) by Siegel & Gale

http://codelab.siegelgale.com/solutions/png.html

> PNG (Portable Network Graphics) is a graphics file format that is sponsored by the World Wide Web Consortium (W3C). It has advantages over other image standards such as JPEG and GIF, such as support for resolutions up to 32-bit, built-in gamma correction, multiple transparency layers, and interlacing. The PNG Live plug-in is available for displaying PNG images within Navigator and Internet Explorer.

Vector Graphics

The other major type of computer graphic is the vector graphic. To understand what vector graphics are, it is best to compare them to bitmap graphics. Bitmap images are composed of a discrete number of colored pixels arranged in an ordered grid. A scanned photograph saved in TIFF file format is an example of a bitmap image. A vector graphic is a mathematical representation of an image, making it resolution-independent. It must be interpreted by the computer in order to be displayed on a computer monitor or printed. Vector graphics are commonly used in illustrations and CAD drawings. Most of the following plug-ins display vector graphics by interpreting a proprietary file format of the company that created the plug-in.

Shockwave Imaging: FreeHand (Macintosh and Windows) by Macromedia
http://www.macromedia.com/shockwave
> Shockwave Imaging for FreeHand allows users to view and interact with dynamic FreeHand graphics over the Web. It provides compression with optional security, zooming (up to 26,500%), panning, support for embedded TIFF images, and an optional Shockwave toolbar for accessing these features. In addition, URLs can be attached to FreeHand objects to create hotlinks.

Corel Visual CADD (Windows) by Corel Corporation
http://www.corel.com/corelcmx/
> The Corel Visual CADD plug-in displays graphics saved in the Corel CMX vector image format.

SVF/DWG/DXF Plug-in (Windows) by SoftSource
http://www.softsource.com/softsource/
> The SVF/DWG/DXF Plug-in displays images saved in the SoftSource proprietary SVF format as well as AutoCad's standard drawing (DWG) and DXF formats.

Intercap Inline (Windows) by Intercap Graphics Systems
http://www.intercap.com
> The Intercap Inline plug-in from Intercap Graphics Systems displays inline images saved using the Computer Graphics Metafile (CGM) format.

Quicksilver (Windows) by Micrografx
http://www.micrografx.com
> The QuickSilver plug-in from Micrografx displays vector graphics created with Micrografx ABC Graphics Suite.

Animation

For many people, animation is synonymous with multimedia. This is because most high-end multimedia presentations include some animation. Also, the term animation covers a broad range of graphic imaging from moving text to 3D flying logos to Saturday morning-style cartoons. Even without plug-ins, Web browsers are capable of displaying animation of a certain limited nature through the use of server-push animation.

Server-Push Animation

Before the advent of plug-in technology, the only way to create an animation in a Web page was to use a technique known as server-push. A server-push uses a CGI (Common Gateway Interface) script to send a series of images from the server to the user's browser. Many people, however, find server-pushes annoying as the process takes away a degree of control over the presentation from the user. Now that Shockwave is available, it is very likely that server-push animations are well on their way to the World Wide Web history books.

If you are interested in creating animations via server-push, a very good Web page to consult is: http://www.emf.net/~mal/animate.html

GIF Animation

Since the release of Netscape Navigator 2.0, another method of non-plug-in animation has been available: the GIF animation. Although GIF has been thought of primarily as a still image file format, since 1989 the GIF standard (GIF1989a) has included the capability to save multiple images within a single file, along with timing information for playback. The animation capability is rudimentary compared to what is possible with Shockwave—although in certain instances it may be appropriate.

GIF animation is a relatively new phenomenon. Although the specification has allowed for animation since 1989, only recently has it found acceptance and is now implemented in Netscape Navigator and Microsoft Internet Explorer. An important difference between a GIF animation and a single GIF image is that the single image can be interlaced and viewed progressively as it downloads. A GIF animation must be downloaded completely before it will play. Several good shareware and freeware utilities for converting multiple images into GIF animations can be found on the Internet. For Macintosh, a very good freeware utility, GifBuilder, by Yves Piguet is available at:
http://iawww.epfl.ch/Staff/Yves.Piguet/clip2gif-home/GifBuilder.html

A comprehensive Web page devoted to GIF animations can be found at:
http://member.aol.com/royalef/gifanim.htm

Animation Plug-ins

Besides Shockwave for Director, at least two other plug-ins are available that allow playback of inline animations at this time. One of these, Astound WebMotion by Astound, Inc. has additional multimedia capabilities, which will be discussed later. The other is Sizzler by Totally Hip.

Sizzler (Macintosh and Windows) by Totally Hip
http://www.totallyhip.com

Sizzler is a plug-in that plays inline animations within Web pages. The distinguishing feature of Sizzler is its capability to stream the animation to the browser. The animation appears progressively, much like an interlaced GIF image (although not as a GIF animation. See "GIF Animation" above.) At this time, Sizzler does not have other multimedia capabilities.

Astound WebMotion (Macintosh and Windows) by Astound, Inc.
http://www.astoundinc.com

Although WebMotion falls into the "multi-purpose" category that appears at the end of this chapter, it does have animation capabilities that can be utilized specifically for the Web. Animations can be authored in the WebMotion application and played back using the Java capabilites of Netscape Navigator and Microsoft Internet Explorer.

Audio

Audio, in the form of music, the spoken word, or sound effects is an integral part of multimedia. In fact, the last major structural change in the development of one of the original multimedia forms, motion pictures, was the addition of audio some 60 years ago. Audio is rapidly assuming a similar role in the development of the Web, however substantial challenges to its full implementation must be overcome first.

The primary impediment is bandwidth. Most users are accessing the Web via a dialup connection with a transmission rate of 28.8 kbps, which allows only enough uncompressed data for telephone quality audio. Another impediment is the asynchronous nature of the Internet; rather than the continuous stream of voltage changes that comprise analog audio, digital audio (like all other digital information) is sent as a series of packets from the server that must be reassembled in the correct order on the client's machine. A goodly amount of the data that is sent down the pipeline is error correction, instructions, and the resending of packets, thus cutting further into the limited amount of information that can be transmitted.

To compound the problem, by its very nature audio demands to be experienced in a continuous stream. The human brain has evolved in such a way that visual data can be broken up spatially and temporally (to a degree) so that the mind can "fill in" missing visual data and create patterns from limited graphic information. Audio information, however, must be heard in a continuous stream if it is to be comprehended. For example, people are generally much more tolerant of snow (the electronic kind) on a television image or the loss of the image altogether, than they are of audio hiss or missing audio.

The available solutions to these, fall into a few basic categories. One is to reduce the dynamic range of the audio (or downsample the data, in digital parlance). Another is to use compression techniques. Yet another solution is to send only instructions that interact with data already stored on the client's machine.

Downsampling is a method that can be used to reduce the dynamic range of a sound file. For example, a 22 kHz, 8-bit monaural sound file is eight times smaller (in terms of file size and consequently download time) than an CD standard 44 kHz, 16-bit stereo sound file. However, the dynamic range of the sound reproduction is reduced commensurately by downsampling—that is, the higher sounds and the bottom, or deeper sounds are lost. Just think of listening to music over a telephone as opposed to headphones attached to an expensive stereo system.

Compression techniques reduce file size via the use of mathematical algorithms. Sound files, however, do not compress as efficiently as graphic files; therefore, the reductions in file size are not as dramatic. Also, most of the better compression techniques are lossy—that is, some sound quality is sacrificed in the compression process (but not as much as downsampling). One of the more popular compression schemes is IMA (Interactive Multimedia Association), which has a compression ratio of 4:1. QuickTime (which we will examine shortly) can utilize IMA compression.

Sending a series of instructions that use resources on the client's machine is another method to create sound. However, only certain types of sound information are amenable to this technique. The primary example of this method on the Internet is the sending of MIDI (Musical Instrument Digital Interface) music files from the server to the client. A MIDI file is analogous to the old player piano paper rolls from days gone by. Just as the holes in the paper instructed the piano the notes to play at what tempo, the digital information in a MIDI file tells MIDI devices attached to the client (such as keyboards and synthesizers), the same kind of information, plus much more (such as key velocity and instrument). And with the appropriate plug-in, the music files can be played directly within the browser. QuickTime also supports its own Music Architecture that is based on MIDI and can be played back over the Internet.

Audio is delivered from the server to the client in one of two ways: either the entire sound file is downloaded to the user's machine and then played from the local hard disk; or the file is streamed and played on-the-fly as the file comes in from the network. One advantage to downloading the entire file before playing it is that the file can be any resolution or format. All that is needed on the client side is an appropriate application or plug-in to play back the sound. The disadvantage is that the user must wait for the sound to download before listening to it, precluding any opportunity to link the sound to another media element. Also, the files are usually short in order to lessen download times. Streaming the file on the other hand, has the advantage of immediacy; the user can view graphics while the file plays. The disadvantage is that because the sound must be continuous, it must be downsampled and compressed in order to meet the bandwidth requirements of a dialup connection; hence, the sound quality tends to suffer. Regardless, streaming opens the possibilities for widely accessible Internet broadcasting.

Several technologies are now available that make sound playback within the browser possible. Helper applications also can be used for certain sound formats.

Sounds

A computer sound file is a digital representation of a recorded sound—just as a sound stored on tape is an electromagnetic representation of a real sound. Like any digital data, sound files are transported easily over networks. The Internet is rife with sound samples from popular music and television shows (some legally recorded, some not) as well as sounds recorded by individual users. Most of these sounds are in .AU or .WAV format and must be downloaded to the user's hard drive before playback. Many freeware and shareware utilities are available that can play these sounds. Additionally, audio-only QuickTime movies can be downloaded and played back or (with certain plug-ins) can be streamed and heard on-the-fly (more on QuickTime when video is discussed below). The release of Shockwave for Director 5 added Streaming Audio, which provides Shockwave with breakthrough technology for streaming high-quality voice, sound effects, and music from the network. Shockwave with Streaming Audio is covered in detail in Chapter 6, "Shockwave Media Creation." The following technologies also offer streaming audio formats for the Web.

RealAudio (Macintosh and Windows) by Progressive Networks
http://www.realaudio.com

> The RealAudio plug-in (and helper application) enables the user to hear a continous stream of digitized audio playing back from a RealAudio-equipped server. The sound stream is highly compressed but, thanks to buffering (reading ahead in the sound file and storing what is read on the client's drive), plays in a continuous fashion much like broadcast radio. RealAudio supports interactive control of real-time processing.

RapidTransit (Macintosh and Windows) by MonsterBit
http://monsterbit.com/rapidtransit

> RapidTransit is a compression scheme for the Web that allows servers to provide full 16-bit, 44.1 kHz CD-quality sound at compression ratios of 20:1 or better. Unlike RealAudio, the sound file does not stream from the server to the client; the file must be completely downloaded before it is heard.

MIDI Music

As described earlier, MIDI files consist only of information which can be interpreted by the client computer as music. This makes MIDI an extremely efficient method of sound transmittal. However, unless the user has an expensive MIDI instrument of some kind attached to his or her system, the quality of sound is limited. Many sound cards on the PC are capable of playing MIDI files directly through the computer's speaker. On the Macintosh computer, plug-ins enable MIDI playback. Additionally, the MIDI file can be converted to the QuickTime Music Architecture format and played back via QuickTime. This gives the file creator some control over how the music will sound when played back on the user's system, as musical instrument sound samples may be assigned to unique tracks of the file.

MIDIPlugin for Netscape Navigator (Macintosh) by Arnaud Masson
http://www.planete.net/~amasson/midiplugin.html
> The MIDIPlugin by Arnaud Masson is a plug-in for Macintosh that enables users to play back MIDI files directly over the Internet.

Crescendo (Macintosh and Windows) by LiveUpdate
http://www.liveupdate.com/midi.html
> The Crescendo plug-in allows Windows and Macintosh users to play back MIDI files directly over the Internet.

Voice

In addition to the use of digitized sound and MIDI music for online applications, a third category of sound-related technologies is emerging: voice. Internet telephony has received a great deal of attention—and with good reason. The ability to make virtually free long distance phone calls anywhere in the world has caught the attention of the major long distance carriers and has raised some concern about the future of their franchises. Real-time telephony is now available. This is still a far cry from the ease of use of a traditional telephone. Additionally, the reliability and sound quality that telephone users are accustomed to is sometimes lacking. However, software and hardware are evolving quickly, so the current situation could change dramatically. A prime example of this new telephony technology is Netscape's CoolTalk.

CoolTalk (Windows 95, Windows NT and UNIX at present) by Netscape
Communications
http://home.netscape.com

> CoolTalk is an Internet telephone tool included with Netscape
> Navigator 3.0 that provides audio conferencing, a whiteboard
> function and text-based communication using a chat tool.
> CoolTalk features full-duplex sound which enables users to speak
> and be heard simultaneously. It is a scaleable technology that allows
> users with higher bandwidth connections to take advantage of
> higher audio quality.

Another voice-related technology is the text-to-voice plug-ins that are available.
A voice plug-in enables a synthetic voice to read ASCII text aloud from a Web
page through the client computer's speaker. At the time of this writing, two plug-
ins for Netscape Navigator are available as well as one Xtra for Shockwave.

ShockTalk (Macintosh) by Digital Dreams
http://www.surftalk.com

> ShockTalk combines the features of Netscape Navigator or
> Microsoft Internet Explorer, Shockwave for Director, and Apple's
> PlainTalk Speech Recognition technologies. ShockTalk is an Xtra
> code module that is called by a Shockwave movie. The Xtra
> invokes a synthetic voice to read a block of text, and allows the
> computer to process and respond to spoken language using Apple's
> PlainTalk technology. PlainTalk is a system extension that ships
> with all Power Macintosh computers. It is available from Apple at
> http://info.apple.com.

ToolVox (Macintosh and Windows) by VoxWare
http://www.voxware.com

> ToolVox is a plug-in for high-end Macintosh and Windows systems
> that reads ASCII text aloud without additional system software.

Talker Plug-In (Macintosh) by MVP Solutions
http://www.mvpsolutions.com

> The Talker plug-in uses Apple's PlainTalk technology to enable
> Netscape Navigator to read ASCII text aloud.

Video

Digital video on the Internet presently suffers from the same bandwidth "challenges" as digital audio—only more so. Digital video must present a continuous stream of images, and it usually incorporates digital audio as well. Consequently, the digital video that is currently available on the Internet is a long way from the highly refined state of broadcast television technology. However, the foundation is being laid for online digital delivery of high quality video images on demand.

Like audio, video must be compressed for delivery over networks. Digital video comes in several compression formats, usually associated with the platform on which the format was originally designed. QuickTime, AVI, VfW, and MPEG are examples of the most common formats found on the Internet. Other proprietary formats are found, as well.

QuickTime is unusual among the formats in that it encompasses several other data types as well as digital video and audio. QuickTime Music Architecture is a data type based on MIDI (and QuickTime can, in fact, convert MIDI files to its own format); however, it extends the MIDI paradigm by providing the sound samples necessary to play the music in a standardized fashion. Additionally, QuickTime can accommodate text tracks for subtitling and another track for time code information. In future versions of QuickTime, developers and users can look forward to MPEG support, full Internet streaming, and an object-based scripting language.

The following is a list of digital video formats and the plug-ins that utilize these formats to play back video within Web pages.

QuickTime

QuickTime is Apple Computer's cross-platform technology for displaying temporal information dynamically. The information can be stored as a variety of different data types that include (not exclusively): digitized video, audio, text, sprites, music data (converted from MIDI), and time code. The data in these various media tracks may or may not be compressed and they are synchronized for consistent playback. The QuickTime architecture is scalable and extensible, allowing for many different compression schemes and data transfer rates. Because of these attributes, QuickTime is an ideal technology for information distribution over the Internet. Several plug-ins that incorporate QuickTime are available, including the official QuickTime plug-in that accompanies Netscape Navigator 3.0. This plug-in can be downloaded from http://quicktime.apple.com.

MovieStar (Macintosh and Windows) by Intelligence at Large
http://www.beingthere.com
>	Movie Star is a plug-in that permits the playing of QuickTime
>	movies within Web pages. The plug-in enables QuickTime movies,
>	which are created with Intelligence at Large tools, to be streamed to
>	the client computer and played on-the-fly.

ViewMovie QuickTime Plug-in (Macintosh) by Iván Cavero Belaúnde
http://www.well.com/~ivanski/download.html
>	ViewMovie is a freeware plug-in that plays back QuickTime movies
>	within Web pages. The files must be completely downloaded before
>	the movie will play.

AVI

Video for Windows is Microsoft's alternative to Apple's QuickTime technology.
Like QuickTime, Video for Windows files (.AVI format) display temporal information dynamically—primarily digitized video and audio.

CoolFusion (Windows) by MDL Information Systems
http://www.iterated.com/coolfusn/download/cf-loadp.htm
>	The CoolFusion plug-in enables .AVI files to be viewed within
>	Netscape Navigator.

MPEG

MPEG, an acronym for Motion Picture Experts Group, is a standard for video
compression and playback. MPEG is a highly asymmetrical file format; that is, it
takes much longer to compress the video than it does to play it back. Also, the
compression algorithms that produce MPEG files compress both interframe and
intraframe. The result is a highly efficient, but inflexible medium for digital video
that is ideal for playback over computer networks.

Microsoft ActiveMovie (Windows) by Microsoft
http://www.microsoft.com/ie/ie3/mmedia.htm
>	ActiveMovie is Microsoft's video technology for playing MPEG-II
>	video over the Internet or on the desktop. Within Microsoft
>	Internet Explorer, ActiveMovie uses an ActiveX control to display
>	streaming MPEG audio and video. With ActiveMovie technology,
>	users also can play back other media formats on the Web, including
>	.AVI, QuickTime, .AU, .WAV, MIDI and AIFF.

Prevu (Windows) by Intervu

http://www.intervu.com/download.html

> The Prevu plug-in plays MPEG movies embedded in Web pages through Netscape Navigator.

Proprietary

Along with open formats such as QuickTime, .AVI, and MPEG, other proprietary encoding schemes have been developed for video compression and encoding.

VDOLive (Windows) by VDONet

http://www.vdolive.com/download/

> The VDOLive plug-in by VDONet provides video streaming using a proprietary format.

VRML

The Virtual Reality Modeling Language (VRML) is a developing standard for describing interactive three-dimensional (3D) scenes delivered across the Internet. At the most basic level, a VRML file is a database of the geometry of a 3D space or object that is interpreted by the computer as an interactive entity. The user may navigate through the space as the plug-in renders the image on-the-fly, giving the illusion of movement within the scene. Texture maps can be applied to surfaces to enhance the illusion. Additionally, various kinds of lighting can be employed within a scene to create mood, or for other aesthetic reasons. Uniform Resource Locators (URLs) can be attached to objects within a scene allowing the user to navigate to other Web pages which may or may not include VRML.

A number of plug-ins and helper applications have been released that enable inline viewing of VRML files. The definitive source of VRML information is the VRML repository at http://www.sdsc.edu/vrml/

The following is a list of some currently available VRML browsers and plug-ins:

Live3D (Windows) by Netscape
http://home.netscape.com/comprod/products/navigator/live3d/index.html
> Netscape Live3D extends Netscape Navigator so that users can experience distributed, interactive 3D spaces with text, images, animation, sound, music, and video. In addition to providing a VRML viewer, Live3D extends Netscape's Java, JavaScript, and plug-in interfaces to enable developers to distribute 3D applications on the Netscape Navigator platform. Live3D is based on the proposed Moving Worlds VRML 2.0 specification submitted to the VRML Architecture Group.

VRML Support (Windows) by Microsoft
http://www.microsoft.com/ie/ie3/vrml.htm
> VRML Support is a fully integrated add-on module for Microsoft Internet Explorer.

WebFX (Windows) by Paper Software, Inc.
http://www.paperinc.com/webfx.html

> Based upon the VRML standard, WebFX is a plug-in for Netscape Navigator that uses Netscape's built-in history, hotlist, security, and caching capabilities.
>
> WebFX is capable of integrating into the Windows 95 Explorer interface, providing standalone HTTP communications independent of any Web browser.

VRealm (Windows) by Integrated Data Systems
http://www.ids-net.com/ids/vrealm.html

> VRealm reads VRML and is available as either a standalone application or as a plug-in.

Virtus Voyager (Macintosh and Windows 95) by Virtus Corporation
http://www.virtus.com

> Virtus Voyager is a VRML browser that can be used as a helper application external to the Web browser.

VR Scout VRML Plug-In (Windows) by Chaco Communications
http://www.chaco.com/vrscout/plugin.html

> VR Scout is a plug-in that displays inline VRML files. VR Scout uses either Intel 3DR or Microsoft Reality Lab 3D graphics engines, allowing it to be hardware-accelerated on a variety of 3D graphics boards.

Whurlplug (Macintosh) by Apple Computer
ftp://ftp.info.apple.com/Apple.Support.Area/QuickDraw3D/Test_Drive/Viewers/

> While not a true VRML plug-in, Whurlplug facilitates inline viewing of 3D objects saved in Apple's QuickDraw 3D 3DMF file format.

Multi-purpose

A multi-purpose multimedia application or plug-in incorporates two or more of the previously mentioned media types and usually has a scripting or programming language.

Java (Macintosh and Windows) by Sun Microsystems
http://java.sun.com

    Java is the best known of the multi-purpose extensible technologies, and it has the unique position of being incorporated into the Netscape Navigator and Internet Explorer browsers. Such an advantage speaks for itself.

    Java is an object-oriented programming language and development environment. It is based on C++, but differs in that it is wholly self-contained. By self-contained, we mean that the applications written in Java run inside a "virtual machine" that handles all of the interaction between the application (or "applet" as they are known) and the operating system. This isolates and protects the operating system from network-borne viruses and makes programming simpler—as the programmer never has to deal with juggling memory.

    Java is complemented by a simpler scripting language, JavaScript. Unlike Java, which must be compiled to be executed, JavaScript is an interpreted language that is written into the HTML of a Web page.

    Java is poised to be the lingua franca of the Web. However, multimedia development in Java is not for the faint-hearted. No development environment on the order of Director is currently available. In a completely subjective review of available Java applets made during the course of the writing of this book, we found Java applets wanting in comparison to the efforts of Shockwave developers. The Java sites we visited usually had very little animation, interactivity, audio or sophisticated graphics. The lack of an authoring environment was more than apparent. This surely will change over time. For now, however, Macromedia Director gives digital artists and designers the best environment in which to express their creativity. Macromedia and Sun Microsystems have announced plans for future compatibility with Shockwave and Java. The coupling of Java's computational abilities and database connectivity with Director's animation capabilities is a powerful and promising combination.

ASAP WebShow (Windows) by Software Publishing Corporation
http://www.spco.com/asap/asapwebs.htm

> ASAP WebShow is a presentation viewer that runs either as a plug-in, or as a helper application for all other Web browsers. ASAP WebShow lets users view and download presentations and reports created with SPC's ASAP WordPower. Reports and presentations that contain graphics also can be printed.
>
> ASAP WebShow uses RealAudio from Progressive Networks (mentioned previously) for audio support.

Astound WebMotion (Macintosh and Windows) by Astound, Inc.
http://www.astoundinc.com

> Astound WebMotion uses Netscape's LiveConnect architecture to present multimedia projects created with Astound's WebMotion application. Astound's WebMotion creates Java-based interactive productions that can be viewed within a Java-compatible browser without the aid of a plug-in or helper application.

Shockwave for Director (Macintosh and Windows), by Macromedia
http://www.macromedia.com/shockwave

> Our final multi-purpose, multimedia technology is the subject of the book you are reading, Shockwave for Director. The following chapters include everything you need to know to create Shockwave movies, along with in-depth case studies of existing shocked sites, sample code for implementing Shockwave's Network Lingo Extensions, and tips and techniques for optimizing your Shockwave movies.

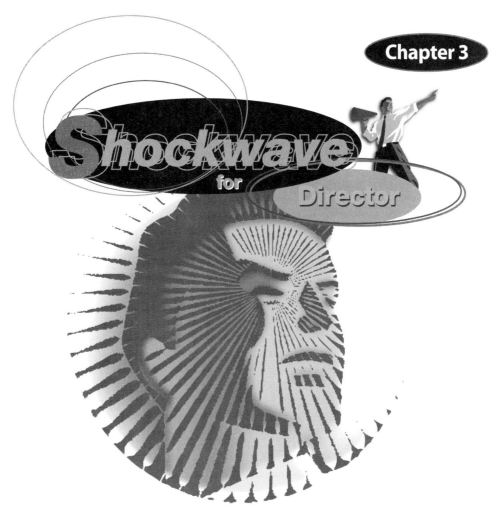

Chapter 3

Author Once, Play Anywhere
Shockwave for Director

In the previous chapter we examined a variety of media elements and plug-ins that bring multimedia and interactivity to the Web. This chapter focuses on Shockwave for Director, and includes the basic information required to begin creating and publishing Shockwave movies.

Director on the Net

The most concise definition of Shockwave for Director could be construed as "Director on the Web," but that would not be an entirely accurate characterization. Being "on the Web" opens up a host of opportunities for Director productions that would not be possible in any other environment. Through the use of network-specific Lingo commands and the inherent possibilities of millions of interconnected computers worldwide, Shockwave makes Director much more of what it already is: one of the best tools for multimedia communication.

Shockwave brings Director productions directly to the user. This means that Director developers can present their work instantly to a worldwide audience. Likewise, in the case of high bandwidth intranets, Shockwave enables Director developers to make presentations available to anyone on a local network, which only would have been previously possible by distribution on floppy disks or CD-ROMs.

The majority of the work involved in creating Shockwave movies occurs within the Director software application. Director is a very robust and flexible authoring tool that can be used to create anything from very simple animations or slideshows to fully interactive multimedia applications. Almost all of the features available within Director are available within the Web environment. (A list of restricted features for Shockwave can be found in Chapter 8, "Shockwave Lingo.") With some knowledge of Director behind you, let's examine the tools you'll need to begin transforming your Director movies into Web-ready applets.

Tools Checklist

To effectively develop Shockwave movies, you will need Director, tools for generalized Web development, and a few programs and files to prepare and display your movies inside a Web browser. You'll also need tools to create and edit the media assets you use in your Shockwave movies. (The nature of these tools may vary widely depending on the types of projects you are producing.)

❏ Director from Macromedia

Version 5.0 of the industry-standard authoring tool is currently available for Macintosh and the Windows operating systems. Version 4.0 may be used for Shockwave movie development, but the enhanced performance and features of version 5.0, which includes Shockwave for Audio compression, are especially useful in the Web environment.

❏ Afterburner Xtra from Macromedia

This Director Xtra converts your Director movies into Shockwave movies. It also compresses files to reduce download time. The Afterburner Xtra is functionally equivalent to, and replaces, the Afterburner application used with Director 4.0 movies.

❏ A Network Web Server

When developing for the Internet, developers have the choice of running their own Web server or establishing an account with an Internet Service Provider (ISP) in order to lease Web server space or gain access to the Internet. As hardware gets cheaper and server software gets easier to use, setting up your own Internet host gives you ultimate control over your site's performance. On the other hand, serving your site through an ISP enables you to get on the Web quickly and cheaply, and leaves you free of network administration responsibilities. If you choose to work with an ISP to serve your Web pages, be sure you consider the type of connection you will have to the remote Web server. While part-time, dial-up connections are fine for browsing the Web and sending electronic mail, you will need access to a computer with a full-time connection to the Internet to publish your Web pages, whether they are shocked or not. Some additional information about getting connected to the Web can be found in Appendix B, "Internet Basics: Getting Connected."

❏ A Shockwave-ready Browser

As of this writing, Netscape Navigator and Microsoft Internet Explorer can be used to view Shockwave movies. Other browsers supporting Netscape's plug-in architecture, such as Emissary from Attachmate and WebSurfer from Netmanage, are also Shockwave-compatible. In addition, Macromedia has announced that Shockwave will be seamlessly integrated into America Online and supported by other Web browsers in the near future.

❏ Shockwave Plug-in or ActiveX Control from Macromedia

The Shockwave plug-in for Netscape Navigator 2.0 or later, or the Shockwave ActiveX control for Microsoft Internet Explorer 3.0 or later, enables your browser to display Shockwave movies. Macromedia provides an installer that places Shockwave into the appropriate directory on the end user's system. The Shockwave installation also creates a Support folder, in which Xtras, external cast libraries, and linked media can be installed by the end user.

For Navigator, the Shockwave plug-in is installed inside the folder named "Plug-Ins," which resides inside the Navigator folder. For Internet Explorer, the ActiveX control is automatically installed. When the Internet Explorer browser first loads an HTML page that references a Shockwave movie, it requests permission from the user to download the Shockwave control. If the user approves, it downloads and installs the control.

❏ A Shockwave-ready Server

The appropriate documents must be stored on a Web server in order to serve Director files to the browser. This involves adding the MIME types (or data types) for Shockwave to your server's configuration files, if they have not been added by your system administrator.

❏ FTP Client Software

FTP, an acronym for File Transfer Protocol, is the standard method for transferring files between computers on the Internet. In most cases, developers need FTP software to transfer Shockwave movies, HTML documents, and related resources to a remote Web server. There are several good shareware FTP clients available for Macintosh and Windows, including WinFTP and CuteFTP (Windows), and Anarchie and Fetch (Macintosh).

❏ Text Editor

A text editor is a simple word-processing application, such as BBEdit from Bare Bones Software (Macintosh) or WebEdit from Nesbitt Software (Windows), that generates a plain ASCII text file. You will use your text editor to write the HTML documents that instruct the Web browser to display what you want on a given Web page. Commercial HTML editors are also available, and offer WYSIWYG display and other features geared toward convenience and ease of use. They can be used in lieu of a plain text editor, but check to ensure that they support the <EMBED> tags that are used to display Shockwave movies and other plug-in reliant media. For developing, managing, and maintaining a full Web site, consider using a site-building tool such as Backstage Designer from Macromedia.

❏ Media Production Tools

These include any tools you may need to create and edit media for use in Director. This might include software for image editing, illustration, and audio editing, for example.

❏ Offline Lingo Scripts (optional)

These Lingo scripts intercept Shockwave network commands that are not understood by Director during Shockwave authoring. (Lingo Network Extensions are supported and recognized by the active Shockwave plug-in or control, but not by Director at this time.) The offline Lingo scripts are used with Director to speed the development process when you are not connected to the Internet. While not an essential component of Shockwave development, the Lingo handlers in the Offline.dir movie included on the *Shocking the Web* CD-ROM can be copied into your own movies.

Shockwave Step-by-Step

Here is the general step-by-step procedure for creating, compressing, embedding, and serving a Shockwave movie.

Creating

Shockwave movies are created using Director for either Windows or Macintosh. One of the most important features of Director files is that they are binary compatible—that is, the same file created on a Windows PC can be opened, edited, and run on a Macintosh, and vice versa, with no conversion necessary. This means that a developer does not need to duplicate her or his efforts in order to port a Director presentation to another platform. The same is true for Shockwave movies.

In order to distribute a Director-based multimedia production in a typical authoring situation, a developer must use Director to create what is known as a Projector application, which is a stand-alone runtime program that is freely distributable with the Director movie files. Projectors are platform-specific and require developers to run separate copies of Director on each platform in order to create the necessary Projector for that platform. So a developer who intends to distribute his or her work on a hybrid CD-ROM (one that will work on either Windows or Macintosh PCs) must create separate Projector files—one for each platform.

On the other hand, for Shockwave productions created using Director, Director's runtime player is incorporated into the Shockwave plug-in or control, so it is only necessary to create one version of a Shockwave file for publication on the Web. The developer is not required to create a player or Projector file.

In theory, any Director file can be converted to a Shockwave movie. However, because of the limited bandwidth available to most users, certain techniques should be employed to ensure that the Director file is as small as possible. Generally, this means using graphics in the movie that lend themselves to compression, using the object-oriented nature of Director (for example, using multiple instances of the same graphic with different ink modes), using Lingo to enhance animations and interactivity, and simply being conservative with the use of graphics and sound.

Fortunately, with the release of Shockwave for Director 5, a major file size impediment was eliminated: the size of sound files. Previously, sounds had to be embedded within the Shockwave movie. Now, thanks to the Shockwave with Streaming Audio Xtra, large sound files can be compressed, downloaded incrementally, and played back from a buffer. This development represents a tremendous savings in the size of Shockwave movies. We will look at other file size reduction techniques in later chapters and throughout the Case Studies in Part II of this book.

Compressing

The conversion of a Director file to a Shockwave movie is very straightforward. Create a Director movie in the normal fashion—just as you would for playback from CD-ROM or floppy. The file must then be "burned" using the Afterburner Xtra, a free utility that can be downloaded directly from Macromedia's Web site. The Afterburner Xtra must be placed in the Xtras folder that resides in the same folder as your Director application (which makes it available to Director). Once installed, the Afterburner Xtra is available from Director's Xtras menu. To burn the Director file, just select the Afterburner Xtra from the Xtras menu. If you have not saved the latest changes to your file, you will be prompted to do so before proceeding.

The term "burning" refers to a process by which the Director file is stripped of any extraneous code, such as the text of any Lingo used in the file (but not the compiled Lingo), and then compressed using a lossless (i.e., without degradation) compression method to make the file as small as possible. This results in a new file that is appended with the .dcr extension. Depending upon the contents of the original Director movie, this file may be as much as 80 percent smaller than the original. When viewed with a Shockwave-ready browser, the .dcr file will play back within the browser exactly as the original file played in Director.

A Director file does not have to be burned in order to be viewed within a browser. In fact, a raw Director file (.dir), or a protected Director file (.dxr) also can be viewed. However, burning provides two advantages: (1) reduced file size; and (2) the file is protected—that is, the file cannot be opened with Director by another user. This means Lingo code cannot be copied out of the file, and the graphics are not in a form that can be retrieved easily by others. In fact, you cannot open your own Afterburned files, so it is necessary to keep a backup of your raw Director files—just in case you need to alter and reburn them.

Embedding

After the Director file has been converted and compressed with Afterburner, it is time to embed the file within a Web page. While this is not strictly necessary (Shockwave movies can be opened directly with a Shockwave-ready browser), doing so puts the movie into the context of a Web page, combining the Shockwave presentation with other media elements such as text and GIF images that can extend and amplify the message of the Shockwave presentation. Also, you can have more than one movie playing within the page. Although technically you can have as many movies as you like embedded within a page, Macromedia recommends that you have no more than three per page for performance reasons.

The HTML <EMBED> Tag

Adding a Shockwave movie to an HTML document is simple; it is accomplished using an HTML tag. The <EMBED> tag is the most common HTML tag used to display any file type that requires the presence of a plug-in to be displayed by the browser. Some Web page creation programs will automatically add the <EMBED> tag, but the tag also can be added easily with a text editor. An example <EMBED> tag that contains the minimum amount of information required to embed a Shockwave movie entitled title.dcr would be:

```
<EMBED SRC="http://www.yourserver.com/movies/title.dcr" WIDTH=335
HEIGHT=108>
```

The SRC parameter defines the URL of the source movie within quotation marks, including the path information—which may be relative or absolute. The pathname listed above is an absolute path that contains the full HTTP path to the movie. A relative path statement, such as <EMBED SRC="movies/title. dcr" WIDTH=335 HEIGHT=108> first points to the folder named movies, which is one level down from the HTML file containing this <EMBED> tag. It then locates the title.dcr file inside of the movies folder.

The WIDTH and HEIGHT parameters tell the browser how large a window to allocate within the page to play the Shockwave movie. Normally, the width and height are equal to the Stage size of the Director movie. Other attributes of the movie can be passed to the browser from within the <EMBED> tag by setting the following optional parameters:

BGCOLOR: You can set the background color of the embed rectangle to a hexadecimal value using this parameter. This helps integrate the rectangle into the Web page while a movie is downloading. The following tag sets the embed rectangle to solid black:

```
<EMBED SRC="http://www.yourserver.com/movies/title.dcr"
WIDTH=335 HEIGHT=108 BGCOLOR=#000000>
```

PALETTE: This parameter specifies whether the HTML page uses the browser's palette or a custom palette contained within the movie. Setting PALETTE equal to BACKGROUND delegates color management responsibilities to the browser and is recommended for most applications. BACKGROUND is the default value used if the PALETTE parameter is absent from the <EMBED> tag.

Setting PALETTE equal to FOREGROUND forces the browser to use the custom palettes specified in the Score of the movie. Note that the use of custom palettes is likely to cause unpredictable changes to the appearance of the windows on the user's monitor. This tag designates the Shockwave movie's palette as the active palette:

```
<EMBED SRC="http://www.yourserver.com/movies/title.dcr"
WIDTH=335 HEIGHT=108 BGCOLOR=#000000 PALETTE=FOREGROUND>
```

Note
The PALETTE parameter is not supported by Internet Explorer.

TEXTFOCUS: This parameter specifies how the Shockwave movie will handle input from the user's keyboard. Setting TEXTFOCUS equal to NEVER ignores all keyboard input; ONSTART responds to keyboard input as soon as the movie has finished loading; ONMOUSE causes the movie to accept keyboard input only after the user has clicked on the movie. The default setting for this parameter is ONMOUSE.

The following tag contains all of the parameters described above:

```
<EMBED SRC="http://www.yourserver.com/movies/title.dcr"
WIDTH=335 HEIGHT=108 BGCOLOR=#000000 PALETTE=FOREGROUND
TEXTFOCUS=NEVER>
```

The <OBJECT> Tag

Shockwave is the first ActiveX control for the Microsoft Internet Explorer browser. Based on Microsoft's OLE (Object Linking and Embedding) technology, ActiveX is the PC and Internet architecture from Microsoft that facilitates communication between Internet Explorer and ActiveX controls on the network and on the user's desktop. In conjunction with ActiveX, the <OBJECT> tag can be used to embed Shockwave movies within HTML documents. Internet Explorer 2.0 (pre-ActiveX) recognizes the <EMBED> tag, and version 3.0 or later recognizes the <EMBED> tag—provided that the Shockwave ActiveX control is installed. On the flip side, Navigator 3.0 or later recognizes the <OBJECT> tag.

So, as a Shockwave developer, which tag should you use? The <EMBED> tag can be used for compatibility with the largest number of installed Web browsers, but if a visitor to your site uses Internet Explorer 3.x without the ActiveX control, your Shockwave movies will not display.

If you opt to use the <OBJECT> tag, Navigator versions prior to 3.0 will not display your Shockwave movies if they are contained within the <OBJECT> tag. A solution to this problem is to include an <EMBED> tag within your <OBJECT> tag to handle this particular situation. (An example tag is included in Chapter 7, "Shockwave Authoring.") In addition, the <OBJECT> tag provides Shockwave developers with access to features that are not directly supported by the <EMBED> tag, such as built-in parameters used for streaming audio. The <OBJECT> tag also provides an identifier that is intended for future uses in communicating between ActiveX objects. Finally, probably the biggest advantage of the <OBJECT> tag is the automatic installation feature. If the ActiveX Shockwave control is not installed, Internet Explorer retrieves and installs the control that is specified in the <OBJECT> tag from the codebase on Macromedia's site.

All in all, your decision to use either <OBJECT> or <EMBED>, or both, must be based on the features required by your particular Shockwave movie and the minimum configuration standards established for your Web site.

The standard <OBJECT> tag syntax is as follows:

```
<OBJECT CLASSID="clsid:166B1BCA-3F9C-11CF-8075-444553540000"
CODEBASE="http://active.macromedia.com/director/cabs/sw.cab#vers
on=5,0,1,61"
WIDTH="416"
HEIGHT="280"
NAME="Shockwave"
ID="titlemovie01">
<PARAM NAME="SRC"
VALUE="http://www.yourserver.com/movies/title.dcr">
<PARAM NAME="BGCOLOR" VALUE="black">
<PARAM NAME="PALETTE" VALUE="background">
</OBJECT>
```

The CLASSID and CODEBASE parameters must be included as shown above in all <OBJECT> tags. All other parameters shown in the tag are specific to the Shockwave movie.

Additional Parameters

It is possible to define additional parameters within the <EMBED> or <OBJECT> tags. These HTML parameters can be accessed by Lingo functions within the Shockwave movie in order to determine or alter the performance of the movie. The Lingo functions available for accessing external parameters are externalParamCount(n), externalParamName(n), and externalParamValue(n). These functions are explained in Chapter 8, "Shockwave Lingo."

One important issue for developers to note is that the <EMBED> tag supports user-defined parameters, but the <OBJECT> tag currently supports a restricted set of pre-defined parameters. Therefore, using the pre-defined <OBJECT> tag parameters will ensure that they are recognized by both Navigator and Internet Explorer. The <OBJECT> tag parameters are listed in Chapter 8, "Shockwave Lingo."

Serving

After the Director movie has been burned and embedded, it's time to post the Shockwave movie on the Web server. Most commonly, the file is copied to the server with an FTP client program. It's important to transfer the file to the server as a binary file in order for the Shockwave movie to play.

One additional step is required for the file to be viewed within the Web browser. The correct Shockwave for Director MIME types (or data types) must be added to the Web server's MIME configuration file. MIME configuration files and formats vary for different servers and platforms. However, on a large number of Unix servers, MIME configuration can be accomplished by editing an .htaccess file at the root level of your public HTML directory on the server. An example of an .htaccess file would be a text document which defines the MIME types for raw (.dir), protected (.dxr), and compressed (.dcr) Director files, and includes the following information:

```
AddType application/x-director dir
AddType application/x-director dxr
AddType application/x-director dcr
```

To configure other types of servers for these MIME types, or if you are unsure about the location of your server configuration files, consult your server software documentation or ask your system administrator to add server support for the Shockwave MIME types. Additional information is available from Macromedia's Web site at http://www.macromedia.com/shockwave/config.html

Extending Shockwave Functionality

Shockwave for Director files can be completely autonomous Director movies playing inline within a Web page. However, Macromedia has designed Shockwave for Director with portals to the world outside the closed Director environment. Through the use of linked media such as audio and digital video, and through the use of Xtras, Shockwave can communicate with the user's desktop environment. Similarly, by combining a Shockwave for Director movie with a CGI script on the server, or by storing user preferences and passing external parameters, or using JavaScript, Shockwave movies can communicate with other movies and other resources on the Internet.

Linked Media

Shockwave for Director now supports linked media such as bitmapped graphics and AIFF sound files. These files may be downloaded by the user and stored in the Shockwave Support folder on the user's local drive. Additionally, now that Director 5 supports multiple casts, linked external casts also may be downloaded and stored in the Support folder. Macromedia is investigating a solution that bundles linked media with the corresponding Shockwave movie in a future Shockwave version in order to simplify the installation process.

The ability to access linked media means that Shockwave can interact with media elements that may be too large to efficiently transmit over the Internet. Media such as digital video can be stored on CD-ROM and accessed from an embedded Shockwave movie. The ideal way to accomplish this would be to store commonly used media elements on a CD-ROM with an alias or shortcut to the files stored in the user's Support folder. This presents developers with the best of both worlds: instantly updateable Shockwave movies from the Internet combined with media-rich content playing from the user's local drive.

Xtras

Shockwave for Director 5 supports Xtras, which are software objects that extend Director's capabilities under Macromedia's open development architecture. These plug-in code modules can be accessed by Shockwave movies if they are stored in the Shockwave Support folder on the user's hard drive. During Shockwave installation, the Shockwave for Audio (SWA) Streaming Xtra and the SWA Decompression Xtra are automatically placed into the Support folder. Although Xtras must be written in a programming language such as C++, many developers are writing Lingo, cast, sprite, and transition Xtras to target the needs of Shockwave developers. The *Shocking the Web* CD-ROM includes a sample of runtime Killer Transitions Xtras from g/matter, inc.

Note
Shockwave for Director 5 also supports XObjects, which were used prior to the release of Director 5 and the Xtras architecture.

Common Gateway Interface (CGI)

Common Gateway Interface (CGI) scripts are server-side programs that return a text result. These programs can be written in any programming language, although a scripting language is commonly used. PERL (an acronym for Practical Extraction and Report Language) is the most popular CGI scripting language.

Note
Under the Mac OS, AppleScript also can be used to write CGI scripts. AppleScript CGI programming tutorials, libraries, and resources can be found at http://www.comvista.com/net/www/ and http://www.scriptweb.com

CGI programs provide an avenue for the browser to send data to and from the network. Simple examples include the use of CGI scripts to return a URL when a user clicks an image map, or to process user input to a form in order to generate HTML on the fly. If, for example, a user submits "Judy" as a first name within a simple form, a confirmation page can be generated to include the message, "Thank you, Judy." The browser triggers a CGI program using a standard GET method to request the URL where CGI scripts are stored on your server, followed by parameters to be passed to the CGI. The parameter portion of the URL is an environment variable. The CGI location is separated from the environment variable by a question mark (?). Within the environment variable, parameters are separated by ampersands, and spaces are designated by plus signs. Non-alphanumeric symbols are converted to a 2-digit hexadecimal code prefixed by a percent sign.

Through the use of network Lingo commands, Shockwave can initiate CGI programs. Using the `GetNetText` or `GoToNetPage` Lingo commands, Shockwave can issue a URL request with an appended environment variable. The result returned by the CGI program can be read into the Shockwave movie using the `NetTextResult()` Lingo function to alter the Shockwave presentation. This capability makes dynamic presentations possible. For example, the following Lingo script uses a `GetNetText` command to call a CGI script that retrieves the name and value assigned to the parameters in the environment variable.

```
on exitFrame
  GetNetText "http://www.yrserver.com/cgi-bin/your.cgi?
Name=nextPage&Value=Total"
end
```

Note
It is necessary to monitor the status of the text retrieval using the `netDone()` Lingo function. The `NetTextResult()` function cannot be called until the operation is complete and `netDone()` returns TRUE. It is also a good idea to build a timeout into your script in case the item is never retrieved from the network.

JavaScript

JavaScript is Netscape's interpreted scripting language for Web client and server applications. JavaScript is supported by Netscape Navigator version 2 or later and Microsoft Internet Explorer version 3 or later. Unlike Java, which is a compiled programming language used to create applets and applications, JavaScript statements are written directly into the HTML page and are interpreted by the browser to perform specific actions such as responding to user events or processing form input. JavaScript can be viewed as an extension language that adds functionality beyond the capabilities of HTML. It has been referred to as the glue that holds HTML, plug-ins, and applets together.

JavaScript and Shockwave are supported by the same Web browsers. JavaScript can be a powerful asset for Shockwave developers because Shockwave movies can be embedded within JavaScripts. For example, under Navigator 3.0, a JavaScript function can be used to return the browser version the client is using to give the developer the opportunity to display or embed different HTTP items based on the user's configuration. In the same environment, a JavaScript function can be used to determine whether the Shockwave plug-in is installed. (These JavaScript functions are included in Appendix C, "JavaScript Reference," and on the *Shocking the Web* CD-ROM.)

Thousands of examples of JavaScripts are available online. Links to a large number of JavaScript resources can be found at:

http://home.netscape.com/eng/mozilla/3.0/handbook/javascript
http://www.yahoo.com/Computers_and_Internet/Programming_Language/JavaScript
http://home.netscape.com/people/jamie/jwd_javascript_QS.html.

With an understanding of how to create, compress, embed, and serve self-contained Shockwave movies, together with an awareness of the options available to you to extend Shockwave's functionality, you are ready to integrate Shockwave with Web tools and technologies in order to build network-dependent applications. In the remainder of Part I, we'll examine Shockwave development and address the issues you will need to consider when managing, designing, creating, and delivering full-blown Shockwave projects.

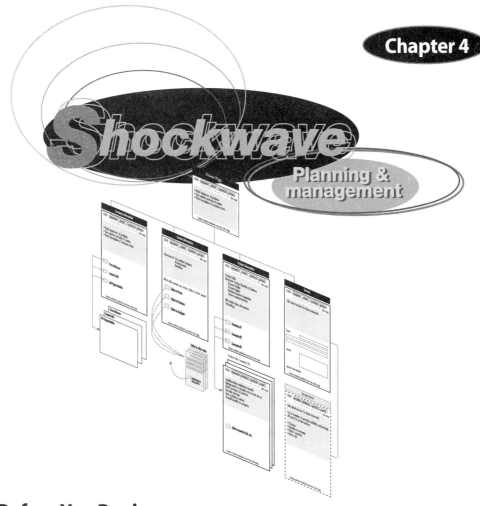

Chapter 4

Before You Begin
Shockwave Planning and Management

Multimedia developers often create and manage full-service design projects from concept through production and final delivery. These projects may involve assembling a team of project managers, art directors, writers, illustrators, photographers, sound designers, programmers, and Web specialists. On smaller projects, the team may consist of a graphic artist, an animator and a programmer— or the project may be assigned to one multi-talented developer. In any case, it is important for both client and developer to clearly define the project. A written proposal or contract should be agreed upon in order to validate each other's rights and obligations.

Proposals, Budgets, and Timelines

Before creating a full proposal, it may be useful to draft a statement of purpose. What is the project? Who is the audience? For which platform(s), browser(s), and minimum connection speed(s) should you design? Why does your client or audience need this application? This one-page, simple outline will help you understand the overall objectives and may help to avoid overlooked issues before getting into the details of the full proposal.

Many Shockwave projects are small-scale productions with budgets in the $500–$3,000 range. If you are simply adding an animated logo to a home page, for example, a simple description along with a total fee or hourly rate and estimated deadline will probably suffice. It is a good idea to clarify payment and ownership terms and to have the document signed and dated by both parties.

Larger Shockwave projects may have budgets ranging anywhere from $10K to $120K, and may require up to six months to complete. These may include shocking an entire Web site, creating Shockwave advertisements, or creating online games. As the pipe gets fatter, so will the budgets. Wherever higher bandwidths are involved (through cable modems, intranets, or CD-ROMs connected to the Internet), Shockwave projects will surely become more like CD-ROM productions in scope—with comparable budgets ranging from $250K–$2 million. Projects of this size typically require complete proposals that include a project overview, budget and payment schedules, ownership rights, terms and conditions.

Together with a proposal, you may choose to include promotional collateral such as articles, reprints, awards, bios, and demo files from your portfolio. Of course, as a Shockwave developer you may simply suggest that the client visit your Web site to see examples of your work. Also, if you are offering design services, always remember that your company's Web site and printed materials reflect your design abilities. So, even though it's often hard to find the time, try to keep your own promotional materials up-to-date.

A sample proposal outline that can be tailored or used as a check-list for building your own Shockwave project proposals can be found on the *Shocking the Web* CD-ROM.

Roles and Responsibilities

A large-scale Shockwave project, like any professional multimedia project, is a team process that requires specialization in the areas of management, design, and production. For smaller Shockwave projects, many of the following roles are combined. Regardless of project size, covering all responsibilities and areas of expertise is essential to the success of any project.

Management Roles

Management roles consist of tasks that are associated with budgeting, scheduling, and client relationships. In most cases, these tasks are handled jointly by the client and a project manager. Larger scale productions may include an executive producer, a producer, and several project managers.

Executive producer

The executive producer, or client, provides project funding. The client often provides the original content and is involved in the conceptual development and design. Client participation varies; ideally, once the client has approved the initial designs, storyboards, and prototypes, you will often be given room to do your job. It is very important that the client and the developer share a common vision before going into the production stage. Do whatever you can to clearly define the scope of the project and the deliverables.

Producer

Most multimedia development groups have producers or project managers that handle client relationships, usually acting as the client's main contact. A producer often attends initial meetings with the client and develops the proposal. Once a project gets off the ground, the project management role involves orchestrating the budgeting, scheduling, staffing, and equipment needs throughout the production process.

Producers or project managers with experience producing multimedia presentations, demos, or CD-ROM titles will easily adapt to managing the multimedia production aspects of a Shockwave project. Multimedia project managers with experience in Web site production are ideal. An understanding of Web issues and trends, authoring tools, design constraints, and HTML is helpful.

Design Roles

Design aspects of a Shockwave project involve conceptualization, visualization, and direction throughout production. Creative directors, art directors, information designers, interface designers, and production artists often are involved in the design stages of the process. In small scale Shockwave projects, one person may cover all roles (including production), while the roles in larger scale productions are usually more specialized.

Creative Director

The creative director, or art director, is responsible for all design-related decisions. This person often has the overall project vision, and must communicate ideas to the entire team. A creative director also supervises all aspects of the character and quality of work throughout production. In addition to understanding aesthetic issues, this person must have a good understanding of technological capabilities and should be able to balance creative goals with technical feasibility.

Information Designer

Information designers, content experts, and writers collect, create, and organize information. The information designer, working closely with the interface designer and creative director, develops treatments, outlines, scripts, and flowcharts to help determine the arrangement and flow of information. Usually, text-based outlines and scripts provide the architectural framework for a multimedia project. A Web multimedia designer can efficiently examine text-based content to determine where Shockwave or other multimedia technologies would be an effective enhancement or replacement for text.

Interface Designer

The interface designer, or interaction designer, focuses on the interaction between the user and the technology. Decisions are made regarding function, aesthetics, and human behavior in order to foster a positive end-user experience. The interface designer often creates navigational maps or diagrams to illustrate information hierarchies and branching structures. In developing multimedia for the Web, a major objective is to build intuitive interfaces that make it easy for users to navigate through a Web site without becoming lost or trapped. Prototypes allow a designer to test interaction designs on the target audience. Rapid prototyping is easy within the Web environment. Before sites are made available to the public, they can be tested on smaller groups to gain feedback. It is important to be willing to change the original design based on this feedback. Like the creative director, the interface designer must understand the design constraints and the technical capabilities. Shockwave interface design issues are discussed in Chapter 5, "Designing for Shockwave."

Production Roles

For the most part, the typical Shockwave production team is equivalent to any multimedia production team. This group of multimedia specialists includes illustrators, 2D animators, 3D animators, musicians, sound designers, and Lingo, Xtras, and C++ programmers. In addition, a Shockwave project may require Web authors, artists, and programmers with a knowledge of HTML, JavaScript, ActiveX, CGI, and Java. In the new Web multimedia authoring environment, the two groups are merging rapidly. Multimedia developers are learning more about Web authoring and vice versa. Web-oriented authoring tools and technologies also are emerging, which will attract both groups simultaneously.

Developer Outlook

For basic Shockwave projects, an experienced team of Director developers and multimedia artists already has the skills required to create compelling multimedia on the Web. Graphic artists, animators, and sound designers simply need to be aware of the issues outlined in Chapter 5, "Designing for Shockwave," and Chapter 6, "Shockwave Media Creation." Lingo programmers must learn the network Lingo commands covered in Chapter 7, "Shockwave Authoring," and Chapter 8, "Shockwave Lingo." The additional HTML skills required to layout a basic Web page or embed Shockwave files are fairly straightforward.

In order to build more sophisticated Shockwave projects, there is a lot to learn about the Web environment. The media creation aspects remain unchanged— but the asynchronous Web environment can be a challenge to most Lingo programmers. Perpetual beta release versions of browsers, combined with the ongoing browser war between Netscape Navigator and Microsoft Internet Explorer, will cause continued compatibility issues and will require multimedia developers to learn ways to create and combine the functionality of Shockwave with JavaScript, CGI, and new Xtras. Until new authoring tools are available, writing Xtras, Plug-ins, ActiveX controls, and Java applets will remain a job for programmers.

**The CSAA
Project Team**

In order to discuss the roles and responsibilities involved in Shockwave development, let's use the project discussed in Chapter 14, "CSAA Case Study," as an example. Organic Online, a San Francisco-based Web developer, completed a Web site for their client, CSAA (California State Automobile Association). Organic contracted DXM Productions to create a Shockwave site tour for CSAA. The following list indicates the roles and responsibilities of the project team.

CSAA

Executive Producer/Web Management

Provided project funding, established deliverables, scheduling, reviews, sign-off, and provided content (in text form).

Organic

Producer/Project Manager

Managed budget and schedule, and hired production team.

Creative Director

Design reviews and sign-off.

Web developer

Integrated final Shockwave and HTML on Organic server for testing, and finally on CSAA server for release.

DXM

Creative Director

Concept, storyboards, prototypes, and animation.

Illustrator

Created stylistic illustrations.

Programmer

Lingo programming, HTML, JavaScript, PERL, and sound integration.

Total 7 team members; about 80-85 total hours.

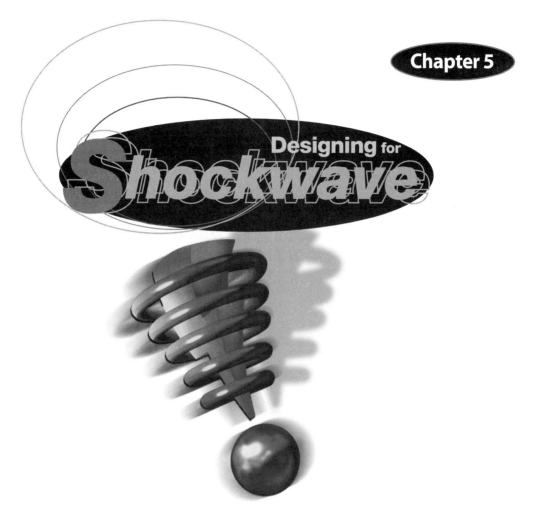

Chapter 5

Designing for Shockwave

Meet the Challenge
Designing for Shockwave

Designing effective Shockwave applications is a challenge for any multimedia developer. Typically, the objective is to create something really cool with lots of animation, graphics, and sound—culminating in a file no more than 50 kilobytes. And, of course, it should download quickly, run fast, look great on all platforms, and perform well in all Web browsers.

Good designers design for the medium! Most Shockwave developers probably have heard statements from clients and colleagues such as, "Oh, I've seen Shockwave movies—but they're so slow." Comments like this can be very frustrating to experienced developers. The perceived speed problem, for the most part, is not a result of Shockwave technology; more likely, the Shockwave developer did not design the project to suit the medium. In many cases, this is simply because the developer refuses to design within the medium's limitations, or is not fully aware of its associated constraints. On the other hand, the developer may have intentionally designed a Shockwave application with high bandwidth users in mind, but failed to communicate this to the low bandwidth user who could have the unpleasant experience of staring at a Shockwave logo for a minute or so during a download.

Due to bandwidth constraints and the variety of platforms and browsers, designing for Shockwave can be complex—and the production process can be sometimes painstakingly slow. In many ways it is also the ultimate design challenge. It is similar to the art of miniature painting. The artist has a very small canvas, a single-hair paintbrush, and uses very little paint. Shape, color, and composition are applied with great consideration, patience, and surgical precision. For Shockwave, you need to think small, and most importantly, design for the medium.

As a Shockwave designer, it is critical to clearly understand the constraints of the networked medium. By defining these constraints, you create the framework for your project and establish boundaries to stay within during brainstorming sessions and guidelines to follow (or break) throughout production. Before designing a Shockwave project, consider the following issues and focus on turning limitations into creative solutions.

Bandwidth

Technically, Shockwave presents no file size limitation. Theoretically, a Shockwave developer could process the entire contents of a CD-ROM title through Afterburner and then post it on the Web. For discussion, let's say Afterburner compressed the 650MB file to about 162MB. For the Web surfer using a 14.4Kbps modem, this file would take about 81 hours to download—just over 3 days! On the other hand, the speed surfer using a dedicated T3 connection could download the entire file in a few minutes.

This scenario makes overly broad assumptions regarding servers, pipelines, Web traffic, user platforms, and browser configurations. All of these variables combine to effect download time. Understanding the factors affecting network performance will help you design appropriately for specific audiences.

Network Performance

The bandwidths and associated download times of your target audience will vary tremendously. Today, the majority of Internet users connect at relatively slow speeds—usually at 14,400 or 28,800 bits per second. At best, the 28.8Kbps modem user can download about 3K per second. This means that a 60K file will take about 20 seconds to download.

Note

Bits vs Bytes: Multimedia developers talk in terms of bytes: kilobytes, megabytes, and gigabytes. A dual speed CD-ROM drive has a data transfer rate of 600 kilobytes per second. The telecommunications industry discusses bandwidth in terms of bits: kilobits, megabits, and gigabits. A 28.8Kbps modem is capable of transferring data at a rate of 28.8 kilobits per second. Eight bits equal one byte, so a 28.8Kbps modem translates to 3.6 kilobytes per second (divide the total bits by eight to convert bits to bytes).

Delivery Medium	Transfer Rate (bits per sec / bytes per sec)
14.4 Kbps modem	14.4Kbps / 1.8KB
28.8 Kbps modem	28.8Kbps / 3.6KB
56 Kbps modem	56Kbps / 7KB
DS-0 / Single ISDN B-Channel	64K / 8KB
ISDN BRI (2 B-Channels)	128Kbps / 16KB
ISDN PRI (23 B-Channels)	1.472Mbps / 184KB
T1	1.544M / 193KB
Ethernet	10Mbps / 1.25MB
T3	44.736Mbps / 5.592MB
Fast Ethernet	100Mbps / 12.5MB
ATM / B-ISDN / SONET OC-3	155.520Mbps / 19.44MB

To further complicate the issue, it is not just the end user's connection that determines download speeds. Client computers also can add delay to transfer time if they are slow machines that are not capable of quickly parsing and displaying data received. Computers with inadequate memory process data more slowly and may cause memory-related errors or crashes to occur.

In addition, overloaded Web servers or servers with slow disk drives can take a long time to process a request. Web servers can handle only a maximum fixed number of connections per second and exceeding this limit results in "Host is busy...try again later" messages. The solution to this problem is to upgrade to faster servers or add mirror sites that contain multiple copies of the site's content to handle the additional requests. This can result in a Catch-22 situation for smaller Web publishers. While it may be technically and economically feasible for a small developer to create a popular Web site that attracts crowds, it may not be possible to upgrade server equipment fast enough (or cheaply enough) to maintain the performance required to keep people coming back to the site.

Lastly, another form of network latency is propagation delay. Propagation delay is a result of the time required for a signal to travel from one point to another. The greater the distance transmitted, the longer the signal takes to reach its destination. This is an inherent physical limitation of all networks, because the speed of every connection is limited to the speed of light. The speed of light is a constant, which means that nothing can be transmitted over 3,000 miles in less than 16 milliseconds. Propagation delay can become an issue for large amounts of international data traffic.

Eventually, high bandwidth networks will become widespread and Shockwave developers will be able to provide media-rich experiences over the Internet. It is easy to imagine the Web evolving from a static page-based medium into an interactive multimedia broadcasting medium, given the Web's bandwidth potential. Until then, Shockwave developers must design for the lowest common denominator, develop exclusively for specific bandwidths, or create scaleable Shockwave projects.

Designing for Average Connection Speeds

In order to appeal to the 14.4 or 28.8Kbps modem user, it is recommended that Shockwave files stay within the 30–50K range. This means that prior to compressing the file using Afterburner, the Director movie should be no more than 200K. Remember that the amount of compression varies depending on the type of media used in the Director movie. It is a good idea to compress files using Afterburner throughout the production process to be sure that you are staying within the recommended range. The following movie demonstrates the amount of media included in a 30–50K Shockwave file in order to help you design accordingly.

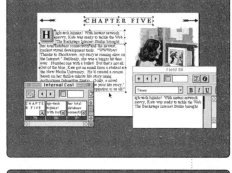

Text: The movie contains two text areas that use field text. Because field text requires that the font be installed on the end user's system, a system font was selected—12 point Times in this example. Director's rich text with anti-aliasing was used for the chapter headings.

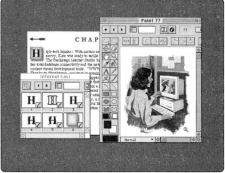

Graphics: The large graphic illustration of the woman sitting at the computer uses most of the memory in this example. It is an 8-bit image that is 192w x 222h pixels, and is 41.6K uncompressed. A small bitmapped animation of the letter H totals 19.4K, and is also indexed to 8-bit.

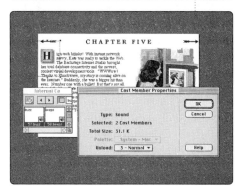

Sound: Two small looping sound effects that total 31.1K uncompressed are included. They are 16-bit mono sounds, downsampled to 22.050kHz, and compressed as internal Shockwave audio (SWA) sounds.

The uncompressed Director file totals 118K. Afterburner compressed the file to 43K. The example movie can be found at
http://www.macromedia.com/macromedia/ investors/annual96/novel/shocking.htm

Designing for Specific Bandwidths

In some cases, you may be designing Shockwave for specific bandwidths only. For example, a high-tech corporation realizing that the overwhelming majority of visitors to its site will be other high-tech corporate users may decide to establish higher file size limits—perhaps designing for ISDN or T1 minimum connections. Refer to the download table above for recommended file sizes and estimated download times for various bandwidths. Also, be sure to clearly communicate that the visitor is entering a high-bandwidth zone that is not recommended for low-bandwidth surfers.

Intranet Bandwidth

High-bandwidth zones also can be found on intranets. Simply put, an intranet is a private Internet. It is a TCP/IP network inside a company or organization that acts as its centrally located source of information, resources, and communication.

Currently, most company employees are connected through an Ethernet local area network (LAN) that transmits information among computers at speeds of up to 10 million bits per second (Mbps). The most recent Ethernet standard is the new 100Mbps Fast Ethernet standard that operates over twisted-pair and fiber optic media.

Theoretically, a 10Mbps Ethernet system can download up to 1.25 megabytes (MB) per second. A 100Mbps Fast Ethernet system can download 10 times that amount (about 12.5MB per second) under ideal conditions. This greatly exceeds today's fastest CD-ROM transfer rates, and obviously could support very robust Shockwave content.

However, it is important to note that the same issues discussed earlier regarding Internet performance and network latency apply to intranets. As multimedia content becomes widespread on the Internet and on proprietary intranets, the infrastructure must be capable of supporting it. For example, a typical Ethernet network for 100 employees may include one server that can effectively support the connections of 10 employees per second with average downloads of 10K. If the average download per connection suddenly increased to 100K, the same server would then only support one employee connection per second. Inevitably, companies will need to upgrade their networks to support extensive media-rich traffic on intranets.

Also, all employees may not be connected to the LAN through Ethernet. Branch offices may have slower connections to the LAN, or they may have their own LANs. Employees also will want remote access to the intranet and probably will connect from home or portable computers with dialup modems. Consider developing lower bandwidth Shockwave versions for this group.

Designing for Scaleable Bandwidths

Some Web sites with audience connections that range from 14.4 to T3 offer a choice of either high or low bandwidth versions of the entire site. However, maintaining multiple versions of a site can be laborious and inefficient. Here are some tips for making Shockwave movies that automatically scale to suit the user's connection speed.

Determining Bitstream

A very small file can be used to test the connection speed of a particular visitor to your site. Once the user's bit rate has been determined, the appropriate small, medium, or large Shockwave file can then be downloaded without requiring the user to make the selection manually. By recording the amount of time required to transfer a fixed amount of data when the user first loads your Shockwave movie, you can index the transfer time to a corresponding list of connection speeds. This technique is useful—but not foolproof, because bitstream often fluctuates during a single connection. For an accurate assessment, it is necessary to repeatedly test the user's bitstream. However, testing repeatedly uses CPU cycles and slows the performance of your Shockwave movie. An example movie that uses this Lingo technique is described in Chapter 7, "Shockwave Authoring." The Director source file named autoDeterminator.dir can be found on the *Shocking the Web* CD-ROM.

Shockwave Support Folder

As discussed in Chapter 3, "Shockwave for Director," Shockwave allows linked media elements and external cast and code libraries to be stored on the user's local disk in the Support folder. This folder can be used as a cache to store commonly used media elements. Any Shockwave movie can be programmed to pull specified media from this pool of resources without download delays. For example, a shocked site with many return visitors could add downloadable Shockwave support files. Unfortunately (for developers), the user must manually choose to download the files and place them in the Support folder. Therefore, you cannot assume that the files were downloaded, and unless you provide a downloadable or

CD-ROM installer, you cannot be sure that the files were put in the proper place. With some clever design and Lingo programming, the same Shockwave file can play seamlessly whether or not the Support files are installed. An example movie that uses this Lingo technique is described in Chapter 7, "Shockwave Authoring." The Director source file named EnhanceMe.dir can be found on the *Shocking the Web* CD-ROM.

Modular Media

If you are designing Shockwave for various bandwidths or eventually plan to offer high bandwidth versions of your movies, pre-production planning and thorough post-production archiving are essential.

It may help to think about the media elements (sounds, animation, graphics, etc.) in your Shockwave files as optional or modular enhancements that can be added or removed to accommodate bandwidth requirements. For example, a large Shockwave movie may contain an animation that includes two key frames and eight "in-betweened" cast members for a total of 10 frames. In order to make a smaller version, the number of "in-betweens" can be reduced. It is much easier to remove media elements than to add them later—so, if possible, create the high bandwidth version first and structure the Score and Lingo code to be flexible enough to easily add and delete elements.

Since higher bandwidth is on the horizon, you may want to archive all original, high-resolution source files in order to easily recreate a broadband version of your work at a later date.

User Platforms

Shockwave movies can be viewed on both Macintosh and Windows computers with basic multimedia capabilities, but the specific hardware and software configurations used by visitors to your Web site will vary widely. In order to target the widest Web audience, it is best to take a lowest common denominator approach to building your site. Consider the following platform differences before designing Web content.

Minimum System Requirements

The following minimum hardware configuration is recommended for playing Shockwave for Director movies:

MacOS

- Macintosh, Power Macintosh, or Power Macintosh compatible running system 7.1.2 or later
- 8-bit display; 256 colors or greater
- 16MB free disk space for installation; 8MB free disk space for local disk cache
- 16MB RAM installed, 10MB free before running Navigator or Internet Explorer
- FPU for streaming audio playback.

Windows PC

- IBM PC or compatible running Windows 3.1, Windows 95, or Windows NT
- 8-bit display; 256 colors or greater
- 9MB free disk space for installation; 8MB free disk space for local disk cache
- 16MB RAM installed.

Display

The majority of computers today are capable of displaying 256 colors or more. Most users will view your site in 256 colors (8-bit), but others may have their display's color depth set to thousands or millions of colors. If your animations do not run smoothly in higher bit depths, consider testing the Lingo `colorDepth` property and then alert the user to set his or her display to 256 colors if necessary.

For example:

```
on startmovie
  if the colorDepth <> 8 then
    alert "For optimal performance, please set
    your display to 256 colors."
  end if
end
```

Note

The Lingo command for setting the `colorDepth` has been disabled in Shockwave—the property can only be tested. See Chapter 8, "Shockwave Lingo," for a list of restricted and disabled Lingo commands.

Before choosing the Stage size for your Shockwave movie, consider that the average display resolution in pixels is 640 wide x 480 high, and the default browser window size (which includes a toolbar, location field, and directory buttons) uses a large amount of screen real estate. If you would like the user to view your Shockwave movie without scrolling or enlarging the browser window, your Stage should be no larger than 464 pixels wide x 310 pixels high.

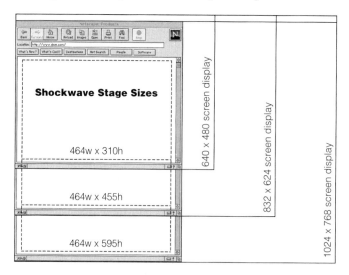

Memory

For playing Shockwave movies,
Macromedia recommends a minimum
10MB of available RAM memory and a
minimum browser disk cache setting of
8MB. The disk cache is a designated portion of local disk space (specified within the
browser's preferences) for downloading
HTTP items to the end user's computer.
Items are retrieved from the cache rather
than from the network—thereby saving
time—if they have been previously downloaded by the browser. If the amount of
available RAM is too low, error messages and crashes will occur. If the disk cache
is set too low, a broken icon will appear in place of the Shockwave movie.

From within Director, it is possible to determine the amount of free RAM on the
user's system (using the `freeBytes` function and other Lingo techniques), but
the amount of available disk cache is totally unpredictable. In most cases,
Shockwave file sizes are so small that they load into RAM memory without a
problem. Data stored in the local disk cache, on the other hand, is not so man-
ageable. The browser flushes cached data whenever space is required by a download. You cannot rely on data that has been stored in the cache—it may not exist
from one session to another.

Processor Speeds

Common processor speeds range from 33 megahertz to 200 megahertz and above.
In order to ensure consistent performance of Shockwave movies (animation playback, sound synchronization, etc.) on various CPUs, there are a few techniques
from which to choose:

- At the start of a movie, test the processor speed using Lingo and set the
  movie tempo accordingly. (See Chapter 10, "Macromedia Case Study,"
  Checking Processor Speed sidebar, for a description of this technique.)

- Use the time functions in Lingo to synchronize key events and audio
  throughout the movie.

- Set the movie tempo to an average rate (8–10 frames per second) and
  design the Shockwave movie to run smoothly at this rate.

Operating Systems

Shockwave movies currently play on the MacOS (68K and PowerPC), Windows 3.1, Windows 95, and Windows NT platforms. Remember that shocked Web sites are accessible to a global audience. ASCII text within a Shockwave file may be illegible on foreign language systems. If you would like to create localized versions of Shockwave movies, consider using bitmapped text in your Director movies.

If you choose to convert ASCII text to bitmapped text, file size will increase. You can reduce the file size of the bitmapped text by converting it to 1-bit, however it still will be larger than the original ASCII version.

If you are incorporating Shockwave movies into a Web site that has been localized for languages other than English, you can create separate Shockwave movies to be embedded into the appropriate localized pages. Alternatively, you could build a multilingual version of a single movie that can display the appropriate language or play the appropriate audio based on external Lingo parameters passed to the Shockwave movie. You also could store external cast libraries for each language in the Support folder, and call them accordingly.

Browser Issues

Shockwave is supported by all prominent Web browsers: Netscape Navigator, Microsoft Internet Explorer, America Online (AOL), and Spyglass, for example. However, end-user distribution and installation of the plug-in is a major barrier to global Shockwave adoption. To ensure the wide distribution of Shockwave technology, Macromedia has announced several partnerships. Netscape currently includes Shockwave in the Netscape Power Pack collection of plug-ins and utilities, and the company has integrated Shockwave into version 4 of Navigator, thereby eliminating the need for users to download and install Shockwave. In addition, Shockwave is the first ActiveX control that Microsoft packages with Microsoft Internet Explorer, the Windows 95 operating system, and the Windows 95 original equipment manufacturers kit. America Online integrates Shockwave seamlessly with new versions of the AOL Web browser. And lastly, Apple Computer is bundling Shockwave with the Apple Internet Connection Kit as an OpenDoc part, which is included in all Internet-ready Macintosh computers.

According to Macromedia representatives, more than 11 million Shockwave plug-ins have been downloaded to date. Of course, this is a total download number that combines Shockwave for Authorware, FreeHand, xRes, and Director (which includes Shockwave for Director versions 4 and 5). Although the actual number of Shockwave for Director 5 downloads is unknown, it clearly is being used by an extremely large and growing number of Web surfers.

While default installation of Shockwave will be included in upcoming releases of prominent Web browsers, there are many people that still use older browser versions or downloaded versions that require the manual installation of Shockwave. Until features from competing browsers standardize and Shockwave technology is ubiquitous, Shockwave developers need to address end-user Shockwave installation and multi-browser compatibility issues.

Get Shockwave

You probably already have seen the small rectangular Netscape, Microsoft, or Get Shockwave logo/button links on numerous Web sites. Nearly all Web sites that require specific configurations include this information on the home page or at the entrance to a specific area of the site. For users that are not properly configured to view the site, links to downloadable browsers and plug-ins are provided. To permit users to download the Shockwave plug-in, provide a URL link to http://www.macromedia.com/shockwave. At this location, the user will find released versions of the Shockwave plug-ins. Macromedia also provides straightforward, step-by-step installation instructions and an excellent troubleshooting guide. Currently, Macromedia does not allow distribution of the Shockwave plug-ins on third-party Web sites.

Recently, Macromedia proposed using the Made With Macromedia logo as an alternative to the Get Shockwave logo. As an incentive, by placing the Made With Macromedia logo on your home page, you are entitled to an "Official Shocked Web Site" listing on Macromedia's site. While this may increase the visibility of your site and help Macromedia build a database of shocked sites, there are interface and graphic design issues related to the logo's use that may make this incentive less than appealing.

- It's big. The Macromedia design guidelines require that the logo be displayed at 99 pixels wide by 73 pixels high. At this size, it looks too big on a page and takes up 2.3 kilobytes. The Get Shockwave version is only 88 pixels wide x 31 pixels high and saves you one kilobyte.

- It's inconsistent with other Web logos. Standard logos used by other companies (such as Netscape and Microsoft) to display this type of information are 88 pixels wide x 31 pixels high (the same as the Get Shockwave version). In cases where several of these appear on one page, it is not easy to group the Made With Macromedia logo with the others.

- It does not communicate the appropriate message. The purpose of this logo is to inform the user about specific technical requirements necessary to view a particular site and to provide access to the technology through a hyperlink. The Made With Macromedia logo doesn't convey to the user that Shockwave is required and, unlike the other logos, it does not look like a button that links to another Web page.

Macromedia does not require that you use the Made With Macromedia logo on Web sites. If the issues listed above are problematic, use the Get Shockwave logo or create your own. Otherwise, full details and design guidelines for the Made With Macromedia logo can be found at http://www.macromedia.com/support/mwmp/shockwave.html.

Scanning for Shockwave

To avoid providing a curtain page that requires the user to make a selection, a "Shockwave scanner" can be used to automatically send the user to the appropriate URL. A small Shockwave movie hidden at the bottom of a Web page can be used to determine whether the user has Shockwave software installed. If Shockwave is installed, the Shockwave movie loads and a simple goToNetPage command in the movie sends the user to a shocked Web page. If the user does not

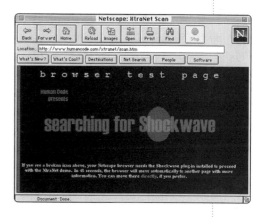

have Shockwave installed, the Lingo command never executes and the user remains on the current page, which then could then act as the first page of a non-shocked version of your site. Alternatively, you could prompt the user to get Shockwave and provide links to the download site, or automatically open the URL for Macromedia's Shockwave download page after a certain amount of time has elapsed.

Note
Depending on which Web browser and which version of the browser is used, the behavior of the browser varies when it encounters a Shockwave movie without Shockwave software installed. In some cases, the browser will prompt the user to download Shockwave. This may interfere with the anticipated behavior of the scanner movie discussed above. Be sure to test your site using shocked and non-shocked versions of the various browsers you intend to support.

A new URL can load automatically after a specified amount of time (or the same document can reload on a regular basis) using "client pull." To achieve this type of client pull, use the META element in your HTML documents. Both Navigator and Internet Explorer support this element. The META element must be included within the <HEAD> tag of the HTML document. For example, the following HTML code automatically loads a new Web page named timeout.htm after three seconds have elapsed:

```
<HTML>
<HEAD>
<META HTTP-EQUIV="REFRESH"
CONTENT="3;URL=http://yourserver.com/timeout.htm">
<TITLE> Temporary Page</TITLE>
</HEAD>
<BODY>After 3 seconds, a new page will automatically load.</BODY>
</HTML>
```

Web Page Integration

Shockwave movies should be considered an integral part of the Web page layout and design. They can be designed to merge with the page background, or stand apart from it. In either case, the placement and implementation of the movies have an impact on the user's experience. The following techniques address the seamless integration of your Shockwave movies within the Web page and browser.

Shockwave Logo

When an `<EMBED>` or `<OBJECT>` tag calls a Shockwave movie, the browser first buffers an area of the screen that is determined by the width and height settings in the tag. Unless otherwise specified in the tag, a white rectangle containing the Shockwave logo is then drawn to the screen as the plug-in is loaded. The Shockwave file then begins downloading from the server and displays the first frame of the Shockwave movie once the entire file has been dowloaded.

The default Shockwave logo that appears during a download can be a source of frustration to many Web page designers. Days, weeks, and months are often spent designing a Web site. Perhaps the designer's objective is to convey a certain mood or atmosphere with meticulous attention given to details such as color, composition, and style to create this type of controlled experience. In some cases, a metaphor is used to establish the illusion of a certain environment. This illusion is greatly hindered during Shockwave downloads by scattered white rectangles that contain the Macromedia logo. Imagine if Unysis was to display its logo every time a GIF file was downloaded. Web pages would start to look like Formula-1 race cars! Here are a few workarounds for dealing with the Macromedia logo.

Use a 1x1 Pixel Movie

One way to hide the Shockwave logo during a download is to create a very small 1x1 pixel movie that contains a simple goToNetMovie command that loads the Shockwave movie you would like to display. To set the Stage size of a Director movie, select Movie from the Modify menu and choose Properties. In the dialog box, choose Custom Stage size and set the width and height to 1 pixel. If the Stage location is set to Centered, you should see a small speck on your screen. This is your Director Stage. If you do not see anything, the Stage may be hidden by menus or windows, but it is still a fully functioning movie. The following Lingo script can be placed in the Movie Script of the tiny movie:

```
on startMovie
  goToNetMovie "myMovie.dcr"
end
```

Be sure to add a Score script that will cause the playback head to loop on a frame. A simple go to the frame script placed in the second frame of the Score will suffice.

The HTML tag for this 1x1 pixel movie should be set to the full height and width of the movie that is being loaded via the goToNetMovie command (that is, myMovie.dcr).

> **Note**
> This technique does not work with the Shockwave for Director 4 plug-in; linked movies with different Stage sizes do not load properly using the goToNetMovie command.

The intro.dcr Movie

In Shockwave for Director 5.0, the logo is actually contained within a Shockwave file named intro.dcr, which is installed in the Support folder on the user's local disk during Shockwave installation. Removing or deleting this file from the Support folder prevents the logo from appearing and does not break anything. However, removing this file is at the end user's discretion. Most people are unaware of its existence and consequently do not remove it.

The file is like any other .dcr file and is referenced by a path and a file name. You may choose to create your own small Shockwave file, name it intro.dcr, and replace the existing file in your Support folder. Your custom file is then displayed every time a Shockwave movie is loaded. Developers also could request that users install custom versions of intro.dcr. However, users then would need to manually overwrite the existing version.

Matching Page and Stage Colors

Another simple technique for facilitating the integration of a Shockwave movie into a Web page is to specify a custom background color in the <EMBED> or <OBJECT> tag using the BGCOLOR parameter (See Chapter 3, "Shockwave for Director" for more information regarding BGCOLOR). Using this parameter allows you to seamlessly match the Web page background color to the Shockwave rectangle that is displayed during a download. Unless one of the techniques described above is used, a Shockwave logo tinted or blended to match the specified color also will appear inside the rectangle.

To seamlessly match the Director Stage color to the Web page background color, you must set the Stage color in Director and write HTML to set a matching background color for the Web page. To avoid dithering in Navigator or Internet Explorer, use a solid color selected from the browser-compatible palette provided on the *Shocking the Web* CD-ROM. The following is a step-by-step explanation of the procedure:

1.   Once the custom palette has been imported into Director, choose Movie and Properties from the Modify menu. In the Properties dialog box, select the browser-compatible palette from the pop-menu and click on the color swatch to choose a color. Note this color's location in the palette for later reference.

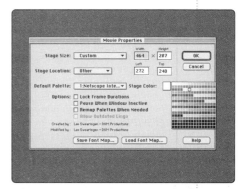

2.   In order to set the Web page background color, your HTML document must include the hexadecimal code (or hex code) for the color you have chosen. To find the hex code for the Stage color selected above, open the browser-compatible palette using Photoshop. With the Info windoid open, click your selected color swatch in the palette and record the RGB values listed. Then use a hex calculator to translate the RGB values to hex code. (A hex calculator is provided on the *Shocking the Web* CD-ROM.)

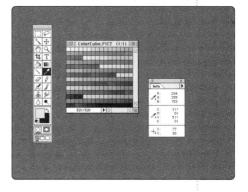

3.   The following HTML sets the Web page background color and the Shockwave <EMBED> tag parameter to match the Stage color previously set in the Director movie.

```
<HTML>
<BODY BGCOLOR="#33FFCC">
<EMBED SRC="Movies/shocker.dcr" HEIGHT=100 WIDTH=200
BGCOLOR="#33FFCC">
</HTML>
```

Shockwave in Tables

Another way to integrate the surrounding Web page artwork with a Shockwave movie is to use tables. Tables are used to layout rows and columns of cell data. Cell data typically consists of text, numbers, links, and occasionally graphics; however, a Shockwave movie also can be embedded into a table cell.

For example, a decorative picture frame graphic could be created using four separate GIF files. Using <TABLE> tags, each side of the frame could surround the Shockwave movie. Aesthetic attributes aside, this method could provide a performance benefit as well. The goToNetMovie command then could be used to load a series of Shockwave movies within the picture frame. If the picture frame had been imported into each Shockwave movie, it would have added file size and extended the load time for each individual movie in the series.

The <TABLE> tag is used to begin a table. Use the </TABLE> tag to mark the end of the table. The <tr> </tr> tag specifies a new row. The total number of <tr> tags will tell you how many rows are in the table. The <td> </td> tag is used to specify the data contained in each cell. These tags must always fall between <tr> table row tags. The total number of cells is determined by the number of <td> tags within the <tr> tags (table data within table rows).

In the following example, the picture frame artwork has been cut into four separate GIF files: top, left, right, and bottom.

The top and bottom sections cover the total width of the movie (320 pixels) in addition to the combined width of the left and right sections. The <td colspan=3> tag allows the first and last row to span the three columns sandwiched in the middle. The size of each data cell is automatically specified by the GIF images and .dcr file embedded within, so be sure to size and crop original artwork carefully. (Optionally, you can specify the height and width of each table cell.)

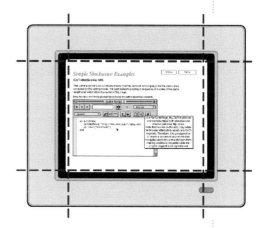

```
<table border=0 cellpadding=0 cellspacing=0>
<tr> <td colspan=3> <img border=0 src="top.gif"> </td> </tr>
<tr>
  <td> <img border=0 src="left.gif"> </td>
  <td> <EMBED SRC="shockpict.dcr" WIDTH=320 HEIGHT=240></td>
  <td> <img border=0 src="right.gif"> </td>
</tr>
<tr> <td colspan=3> <img border=0 src="bottom.gif"> </td> </tr>
</table>
```

Web Page Rollovers

Another clever trick relating to Shockwave and tables discovered by Eric Fixler, a Web multimedia developer, involves using Lingo to track the mouse location outside of the Shockwave movie area and to trigger events accordingly. The `mouseH` and `mouseV` Lingo functions indicate the horizontal and vertical position of the mouse cursor. The values returned by these functions are based on the number of pixels from the top, left of the Director Stage (0,0 is the top left coordinate of the Stage). Because Director also returns coordinates outside of the Stage area (negative values are also returned), you can use the Lingo `rollover` function to determine whether the cursor is within a specific region of a Web page, and then trigger events such as sounds or animations.

Of course, there is no way to control the user's browser settings or window placement, so you must very carefully align the Shockwave movies to the "hot areas," or use tables to ensure that the Shockwave file always remains relative to the area for which you are testing. This technique works best when using images as hot areas. If you would like to use HTML text as a hot area, be aware that HTML text is displayed at different sizes on Macintosh and Windows computers, and that the user may not be using the default browser font. Locking the text within a table will help. You then can use the `machineType` Lingo function to test for the Macintosh or Windows platform, and set the appropriate list of coordinates for the hot areas. Examples of this technique can be found at http://www.outerband.org and http://www.macromedia.com/macromedia/investors/annual96/index.html.

Covering Load Times

Hiding the fact that a file is downloading is nothing new to multimedia developers—especially CD-ROM title developers. Many of the same tricks (and a few new ones) also apply to authoring multimedia on the Web. As discussed in the bandwidth section, a Shockwave file designed for the 14.4 or 28.8 modem user should be no more than 50K, which can take 30 to 60 seconds to download. In order to provide a more pleasurable experience to the user, consider the techniques discussed below.

Now Loading

If there is no way to squeeze your Shockwave file down to the size limits you have established, consider first loading an extremely small file that informs the user that a download is taking place. This file can immediately use a `goToNetMovie` command to load the next movie. Because this "goer" file is in memory, a looping animation can play continuously as the new file is being downloaded. It is important to realize that this file can be interactive as well. Perhaps a simple game or activity could be used to disguise the download entirely. These techniques can help make long downloads less painful for the user.

Preloading

For large Shockwave movies, consider ways to break the files up into smaller chunks. By using `preloadNetThing` with `goToNetMovie` or `goToNetPage`, you can load the next file while the user interacts with the movie that has downloaded already. This works well for more-or-less linear structures such as an interactive storybook. However, with more complex branching structures, it is not easy to predict where the user will go next. This makes preloading difficult.

Buried Treasures

A simple but often effective way to cover load time is to embed a Shockwave file at the bottom of a Web page. By the time the user scrolls to the bottom, the movie may have had adequate time to load.

Interface Design

Interface design on the Web is complicated, and Shockwave adds yet another layer of complexity. There are three unique interfaces to deal with that include the browser interface, the Web site interface, and the Shockwave interface—an interface inside an interface that is inside another interface.

Most browsers provide common navigational controls that use Forward and Back buttons, a Bookmarks menu, and the Location field for entering and displaying a URL. As a user surfs the Web, a record or history of previously visited URLs is maintained and can be used to quickly navigate to any URL in the list. Other browser interface elements act as controls to open files, to print, to stop an operation, and so forth.

While Web site interfaces vary, there are common navigational structures, which include a main menu that provides access to all key areas of the site. This menu is often carried throughout all Web pages in order to allow branching from every page. It is common to see a graphical version of this menu somewhere within the upper portion of the page with a text link version at the bottom of the page. In addition, site maps that illustrate, summarize, and link to all key sections and subsections are often provided. And, of course, hypertext links are used throughout a site to connect related content both within and outside the site. Also, anchor tags can be used to link and scroll to a specific location within a page.

When designing the interface for a Shockwave project, consider the behavior, style, and function of the browser and Web site interface that will contain the Shockwave movie. In some cases, the Shockwave interface may be completely unrelated to the Web site interface. A Shockwave game is a good example. To avoid clutter and interface clashes it may help to clearly differentiate the game from the rest of the site by locating it on a separate page, or within a new browser window. Other Shockwave applications, such as tutorials or online presentations, may be designed to integrate with the rest of the Web site. In both cases, try to be consistent when possible and avoid contradictory button or icon styles and behaviors.

Using Shockwave to Enhance Web Site Interfaces

Shockwave can be used in place of HTML links and image maps to navigate through a site—and in many ways it can be more effective. A common problem with imagemaps is the lack of user feedback or status. Using Shockwave techniques, the interface enhancements discussed below are possible.

Standard Button Behavior

Shockwave buttons can highlight when clicked and remain highlighted while the mouse is down and the cursor is over the button area. If a user moves the cursor outside the button area, the button can be deselected. Director includes some standard button styles (such as radio buttons, push buttons, and checkboxes) and provides Lingo control over their properties. Custom buttons also can be created from any cast member to look and behave as you wish.

Rollovers

Rollovers can be used to highlight tightly arranged buttons or text items from a list before the user makes a selection. This reinforces the area under the cursor as "hot" or active, and often provides confirmation to the user that the selection they are about to make is correct. Rollovers also can be used to provide additional information about an icon or button selection before making the selection. MacOS Balloon Help and the Windows 95 operating system use this interface technique. Refer to Chapter 11, "Earshot SFX Case Study" for a Shockwave example that provides rollover help.

Audio Feedback

Sounds are often used to indicate right and/or wrong answers, or to act as alarms that indicate an error or illegal mouse click has taken place. A small sound also can be used to indicate that a button selection has been made.

Status Message

Use the Lingo `netStatus` command to display a text message to the user. This message appears in the lower left corner of the browser window, and can be used to reinforce user selections or display the status of background operations. (Note that this command is not currently recognized by Internet Explorer 3.0.)

Cursor Icons

Director has a built-in set of cursors that can replace the standard arrow cursor. You also can create your own artwork to be used as a custom cursor (such as the hand cursor used to identify links on the Web), or create your own animated cursors. The cursor also can be hidden within a Director movie using the `cursor 200` Lingo command.

Menus

The menu and installMenu Lingo commands can be used to create a custom menu bar containing your own custom menu options (which could include HTML links). Unfortunately, at the current time, these commands are not supported in Shockwave movies and are listed on Macromedia's Web site under "Features Not Yet Available." However, custom pop-up menus can be created in Shockwave using Lingo. See http://www.mcli.dist.maricopa.edu/director/tips/shocktip/popper.html for a step-by-step example. More sophisticated custom pop-menus also can be created using the PopMenu Xtra from g/matter, inc. Information about this Xtra can be found in the g/matter electronic catalog on the *Shocking the Web* CD-ROM. As a non-Shockwave alternative, an ActiveX control that adds pop-up menus to Web sites is available from Microsoft at http://www.microsoft.com/activex/controls.

Sliders

Custom sliders are commonly used to control sound volume or animation speed, and can be used to enhance a Web page interface. Variations of the Lingo code used to create sliders can be used to create custom scroll bars. An example file named Sliders.dir can be found on the *Shocking the Web* CD-ROM.

KeyDown Events

Lingo handlers can be used to determine whether or not a specific key was pressed by the user. Keyboard input then can be used to control a game or play sounds, for example. Refer to Director's online help, or to the Lingo Dictionary that ships with Director, for more information about related Lingo such as: the key, the keyCode, on keyDown, the keyDownScript, the keyPressed, the keyUpScript, the commandDown, the controlDown, and the optionDown.

A simple example of how to to use a Lingo handler to determine user input follows:

```
on keyDown
  if the key = RETURN then beep
end
```

The TEXTFOCUS parameter can be set in the HTML <EMBED> tag to control when a Shockwave movie will respond to keyboard input. Available options are ONSTART, ONMOUSE, and NEVER. See Chapter 3, "Shockwave for Director" for descriptions of these parameters.

Frames

Some Web sites use frames as a way to navigate through a site or quickly browse through an index that displays selections in a nearby frame. Shockwave menus can be embedded within frames to provide the type of user interface enhancements discussed above. To implement frames, you create an HTML document that uses the <FRAMESET> and <FRAME> elements to divide the browser window into rectangular frames. Next, you specify an HTML document as the source file for each frame. A Shockwave movie would be embedded within one of these HTML source files using the <EMBED> or OBJECT tag. Here's a simple HTML document that establishes two frames within the browser window. The first frame, which contains the source file ShockMenu.htm, occupies 25 percent of the window (vertically); the second frame, which contains the source file InfoPage.htm, occupies the balance of the window (designated by the asterisk):

```
<HTML>
<HEAD>
<TITLE>Frame SetUp</TITLE>
</HEAD>
<FRAMESET COLS="25%,*">
<FRAME SRC=ShockMenu.htm>
<FRAME SRC=InfoPage.htm>
</FRAMESET>
</HTML>
```

While using frames can complicate the interface by adding hierarchies of information within a single Web page, frames have attributes that make them very attractive to Shockwave developers. For example, a Shockwave movie can be downloaded into a frame as an index or site menu to content that is displayed in a nearby frame. The Shockwave index, or menu, is downloaded once and the plug-in does not need to be reloaded each time the user updates content in the nearby frame. By using a single Shockwave movie as a menu, it is easy to store global variables for highlighted states and user tracking within the same movie, rather than passing this information from one movie to another as new pages are loaded. Lastly, only the targeted frame is redrawn on your computer display. The Shockwave index movie also does not have to be refreshed when the nearby frame is targeted.

Netscape Navigator 3.0 and Internet Explorer 3.0 maintain a history for frames. If you click on a link to update a frame, subsequently pressing the browser's Back button will return you to the previous state of the frame. In browser versions prior to 3.0, this action would have returned you to the previous URL—completely ignoring the nested frame structure and history. Frame navigation must be considered when using the GoToNetPage Lingo command to target frames from within a Shockwave movie. If you wish to exit the nested frame structure from within a Shockwave movie, be sure to use the appropriate parameter when targeting a new window or frame. See Chapter 8, "Shockwave Lingo" for a listing of available target attributes.

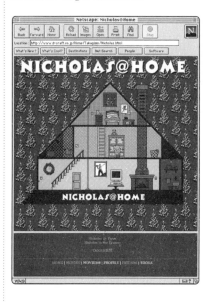

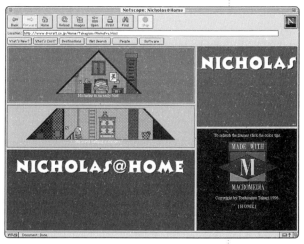

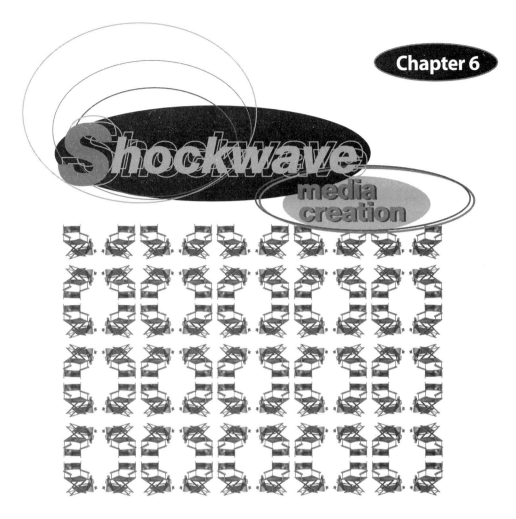

Chapter 6

Facing the Elements
Shockwave Media Creation

Prior to the popularity of CD-ROM, the floppy disk was the key distribution medium for multimedia projects. Director developers with experience squeezing compelling multimedia content onto a 1.44MB disk are well suited to Shockwave development. Many of the same tricks and techniques apply, and are even more critical when developing low bandwidth 30–100K Shockwave files. In addition to the importance of small file sizes, issues related to compression, cross-platform playback, and new technologies affect the way media elements are created for Shockwave files. This chapter will help you to squeeze the most out of various media elements in your Shockwave projects. Production tricks and techniques will ensure that you are getting the most bang for the byte.

Repurposing Media Elements

In general, all media elements in a Shockwave movie should be used efficiently. In order to determine which elements are essential, think about the key objectives and the message you are trying to communicate. Think like a minimalist—and eliminate excess media.

One of the best ways to add breadth to a Shockwave movie is to repurpose the essential media elements within the movie. When a Shockwave file downloads, all internal media elements are stored in memory or in the local disk cache. These elements then can be displayed, animated, or interacted with indefinitely. Through clever manipulation of just a few simple images, animations, and sounds, a small 30K file can engage the user for several minutes and provide a surprisingly robust experience.

Note

Remember to take advantage of the period of time during which a user engages in an activity. This time can be used to preload a new Shockwave file in order to provide a seamless transition from one movie to the next.

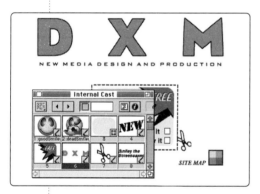

The Shockwave movie named Smiley.dir, which is located on the *Shocking the Web* CD-ROM, is a good example of repurposed media. The file contains just a few graphical elements, one animated sequence, and three small sound effects. It is under 30K. The main graphic in this movie is a small, 3D bitmap of the Smiley character.

Before playing the game, the Smiley graphic is the main graphical element within a poster that promotes the game and prompts the user to click to begin the game.

When the user clicks "try me" to begin the game, the same Smiley graphic becomes the main graphical element for the game. The object of the game is to simply click on Smiley as it moves around the screen. As the cursor rolls over Smiley, the graphic "jumps" to another random location.

If the user is quick enough to click on Smiley, the character is crushed. A second crushed and bloodied Smiley graphic appears, and a short splat sound plays. The game then returns to the poster screen.

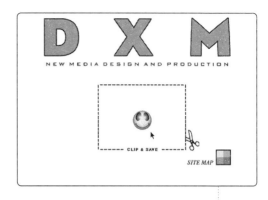

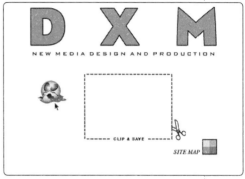

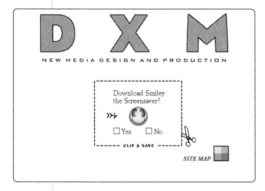

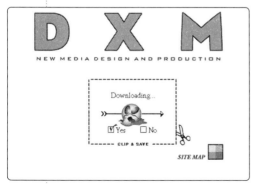

Finally, if the user clicks on the button labeled "I'll take it," the same Smiley splat sequence and sound effect play as the arrow-shaped progress bar pierces Smiley.

By reusing the same media elements in three different situations that serve three different purposes, a fairly complete interactive experience (with a beginning, middle, and end) was created within a very small file size.

The following sections provide specific techniques for manipulating each media type.

Text

There are three different types of text available in Director: rich text, fields, and bitmapped text. In a Shockwave project, there are distinct advantages for each that depend on the application. Knowing when to use the appropriate type of text can save time and file size.

Rich Text

The standard rich text format (RTF) supports spot kerning, tracking, line spacing, tabs, and indents, and files can be imported into Director from other word processing applications. Imported text documents are divided automatically into multiple cast members based on page or column breaks.

In addition to offering text formatting features, rich text can be anti-aliased in Director. Large text can be easily anti-aliased in order to smooth out edges and composite text to the background(s). Rich text is fully editable during authoring. By simply returning to the Director source file, anti-aliased text can be quickly and easily modified. However, when a projector or .dcr file is created, the text is converted to a bitmap and is no longer editable. Even though rich text appears to take up very little file size while authoring in Director, when it is converted to a bitmap it takes up a little more storage space than a typical 8-bit anti-aliased bitmap.

Some of the advantages of using rich text for Shockwave development are
as follows:

- Rich text ensures consistent cross-platform paragraph formatting
  (tabs, indents, line spacing, etc.).

- Because text is converted to bitmaps in .dcr files, it is not required that
  custom fonts be installed in the end user's system.

- Anti-aliasing rich text is more efficient than creating anti-aliased
  bitmaps. (See the following section, "Which Type of Text to Use in
  Shockwave Movies.")

- Even though rich text can be larger in file size than bitmapped text, rich
  text easily composites or anti-aliases to a variety of backgrounds, colors, and
  textures without significantly increasing file size. Creating multiple versions
  of bitmapped text that is anti-aliased over a variety of backgrounds is an
  inefficient production process, and file sizes increase dramatically.

Disadvantages of using rich text for Shockwave development:

- Rich text is not editable during playback, and Lingo control over rich text
  cast member and sprite properties is limited.

- Rich text cast members support only three inks effects: Copy, Background
  Transparent, and Blend. Set these inks in the Score or through Lingo by
  using the ink of sprite sprite property.

- Rich text file sizes are larger than field text and in some cases larger than
  bitmapped text. (See the following section, "Which Type of Text to Use
  in Shockwave Movies.")

Fields

Field text takes the least amount of space and is editable in Shockwave. These attributes make field text very useful. To create field text, use the Field tool on the Tool Palette or choose Insert, Control, Field from the Director menu.

Advantages of using fields for Shockwave development:

- Fields use much less storage space than any other type of text.

- There is robust Lingo control for manipulating text in fields. It is possible to manipulate field properties such as the text of member, alignment of member, font of member, and lineHeight of member. Using Lingo adds nothing to file size. (See the example file named textChanger.dir on the *Shocking the Web* CD-ROM.)

- Unlike rich text cast members, fields can be specified as editable. This enables users to enter or edit text in fields, and can be used to create forms.

Some of the disadvantages of using fields for Shockwave development:

- Text in fields requires that system fonts be installed on all playback computers. To be sure that your text will appear as intended, use standard system fonts. Windows system fonts include Arial, Courier New, Symbol, Times New Roman, and Wingdings. MacOS system fonts include Chicago, Courier, Geneva, Helvetica, Monaco, New York, Palatino, Symbol, and Times. Director automatically substitutes missing fonts with a standard system font. Also, standard Windows system fonts are substituted automatically with a similar Macintosh system font during playback on a Macintosh—and vice versa.

- Paragraph formatting is not supported in fields.

- Fields animate slower than bitmapped or rich text.

Bitmapped Text

Bitmapped text can be created in a variety of ways. Illustration software and image processing software is used to create text effects and anti-aliased text. In Director, fields and rich text are easily converted to bitmaps by selecting the text member in the Cast window and choosing Modify and Convert to Bitmap from the Director menu.

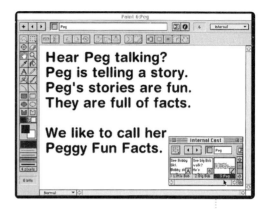

Advantage of using bitmapped text for Shockwave development:

- Dramatic text effects can be applied using image processing software or Photoshop filters. This is not possible using other Director text types.

Some disadvantages of using bitmapped text for Shockwave development:

- Bitmapped text is not editable during playback and, unlike rich text, is not easily editable during authoring.

- Bitmapped text files are larger than rich text or fields.

Which Type of Text to Use in Shockwave Movies

If file size is the overwhelming priority for a particular project, and you are willing to sacrifice graphic quality, then use only field text in a system font to achieve the smallest file sizes possible.

If you are not using field text, then it is safe to make one assumption: As a Shockwave developer, you will probably want to use anti-aliased text for any font size over 12 points to achieve a high level of graphic quality. This means that you have the choice of using bitmapped or rich text for these larger point sizes. For Shockwave movies, we recommend using rich text in this scenario (unless you want distorted text that, in effect, becomes a graphic image).

The best solution, in order to achieve an effective tradeoff between quality and efficiency, is to use rich text for text that requires anti-aliasing, and field text in a system font for body text—that is, text that is 12 points or smaller. Both of these text formats are editable during authoring. In addition, for text that is 12 points or smaller, the jaggies associated with field text are not noticeable. An added advantage is that you can use Lingo to manipulate field text properties and the text can be editable at runtime.

If a custom font must be used for body text, then convert the body text to a 1-bit bitmap. However, remember that you cannot use Lingo field properties once you convert the field text to a bitmap. One caveat is that bitmapped body text cannot be set to scroll. If you require a custom font in a scrolling window, build a custom scroll bar using Lingo, or use rich text with the scrolling option selected.

Scaleable Fonts

Another method for creating low bandwidth text effects can be found in an experimental Shockwave file named scaleable.dir on the *Shocking the Web* CD-ROM.

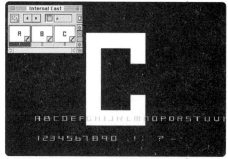

In this example, a tiny 1-bit, bitmapped alphabet was created pixel by pixel. The .dcr file containing the entire alphabet, numbers, and punctuation marks is only 5K. By grouping letters together, words are created and any of the 256 colors in the palette can be applied to the text. Each letter was created without using diagonal lines. This allows the text to be scaled and distorted without requiring anti-aliasing.

Taking the process a step further, Fontographer was used to create a scaleable TrueType font from the artwork. DXM used this font within Director for the opening sequence of a Shockwave movie that was created for the Informix, Inc. 1996 User Conference Web site.

Printing

The printFrom Lingo command is disabled for Shockwave movie development (see Chapter 8, "Shockwave Lingo" for a complete list of disabled Lingo commands) and—unlike HTML text—Shockwave text cannot be copied from a Web page within a Web browser. Currently, the only option for printing from a Shockwave movie is to use an Xtra, such as the PrintOMatic Xtra from g/matter, inc. The *Shocking the Web* CD-ROM includes a demo version of the PrintOMatic Xtra.

Color Palettes

Full-color (or true-color) images in RGB format contain 8 bits of information for each of the red, green, and blue values of a single pixel (8+8+8=24 bit). A 24-bit image can include over 16.7 million color variations. An 8-bit image, on the other hand, contains only 256 color variations, and each pixel is "indexed" to a palette color using a color lookup table (or CLUT).

Most Director developers have become accustomed to creating graphics and animation using 8-bit color palettes. This is because the majority of end users have Windows and Macintosh computers capable of displaying no more than 256 colors (8-bit). Graphics and animations in 8-bit color also take less storage space, load quicker, and run much faster than higher resolution images. For the same reasons, images in Shockwave movies are indexed to 8-bit (or lower) palettes.

In order to create cross-platform, cross-browser Shockwave movies, it is important to use the appropriate 8-bit palette for media creation. A browser-safe palette is typically used. The browser-safe palette is compatible with the Windows and MacOS, and with the Navigator and Internet Explorer browsers.

The Browser-Safe Palette

On a Macintosh computer that is set to display 8-bit, 256 colors, the Netscape browser displays all 256 colors without dithering. On a Windows system, 40 colors are used by the Windows system, other programs, and the desktop. This leaves only 216 colors for the browser.

Netscape developed a 6-bit color cube to draw 216 colors. The 6-bit color cube is supported by most browsers, including Microsoft Internet Explorer. It is the recommended palette for Shockwave use. The colors in the 6-bit color cube are essentially the first 215 colors, plus black in position 255, of the Macintosh system palette. By using these colors in your Director movies, you ensure that colors will not dither and that they will display properly in the browser on both Macintosh and Windows playback platforms.

Director 5 ships with the Netscape color cube palette. It is stored in an external Cast inside the Xtras folder for your convenience during authoring. On a Windows computer, select Palettes from the Xtras menu. Under the MacOS, select Palette.cst from the Xtras menu. This opens an external Cast that contains a palette named Netscape. Copy and paste this palette from the external Cast into your movie's internal Cast and use it as your Shockwave palette. If you are repurposing Director files and have images that are already indexed to the Macintosh or Windows palettes, select Transform Bitmap from the Modify menu to remap the artwork to this color cube. Because these palettes share many of the same colors, remapping usually works well.

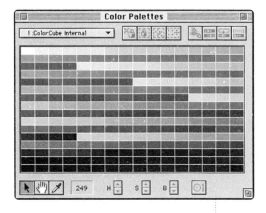

Custom palettes can be used in Shockwave movies, but are not recommended. By setting the PALETTE parameter in the <EMBED> tag equal to FOREGROUND, Director's current palette becomes the active palette for the entire screen. However, if system colors are not preserved in the custom palette, the browser window and desktop colors will remap incorrectly and may cause undesirable effects. Also, Internet Explorer does not support custom palettes or the use of the PALETTE parameter in the <EMBED> tag. So, designating a custom palette in Director is rarely useful.

Note

If you look closely, the Netscape palette within Director is slightly different from other browser-safe palettes you may have seen. It includes the same 216 colors used by the Netscape color cube, with the additional 40 entries set to near-black. Only the last position is true black. This ensures that artwork indexed inside Director will always map to the black in this last palette position. This is important when working with inks and color cycling.

The palette files listed below are included on the *Shocking the Web* CD-ROM for your convenience. The ColorCube palette is identical to the Netscape palette, but is renamed to be less browser-specific. More information regarding ways to use these files is included in the "Graphics" section of this chapter:

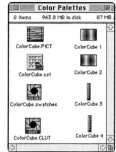

- ColorCube.PICT—This is a PICT file version of the color cube. It can be used to make color selections within various programs, such as FreeHand, PhotoShop, and xRes.

- ColorCube.cst—This is an external Cast file for Director that can be added to your Xtras folder and used during authoring. It is the same as the Netscape palette provided in the Xtras folder with Director 5.

- ColorCube.CLUT—This color lookup table can be used in Photoshop when indexing RGB files to an 8-bit palette.

- ColorCube.swatches—This file can be loaded into the Swatches Palette window in Photoshop and used to make color selections.

Graphics

The graphics in a Director movie can be created using the Paint window or Tool Palette, or they can be imported directly into the Cast, or linked as external files. Graphics created in the Paint window are bitmaps. The Tool Palette creates simple shape members, which are vector graphics that can be colored, filled with patterns, and resized. For importing graphics, Director supports the PICT and BMP (bitmap) file formats. Files of either format can be imported at their original color depth or at the color depth of the monitor. To import linked, external files into a Director Cast, select the Linked checkbox in the Import dialog box when importing a PICT or BMP file. In this case, Director saves only the link to the external graphic as part of the movie.

> **Note**
>
> *Graphix Importer Xtras links other graphics file formats to a Director movie. Using QuickTime 2.5, Graphix Importer enables the importing of Photoshop, GIF, JPEG, MacPaint, and SGI image files via Lingo, and dithers them to the current active palette. The GIF Xtra can dynamically load GIF images into a Shockwave movie's Cast at runtime. A downloadable version of this Xtra is available at http://www.ddce.cqu.edu.au/imu/tools/director/xtras/*

Graphics are usually embedded in Shockwave files—they are not linked. This keeps .dcr files self-contained without requiring the user to install external media into the local Shockwave Support folder. However, keep in mind that you can develop more dynamic Shockwave applications using linked media.

In order to optimize file size and get the highest compression ratios for your Shockwave graphics, consider the following Director features and techniques.

Color Depth

Reducing color depth (or bit depth) of bitmaps in Director files is common practice for multimedia developers. Typically, presentations and CD-ROM titles contain bitmapped graphics that are dithered and indexed to an 8-bit color palette for improved performance and platform compatibility.

Determine the file size of a bitmapped graphic (in total bits) by multiplying height by width (in pixels) by bit depth. Eight bits equal one byte, so divide the total bits by eight to determine total bytes ((HxWxBit Depth)/8 = number of bytes). Just one small image bitmap that is 100x100 pixels with a 24-bit color depth consumes 30K of memory (100x100x24)/8 = 30,000 bytes). The same image indexed to an 8-bit palette is only 10K (100x100x8)/8 = 10,000 bytes).

Reducing color depth also greatly reduces file size and improves performance of Shockwave movies. However, in order to get the most out of Afterburner compression, there are specific indexing techniques to consider.

Afterburner compresses bitmaps using a lossless (without degradation) technique. Depending on the contents of the original bitmap, Afterburner compression can range from about 60–90%. In order to get maximum bitmap compression, avoid dithering when possible. Graphics with flat, solid areas of color or repetitive patterns compress well in Afterburner. Additionally, using fewer colors translates to better compression. If you are including complex bitmaps that contain a wide variety of colors, such as photographic images, dithering will be necessary.

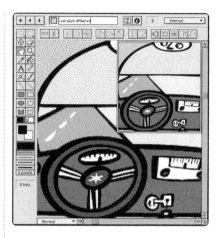 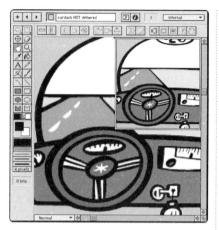

Here are two sample files for comparison. The image on the left is dithered; the image on the right is not.

Tools Used to Reduce Color Depth

It is always best to edit and process images in RGB mode at the highest possible resolutions. Before reducing color depth, save all original high-resolution files as further editing may be required.

Graphics can be indexed using image processing software such as Photoshop, xRes, and DeBabelizer, or they can be indexed by Director. The resulting quality of the indexing and dithering from each software tool varies—depending on the source files used.

Differences in the dithering quality of Director—compared to the quality of Photoshop or DeBabelizer, are often insignificant. Photoshop is slightly better than Director at standard 8-bit dithering, but Director is better at dithering dark colors—especially gray-colored gradients. Photoshop often causes banding in 8-bit gradients, while Director's gradients tend to be very smooth.

When dithering is not required, Director seems to be slightly better than Photoshop at indexing, but the results are very similar. Because non-dithered bitmaps compress better in Shockwave, non-dithering is the preferred indexing technique for reducing file size.

Which indexing method should you use? It can be fast and efficient to index images within Director if the quality is acceptable. Simply create and save a high-resolution version of an image using an image processing tool, and index the image during import into Director by choosing settings in the Image Options dialog box.

Indexing results vary depending on the graphic style of the original high-resolution image. If you do not achieve the desired indexing result for a particular graphic using Director, try using image processing software like DeBabelizer, Photoshop, or xRes. For a large sequence of images, consider using DeBabelizer for batch conversions. (DeBabelizer Lite, which does not support batch conversion, is included on the *Shocking the Web* CD-ROM.)

The following procedures outline dithering and non-dithering options for reducing color depth.

Non-dithered Indexing to 8-Bit, 256 Colors

Non-dithered indexing works well when applied to images with graphic styles such as comic book illustrations, mosaics, geometric patterns, and posterized images. The following procedure demonstrates a non-dithering technique.

1.   If original artwork is created in a vector-based program such as FreeHand, try to use the Shockwave palette colors from the start. (If you are not using a vector-based drawing program, skip to Step 7.)

2.   To add colors from the Shockwave palette to a vector-based illustration, choose File, Open from the FreeHand menu, and import the PICT image of the Shockwave palette named Shockwave.PICT (available on the *Shocking the Web* CD-ROM).

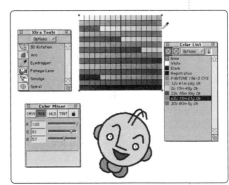

3.   Choose Window, Other, Xtra Tools from the FreeHand menu and select the Color Picker tool from the Xtra Tools window.

4.   Use the Eyedropper tool to select swatches of color from the Shockwave palette and simply drag them into the Color List window. Then use the colors in the Color List window to fill areas of your illustration.

Note
The Color Mixer window in FreeHand also displays detailed information regarding the CMYK and RGB values. These values can be applied to a hex calculator to obtain hexadecimal equivalents if necessary.

Using only browser-compatible colors ensures that dithering is not required when the image is later converted to an indexed bitmap. Adding color to the vector art is preferable to adjusting colors after rasterization. This results in very clean lines, smooth anti-aliased edges, and solid areas of color for better compression. For optimal compression, avoid using gradients. When you are satisified with your color selections, save the FreeHand file.

5. Now we are going to rasterize the illustration in Photoshop. Choose Export from the FreeHand File menu, and select the Illustrator 5.5 format from the Format pop-up menu. Save the file.

6. Open the file in Photoshop. When the Rasterize dialog box appears, you normally can use the default settings. Make sure the anti-aliased setting is selected and that the dots per inch (dpi) setting is 72. The default dimensions are fine unless you want to enlarge the image; if so, increase the dimensions before rasterizing.

7. Complete any image processing in Photoshop that is needed (in RGB mode); adjust the size of the image, add layers if needed, apply filters, and so forth.

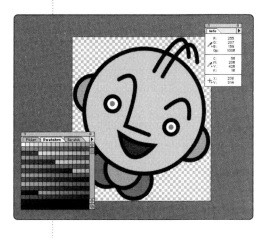

8. If it is necessary to apply color to the image again, only browser-compatible colors should be used. Choose Window, Palettes, Show Swatches, and select the Swatches tab in the Palette windoid. From the pulldown menu, select Load Swatches. Load the PICT image of the Shockwave palette named Shockwave.PICT, which can be found on the *Shocking the Web* CD-ROM. When you have finished editing the image, save the Photoshop file as a high-resolution PICT image.

Note
Choose Window, Palettes, Show Info to display detailed information regarding CMYK and RGB color values. These values can be applied to a hex calculator to obtain hexadecimal equivalents if necessary.

9. Launch Director. If you have not already copied the Netscape color cube palette from the external cast that ships with Director, select Palettes.cst from the Xtras menu. Copy and Paste the Netscape palette from the external cast to the internal cast.

The ColorCube.cst external cast file on the *Shocking the Web* CD-ROM is the same as the Netscape palette mentioned above. If you do not have the Macromedia external palette cast, simply add ColorCube.cst to the Director Xtras folder.

10. Open the Score window and double-click the Palette channel in the first frame. Choose the Shockwave palette from the pop-up menu. This is now the active movie palette.

11. Set your display to 256 colors and select Import from the File menu. When the Image Options dialog box appears, set Color Depth to 8-bit and choose the Remap palette option. From the pop-up Palette menu, select the Shockwave palette. Make sure that the Dither option is deselected, and then click OK. If you have used only the Shockwave palette colors without gradients or drop shadows, the image will map perfectly to the Shockwave palette in Director and the file will compress well using Afterburner.

See Chapter 15, "DXM Productions Case Study," for more information on color related issues.

Note
A timesaving technique is to use the Clipboard to copy artwork directly from Photoshop and to paste it into a Director cast member. Indexing can be accomplished before or after the image is pasted into Director.

Dithered Indexing to 8-Bit, 256 Colors

If the quality of non-dithered artwork is unacceptable, it may be necessary to use dithering. Generally, dithering is required in order to achieve adequate results for photographic images, gradients, 3D artwork, and images with drop shadows. As mentioned above, dark-colored gradients dither well in Director; but in most situations, Photoshop's dithering provides slightly better quality. The following procedure demonstrates a dithering technique using Photoshop.

1. Create or open a high-resolution image in Photoshop. Manipulate the image in RGB mode and save a high-resolution version when you have finished.

2. Select Indexed Color from the Mode menu. Choose the Custom… Palette option and the Diffusion Dither setting. Click OK.

3.   When the Color Table dialog box appears, choose Load and open the Shockwave.CLUT file on the *Shocking the Web* CD-ROM to dither the file to the Shockwave palette.

4.   Save the file in PICT format and import it into Director. Set your display to 256 colors and choose Import from the File menu in Director. When the Image Options dialog box appears, set the Color Depth to 8-bit and choose the Import palette option to import the Shockwave palette with the image.

67.2K

54.1K

41.6K

To improve compression of dithered images, consider ways to simplify the image stylistically. For example, Photoshop filters can be applied to photographic images in order to reduce complexity, create flat areas of color or patterns, and reduce the total number of colors used. The images at left show size reduction of Afterburner files as a result of image simplification.

Bitstripping

Reducing the total number of colors in an image (or bitstripping) also increases compression ratios. Depending on the image, acceptable quality may be achieved using very few colors. For example, the art used in the non-dithered example above can be indexed to a 4-bit adaptive palette (16 colors) for additional savings. If images are indexed to a 4-bit palette, it is still a good idea to convert them back to the 8-bit Shockwave palette. A 16-color adaptive palette may contain colors that are not in the Shockwave palette—and these colors will be remapped by the browser. Also, because Director remaps 4-bit images when they are played back on an 8-bit display, performance is negatively affected. Animated 1-bit and 4-bit sequences play faster if they are reconverted to an 8-bit palette.

Reducing Color Depth to 1-Bit

To achieve maximum compression, images can be downsampled to 1-bit color. Of course, 1-bit images are black and white and cannot have smooth anti-aliased lines or edges—but through a combination of techniques, a 1-bit image or animation can appear to be very complex and colorful.

Dithering is usually required to achieve adequate 1-bit quality. Photoshop and DeBabelizer yield better 1-bit dithering results than Director. Before reducing an image to 1-bit, we recommend that you use filters for different dithering effects and adjust contrast levels.

1.   In Photoshop, select Grayscale from the Mode menu, and apply filters if desired. (The next section, "Using Filters for 1-Bit Special Effects," introduces Andromeda's Series 3 Filters, which are excellent filters for creating unique 1-bit dithering effects.)

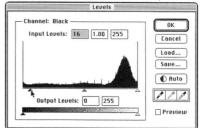

2.   Select Adjust, Levels from the Image menu to adjust the contrast. The Levels dialog box displays a histogram of the image that plots the brightness values and the number of pixels at each level. The darkest pixels appear at the left of the histogram; the brightest pixels appear at the right. To reduce the contrast in the image use the Output Levels slider controls at the bottom of the Levels dialog box. To increase the contrast use the Input Levels slider controls directly below the histogram.

The amount of contrast effects dithering results. Dithered, low-contrast images appear flat and less defined, with an even disbursement of black and white pixels. Dithered, high-contrast images are more defined, with black pixels concentrated in dark areas and shadows, and white pixels concentrated in light, highlighted areas.

3.   Select Bitmap from the Mode menu, and choose a method in the dialog box to convert the image to 1-bit. The Diffusion Dither method usually produces the best results.

4.   Import into Director. Click the cast member Info button to confirm that the color depth is 1-bit. If it is not, select the artwork in the Cast window (use the Shift and Command keys to make multiple selections). Choose Transform Bitmap from the Modify menu, and select 1-bit from the Color Depth pop-up menu. Click OK.

5.   The foreground and background colors of a 1-bit cast member can be set to any of the active palette colors by selecting a bitmap sprite on the Stage or in the Score and choosing a color chip on the Tool Palette. Lingo sprite properties (the foreColor and the backColor) also can be used to set colors. Inks also can be applied in the Score or by using the ink of sprite Lingo property for a variety of effects.

Combining foreground color, background color, and matte ink allows you to create a complex, low resolution, 1-bit graphic. The foreground color is used to define the image, and the background color fills enclosed areas. In the image to the left, the drop shadow is not filled with the background color because there are no enclosed areas and matte ink was applied. The dolphin.dir animation by Erik Bryan on the *Shocking the Web* CD-ROM also uses this technique.

Using Filters for 1-Bit Special Effects

The Andromeda Series 3 filters can be used to create a variety of unique dithering effects that resemble mezzotints, etchings, and engravings. The following examples show the results of some of the available filter settings. A demo version of Andromeda Series 3 filters is included on the *Shocking the Web* CD-ROM.

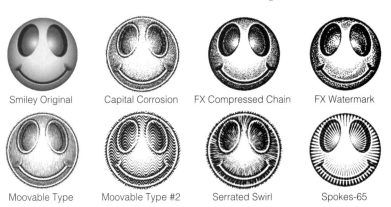

| Smiley Original | Capital Corrosion | FX Compressed Chain | FX Watermark |
| Moovable Type | Moovable Type #2 | Serrated Swirl | Spokes-65 |

Note

Photoshop filters (or plug-ins) can be used inside Director during authoring by simply placing the filters in the Xtras folder inside the Director application folder. Additionally, you can use the same filters in all other Macromedia applications by placing them in the Macromedia folder inside the Windows System folder or in the Macintosh System Folder. Apply filters to a selected area of a specific cast member or to the entire member. They also can be applied to multiple selected cast members simultaneously. Not all filters work—so test them first and, as in Photoshop, apply filters to high resolution bitmapped images for best results.

Ink Effects

Use ink effects in Shockwave movies to modify the appearance of cast members without increasing file size. There are 18 different ink effects in Director that can be applied to sprites in the Score, or by using the ink of sprite Lingo sprite property.

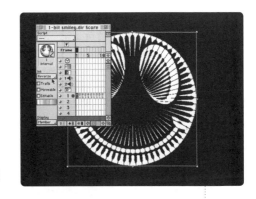

The following techniques identify practical uses for inks in Shockwave movies. In general, you should experiment with ink modes. Before creating a new cast member, consider applying an ink effect to an existing cast member in order to save space.

- Use ink effects as highlight states for bitmapped buttons (rather than creating new cast members). Results vary depending on the style of artwork; however, Reverse, Lightest, and Darkest inks tend to work well as highlight states. Bitmaps also can be set to highlight automatically—without Lingo scripting—by selecting the Highlight When Clicked checkbox in the cast member properties dialog box.

- Use a series of frames in the Score or a simple Lingo handler to cycle through ink effects for an interesting montage or strobing effect. In addition, apply quick transitions between inks to add an animated effect.

- Using Darkest ink can create an interesting transparency effect. The Smiley.dir movie on the *Shocking the Web* CD-ROM uses this technique. (The logo is set to Darkest ink and a graphic animates *underneath* the logo.)

- Blend ink can be used to create a true dissolve effect. By choosing In-Between Special from the Modify menu, apply a range of blend values to a sequence in the Score. This ink effect can be slow, so it should be applied only to small areas on the Stage. See the movies provided in the ShockingNovel folder on the *Shocking the Web* CD-ROM.

Note

Using the Trails sprite option (which is not considered an ink in Director) is another way to create a variety of effects without requiring multiple cast members. Turning on the trails option in the Score window, or setting the trails of sprite Lingo property to TRUE, causes a sprite to leave a trail of images along its path as a movie plays.

Shapes, Lines, Patterns, and Buttons

In addition to creating text and fields, the Tool Palette can be used to create simple rectangular and oval shapes, lines with varying widths, colorful patterns, and standard buttons. A shape cast member is similar to a vector object found in

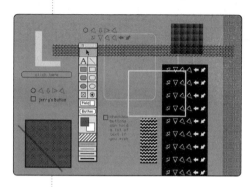

drawing programs. The advantage of using shape cast members in Shockwave movies is that they take up very little storage space. In fact, regardless of size and shape, they are only 64 bytes per cast member. Patterns, inks, and foreground and background colors can be applied without increasing file size. Consider using shape cast members rather than bitmaps whenever possible.

Button Options

The button tools on the Tool Palette are usually overlooked, but are great shortcuts for creating simple buttons that are only about 240 bytes (including highlight states). If handled with care, they also can be aesthetically pleasing. These built-in buttons (which include pushbuttons, radio buttons, and checkboxes) behave like standard buttons, with highlight states that toggle. Foreground and background colors can be set, and Background Transparent, Ghost, and Reverse inks create interesting results. Button text has the same properties as field text; the font, the fontStyle, and the fontSize Lingo properties can be used to change button text. However—like fonts used for field text—button fonts must be installed on the end user's system in order to display correctly. The checkBoxType property can be used to select from three different styles of checkboxes.

The default checkBoxType setting is 0. Because the checkBoxType setting is a movie property, its setting globally affects all checkboxes. The following examples show the results of setting this property:

```
set the checkBoxType to 0
```
⊠ checkBoxType 0

```
set the checkBoxType to 1
```
■ checkBoxType 1

```
set the checkBoxType to 2
```
■ checkBoxType 2

Use Lingo to monitor button member states and to control how they respond to user input. The hilite of member property is set to TRUE if a checkbox is selected; otherwise it is FALSE. The following script tests whether a checkbox button is selected. If so, the button text style is set to bold.

```
on mouseup
  if the hilite of member "CheckBoxButton"= TRUE then
    set the fontStyle of member "CheckBoxButton" to "bold"
  else
    set the fontStyle of member "CheckBoxButton" to "plain"
  end if
end
```

Shape Cast Member Lingo Properties

In addition to Lingo sprite properties such as forecolor, backcolor, ink, and trails, there are specific cast member properties that can be controlled to create dynamic, interactive Shockwave effects for simple, 64-byte shape cast members.

the filled of member

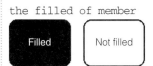

This shape cast member property indicates whether the enclosed area of a shape is filled. It can be tested and set.

Example:
```
if the filled of member "shapeCast" = FALSE then ¬
set the filled of member "shapeCast" = TRUE
```

the lineSize of member

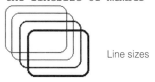

Line sizes

This shape cast member property determines the pixel thickness of the border of a shape cast member. It can be tested and set to a thickness of 0 to 5. Lingo also includes a sprite property called the lineSize of sprite, which has one undocumented benefit: it allows pixel thickness to range from 0 to 14, and it performs better than the cast member property. To set a sprite property using Lingo, first puppet the sprite. See the lineSize of sprite property in your Lingo dictionary.

Example:

```
if the lineSize of member "shapeCast" = 0 then ¬
set the lineSize of member "shapeCast" = 2
```

`the pattern of member`

Patterns and tiles

This shape cast member property determines the pattern associated with a cast member. Possible values correspond to the 64 pattern variations found in the Tool Palette's pattern chips. The 0 setting is solid (no pattern), 1 through 56 are the remaining patterns, and 57 through 64 are 8-bit tiles. This property can be tested and set.

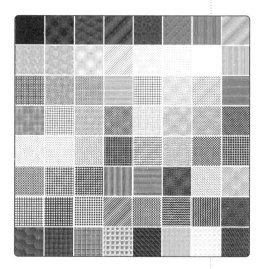

Note

Use this property to animate through a sequence of patterns. Create custom tiles from existing cast members in order to animate through a sequence of up to eight custom tiles. (See "Tiles and Animated Tiles" below.)

Example:

```
if the pattern of member "shapeCast"= 12 then ¬
set the pattern of member "shapeCast" = 64
```

`the shapeType of member`

Types of shapes

This shape cast member property determines a shape's type. The four types are #rect, #roundRect, #oval, and #line.

Example:

```
if the shapeType of member "shapeCast" = #oval then ¬
set the shapeType of member "shapeCast" = #rect
```

See the Wallpaper.dir and ToolPalette.dir movies on the *Shocking the Web* CD-ROM for examples that control shape member properties.

Note
Setting the stage color *property is a way to add color to the entire Stage without adding file size. This movie property is set using Lingo, or by choosing Movie, Properties from the Modify menu. See Chapter 5, "Designing for Shockwave," for information about matching Web page and Stage colors.*

Tiles and Animated Tiles

In the bottom row of the pop-up Pattern window, there are eight default tiles. Up to eight custom tiles can be created from existing cast members without adding file size to a Shockwave movie. Tiled cast members, like all shape cast members, can be set to any size on Stage—and they remain only 64 bytes.

Creating Custom Tiles from Existing Cast Member

Any cast member in a Shockwave movie can be made into a variety of tiled backgrounds. Here's the procedure for creating a custom tile:

1. Click the Pattern chip on the Tool Palette and choose Tile Settings from the bottom of the pop-up Pattern window. Select the built-in tile chip that you would like to replace.

2. Select the Cast Member radio button and use the forward and reverse arrows to choose the cast member from which you want to create a tile.

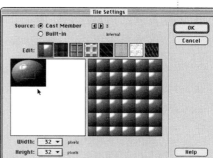

Note
Tiles can be made only from cast members with color depths greater than 1-bit.

3. Choose the tile size using the Width and Height pop-up menus. The rectangular selection marquee will adjust accordingly, and can be dragged over different areas of the cast member. When you see the pattern you like in the right window, click OK.

4. The tile now displays in the bottom row of the pattern window and can be used just like any other pattern or tile.

Note
The current foreground and background colors have no effect on the color of tiles, but inks can be applied.

It is possible to create a sequence of up to eight custom tiles. The tiles then can be animated using the Score, or through Lingo using the pattern of member property. The procedure is the same as those used in Steps 1 through 4 above to create custom tiles from an existing cast member with one exception: in Step 1, before creating a new tile, be sure that you select the next tile chip from the Edit category, or you will overwrite the current tile.

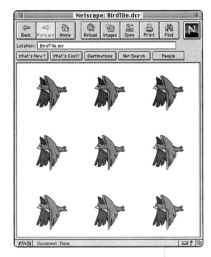

Note

Registering animated tiles is difficult. In the Tiles Settings dialog box, the cast members are aligned to the upper left coordinate, and registration points are ignored. Therefore, it may be necessary to add a bounding box, or a registration pixel to each cast member, which acts as a common registration point for all members in the sequence. By using a color that does not appear within the images, you can set the background color chip on the Tool Palette to this color, and then apply Background Transparent ink to hide the bounding box or pixel.

Creating Seamless Custom Tiles

Photoshop, xRes, and Painter can be used to create seamless tiles. However, the ultimate seamless tilemaker is the Terrazzo filter from Xaos Tools. The patterns you can create with Terrazzo are based on 17 symmetries, which are named after American patchwork quilt patterns: Gold Brick, Pinwheel, Primrose Path, Turnstile, and so forth.

Each Terrazzo-generated pattern is made from a motif, which is the shape that builds a tile when a symmetry is applied to it. The tile, in turn, repeats to build a regular pattern. It may be helpful for you to think of a motif as a type of selection marquee. The area that is enclosed by the motif is the foundation for the tile.

A tile created using Terrazzo can be saved and imported into Director as a bitmapped cast member. The procedures described above then can be used to create custom tiles in Director. When creating a tile using Terrazzo, it is important to use the dimensions supported by Director in the Tile Settings dialog box (widths and heights of 16, 32, 64, and 128 only).

Unfortunately, Terrazzo version 1.0 does not provide numeric control of the marquee, so you will have to click and drag the marquee to change the size of the motif—and it is not always possible to create tiles using the Director dimensions. In this case, you can create a large tile and resize it to the closest Director tile dimensions; however, the quality of the results will vary. (See the Terrazzo.dir example file on the *Shocking the Web* CD-ROM.)

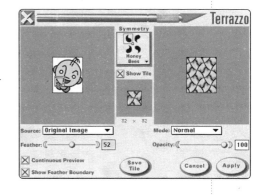

Note

The Terrazzo filter works with any application that supports Adobe Photoshop plug-ins. Such applications are known as "host applications" and include Macromedia Director 5.0, xRes 2.0, Freehand 5.5, and DeBabelizer 1.6.5, among others. Installation instructions for using Terrazzo inside Director 5.0 are included in the Terrazzo Demo Read Me file on the Shocking the Web *CD-ROM.*

For more information regarding Web graphic techniques for static images, visit the Web Graphics sites that are listed in the Bookmarks file on the *Shocking the Web* CD-ROM.

Animation

The Director software application has evolved over the years from a desktop animation tool to a full-featured multimedia authoring tool. The program's animation roots are deep, and Director's strengths as an animation tool are now available for creating and manipulating 2D and 3D Web graphics via Shockwave. In order to create low-bandwidth Shockwave animations, consider the following techniques.

Animated Shapes & Patterns

Animated sequences of shapes, patterns, lines, and custom tiles can be created in the Score, or by controlling Lingo properties covered in the previous "Graphics" section. A shape cast member is 64 bytes regardless of it's size, shape, pattern, or color. It is possible to create elaborate, low-bandwidth Shockwave animation by animating a single shape cast member.

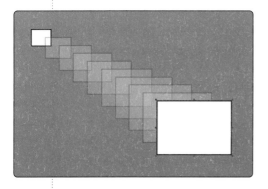

Create or select an existing shape cast member in the Cast window, and click the Info button (or type command-I) to open the Properties dialog box, which displays the size of the member. Although the shape cast member is 64 bytes, a small amount of data is required to define other attributes, such as Cast properties and Score data. In a simple test, we scaled and repositioned a shape cast member across several frames in the Score and found that this added about 6 bytes of data per frame to a Shockwave file that was processed using Afterburner. Even though this is a very small amount of data, a 100-frame animation would add 1 kilobyte per cast member to total file size.

Shape cast member animations can be created quickly in the Score using In Between and In Between Special techniques. In Between Special can be used to transform a shape based on position, size, foreground color, background color, and blend values.

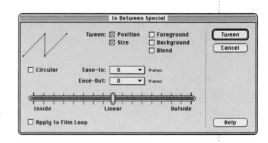

To use In Between Special, create a shape cast member using the Tool Palette. Open the Score and copy the sprite cell; paste it into frame 10 in the same channel. Resize, change the position, and select another foreground color for the sprite in frame 10. Select both sprites and all frames in between the selected sprites. Choose In Between Special from the Modify menu, and select the position, size, and foreground checkboxes in the dialog box. Click Tween. Director automatically calculates the in-between frames and, based on the Tween settings, transforms the sprite in each frame incrementally. For more about In Between Special, see the Using Director manual that ships with Director. Applying blends to the in-between frames of an animation can be used for an interesting transition effect.

Transforming the size and location of a sprite is easy using the Score (as described above). In addition, Lingo can be used to control sprite and member properties in situations when more control is desired.

Here is a script for a button that consists of a small group of shape cast members. While the mouse button is pressed, the movie cycles randomly through a list of forecolor values.

```
on mouseDown
  set colorcycle = list(156,76,19,96)
  set spriteList = list(40,41,42,43)

  repeat while the mouseDown
    set the forecolor of sprite ¬
      (getAt(spriteList,random(4))) to ¬
      (getAt(colorcycle,random(4)))
    updatestage
  end repeat
end

on mouseUp
  go frame "SiteMap"
end
```

Simulated Motion

Obviously, the more cast members that are used in an animated sequence, the larger a Shockwave file becomes. In film and video, 24 to 30 frames per second are often used to generate smooth animation. In order to ensure that animations for CD-ROM titles run smoothly on end-user machines, developers typically design for 10 to 12 frames per second. Ideally, Shockwave developers should optimally try to create 2 to 3 frames per *animation*. Of course, there are exceptions. Limiting the animated areas of the Stage, converting artwork to 1-bit, and using preloading to cache sequences helps and may allow you to add more animation frames. But, in general, avoid unnecessary artwork when you can.

Two-frame animations are ideal. Many events occur faster than the eye's ability to detect them. For example, the blink of an eye could be represented by a single cast member for the open eye, and one additional cast member for the closed eye. The same open-eye cast member is reused to end the sequence. Other example animations that could be represented in two frames include a gunshot, a light switch, a firecracker, a mousetrap, a blinking stoplight, etc. Simple animations like this are often loopable or repeatable, and can be extremely effective when short sound effects are added.

Another good way to fake an animated sequence is to use the Photoshop motion blur filter. For example, a typical rotating 3D logo can animate smoothly using as few as 10 frames—but this requires a lot of storage space. To create a two-frame version, use the first frame to start and end the sequence. Select an in-between frame (7 or 8) and apply a motion blur in the same direction as the rotation. If this animation occurs too quickly, consider creating another blurred image from in-between frame 3 or 4. You then can start the sequence with the first frame logo image and loop the two blurred images to simulate continuous rotation.

Animating a Single Graphic

Of course, the most efficient animation consists of only one image. Rather than create additional bitmaps, consider simply moving, scaling, or distorting a single graphic. In Chapter 10, "Macromedia Case Study," the Hot Contents movie uses Lingo to simply jiggle icon images on rollover. The Smiley.dir movie, described in the "Graphics" section above, uses Lingo to move a bitmap to a random location upon rollover. Both of these movies are included on the *Shocking the Web* CD-ROM.

Looping Animations

Looped animation sequences, such as a bouncing ball, a walking person, or birds in flight, also can be an efficient use of memory. Complete animated sequences may require up to 6 to 8 frames in order to playback smoothly; however, the ability to loop them and move them around the Stage in a variety of ways make them useful in Shockwave productions. Also, in the case of a flying bird sequence for example, it is important to realize that whether you have one bird—or 48 birds—on the Stage, file size remains basically the same.

To avoid redundancy, it may be necessary to randomize playback of the sequences using Lingo. This makes looping animations seem less repetitive and more realistic.

Color Cycling

Palette color cycling is another animation technique that does not increase file size. However, it is tricky to implement color cycling effectively within Shockwave movies for the Web environment. Because Shockwave movies are usually a component of Web pages that are displayed within a browser on the user's desktop, color cycling a range of colors within a Shockwave movie effects all of the other elements that are outside the Shockwave movie.

Results can be unpredictable. If you want to explore a shocked site that uses a large number of unique color cycling and low-bandwidth animation effects,

visit http://www.sirius.com/~shag to view Shockwave movies created by Terbo Ted. Ted provides a library of experimental movies at http://www.sirius.com/~shag/shock/ —enter at your own risk.

See Chapter 13, "Levi Strauss & Co., Inc Case Study," for related color cycling information.

Using Transitions

Director transitions can be used in place of lengthy Score sequences to create basic animations. For example, the Cover Left transition is commonly used to animate type or text bullets onto the stage.

Note
Transitions prevent execution of other events in a movie, so it is important that they occur quickly. Be sure that you avoid looping on a frame that contains a transition.

New Xtra transitions, such as Killer Transitions from g/matter, inc., can be used as efficient Shockwave animation tools. For example, to create a glass-breaking effect using a series of bitmaps in Director would require far too much memory for a Shockwave movie. However, the Shatter transition, which is included with Killer Transitions, adds only 150 bytes to a Shockwave movie.

The problem with using Xtras is that the end user must install the runtime Killer Transitions Xtra (which is available free of charge from g/matter, inc. and is provided on the *Shocking the Web* CD-ROM) into the Shockwave Support folder in order for the transitions to work. It is possible, however, to design Shockwave movies that can play back smoothly whether or not the Transitions Xtra is installed. A custom transition that is referenced in the Score will be ignored if the transition Xtra is not found in the user's Support folder. No error message is displayed.

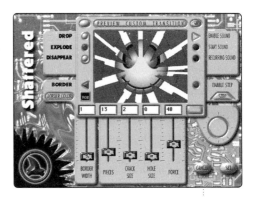

If the user does not have the custom Killer Transitions Xtra installed and you would like to substitute a built-in Director transition, Terry Schussler, of g/matter, recommends the following procedure for gracefully handling the situation:

1. When the user downloads the runtime Killer Transitions Xtra, include an external cast library to be downloaded simultaneously that contains all of the Killer Transitions. The user then must place both of these files in the Shockwave Support folder (unless an installer is provided).

2. At the start of your Director movie, include a Lingo script that checks the number of members in the external transitions cast library. If the number is greater than 0, it means that the cast library was found, and a global flag is set. If the cast library is not found, the flag is not set and the default value remains zero.

3. A `puppetTransition` command is issued to trigger the appropriate transition effect. If the global flag was previously set, a transition from the external cast library is puppeted. Otherwise, the script puppets a built-in Director transition.

The scripts for this procedure can be examined in the Enhance.dir movie found on the *Shocking the Web* CD-ROM.

Digital Video

The large file sizes and associated bandwidth of digital video files make downloading digital video movies to the local disk cache prohibitive. There are plugins and controls available for playing digital video over the Web, but none currently offer interactive capabilities. At the present time, Shockwave does not yet support streaming of digital video over the Internet.

The solution currently available for Shockwave movie development is to integrate QuickTime or Video for Windows movies as linked media, which must be stored locally in the Shockwave Support folder or referenced by aliases (Macintosh) or shortcuts (Windows) to a CD-ROM or local disk. An example movie named Video.dir that contains linked digital video is included on the *Shocking the Web* CD-ROM. You can also drag the video.mov file to your Support folder and open the Video.htm file to view the Shockwave version.

Macromedia has previewed an intranet solution for streaming digital video from an Oracle video server using a Director Xtra. Look for streaming capabilites in Shockwave in the near future.

Shockwave Audio

With the advent of Shockwave Audio (SWA) compression, it is now practical to use high quality sounds within your Shockwave movies. Shockwave Audio files (referred to as SWA files) are highly compressed audio files that can be streamed from a Web server using net Lingo commands. The quality of SWA files is highly impressive, and we strongly recommend that you use SWA technology to enhance your Shockwave movies with sound.

Shockwave Audio supports all of the sound formats that are supported by Director—from 8-bit/11kHz mono to CD-quality 16-bit/44kHz stereo. Internal sounds that are imported directly into Director Casts, as well as external sound files stored on a Web server, are supported by Shockwave Audio.

Using SWA for Internal Sounds

SWA compression can compress internal audio files that are embedded in your Director movies. This approach is generally recommended for short, high-quality audio clips that must be played immediately when needed. The recommended format for internal high-quality sounds is 16-bit/22kHz mono because internal sound data must decompress into available RAM before playing back. This format is acceptable for just about all voice clips and sound effects, as well as music clips with primary content concentrated along the tonal midrange.

To use Shockwave Audio Compression on internal sound cast members, you need the SWA Compression Xtra and the SWA Settings Xtra for Director 5, which are available in the Shockwave Developer's section of Macromedia's Web site (http://www.macromedia.com/shockwave).

Compressing your internal audio cast members with the SWA algorithm is easy and provides compression ratios of up to 44:1—that is, the file size of your compressed audio may be as small as ¼₄th the size of the original. The embedded audio cast members in your Director source file are not affected by SWA compression. Since SWA compression is lossy, Afterburner processing ensures the integrity of your source file, so you will hear only the results of the audio compression process when listening to your .dcr file after it has been processed.

Follow these steps to compress internal audio cast members:

1.   While in Director, select Shockwave for Audio Settings from the Xtras menu.

2.   Check the Compression Enabled checkbox.

3.   Select a bit rate for your internal audio using the Bit Rate pull-down menu. Bit rate choices vary from 32 to 160 kilobits per second. Lower bit rates create smaller files, at the expense of some audio quality. We recommend starting with the low bit rate settings first; if you find that the quality of the sound clip is too degraded as a result of the compression, increase the bit rate incrementally, and then check the results.

4.   Choose Normal or High Accuracy. High Accuracy produces higher sound fidelity, but Afterburner processing takes slightly more time. When creating lower bit rate SWA files, selecting a higher quality setting usually yields a noticeable improvement.

5.   Choose Stereo or Mono output. Lower bit rates (less than 48 Kbps) automatically result in stereo file conversion to mono.

6.   Save the file.

7.   Lastly, create a Shockwave movie using the Afterburner Xtra. The sounds in your Shockwave movie are compressed using SWA. If you are not satisfied with the results, you can change the compression settings in the Shockwave for Audio Settings dialog box, and re-burn the movie.

Note

If you experience an Afterburner Error (80040054) when processing a Shockwave file, this means that the Macintosh Afterburner Xtra is attempting to compress a movie that contains sound resources of the Hypercard 1.x resource format, which is not supported. In order to resolve the problem, the resource needs to be updated. Double click the sound cast members in your movie to launch SoundEdit 16. When each audio cast member is opened using SoundEdit, SoundEdit automatically converts the older sound resource to the AIFF format and saves the change to your Director file. Then, simply quit SoundEdit. Afterburner will be able to compress the file.

Streaming Shockwave Audio Files

Shockwave is also capable of playing streaming audio files. Streaming means that the sounds are played as they are downloaded. In other words, users do not have to wait for a sound to download before they can begin listening to it. (A few seconds of the audio should be downloaded, however, before playback begins to buffer the sound file against unexpected network speed bumps.) With streaming audio, Shockwave movies can play high-fidelity versions of complete songs or other linear audio material over dialup Internet connections, without increasing the file size of the Shockwave movies. While modem-based connections are sufficient for most purposes, higher bandwidth connections allow stereo and increased dynamic range in sound files.

With Shockwave, streaming audio can be played inside elegant user interfaces. It is also possible to make a 1 x 1 pixel movie that automatically plays sound files to provide ambient music (an example movie is provided with the SWA Xtras from Macromedia). Complicated or expensive server-side technology is not required. Your audience needs only the Shockwave plug-in or the ActiveX control to play Shockwave streaming audio.

To work with streaming audio in Shockwave, you must compress an audio file, create a cast member in your Director movie as a placeholder for the audio file, and configure Lingo scripts to control and monitor streaming audio playback.

Processing sounds for streaming playback is somewhat more complicated than compressing embedded audio files. Audio files must be compressed using the SWA Export Xtra for SoundEdit 16 under the MacOS, or the SWA Converter Xtra for Director under Windows 95 and Windows NT (both are available at http://www.macromedia.com/shockwave). SWA files are controlled using Lingo. Most of the Lingo used to control streaming audio is fairly simple and is reuseable for different situations and movies.

Converting Audio Files to SWA Format Using SoundEdit 16 for Macintosh
Streaming audio files can be compressed to various bit rates—just like embedded
Shockwave audio. The bit rate you choose will depend on the bandwidth available at delivery. Generally speaking, bit rates of 16 Kbps can be considered the
lowest-common-denominator for Internet delivery, and higher rates are appropriate for intranet delivery. Here are the streaming audio bit rate recommendations
from Macromedia:

End User Connection	=	Suggested Bit Rate
T1		64 Kbps–128 Kbps
ISDN		32 Kbps–56 Kbps
28.8 modem		16 Kbps
14.4 modem		8 Kbps

As with any media component, it's important to start with the best quality audio
possible—for audio files, that means 16-bit/44.1 kHz. Audio files sampled at 16-
bit/22.050 kHz are also acceptable. Macromedia's developer documentation recommends that files sampled at 8-bit resolution and/or at a sample rate of less than
22.050 kHz be resampled to 16-bit/22.050 kHz before processing; this is not
mandatory, but should be considered if you are having problems playing a SWA
file. Upsampling can be accomplished easily in SoundEdit 16 by selecting Sound
Format from the Modify menu.

Audio tracks from audio CDs can be imported into SoundEdit 16 by choosing
Convert CD Audio from the Xtras menu. Before converting a CD audio track,
make sure that the default document format is set to 16-bit/44.1 kHz, and stereo.
Choose Preferences from the File menu to set the default document format.

Since streaming audio files are transmitted over the Internet to various playback
platforms, filenames should conform to established naming conventions. For
compatibility with the widest range of operating systems, streaming Shockwave
Audio files should have a descriptive name of no more than eight characters (for
compatibility with Windows 3.x), followed by the .SWA suffix. Spaces and special characters should not be used in file names. Filenames are case-sensitive, and
references to SWA files in your Lingo scripts are also case-sensitive. SWA files
are named at export from SoundEdit 16 for Macintosh. SoundEdit 16 also
includes a drag-and-drop AppleScript utility named SWAtomator Droplet, for
batch processing SWA exports. The SWA Converter Xtra for Director provides
automatic naming and batch processing capabilities under Windows 95 and
Windows NT.

Here is a step-by-step rundown of the SWA conversion process using the SWA Export Xtra for SoundEdit 16:

1.   Open a sound file or audio CD track. Make sure that the sound format (resolution/sampling rate) conforms to the guidelines listed above.

2.   Set the bit rate for the SWA file using the Shockwave for Audio Settings option under the Xtras menu. If the bit rate you choose is 48 Kbps or higher, you will have the option of selecting mono or stereo formats for the output file. All files compressed using a lower bit rate than 48 Kbps must be mono.

3.   Save the file using Save As... before you modify it any further, and work with a duplicate version of the file. (You may want to save your original file for future use.)

4.   If the source file is stereo and the output file will be monophonic, convert the sound to mono. Any stereo file that has very different content in it's tracks should be mixed to mono.
- Choose Select All from the Edit menu.
- Choose Mix from the Effects menu. This brings up the Simple Mixer dialog box.
- From the Mix To... pulldown menu, choose the name of the current sound file.
- Choose Mono.
- Click OK.

If you are planning to deliver your sound to only ISDN lines or better (32 Kbps or above), skip to step 8.

To maximize fidelity when delivering audio at modem rates (8 and 16 Kbps), Macromedia suggests that you preprocess the sound before SWA export.

Steps 5 and 6 assume that the entire contents of the sound file are still selected.

5.   Equalize the sound using the Equalizer, which can be found under the Effects menu. For 8 Kbps delivery, attenuating the frequencies above 4 kHz is generally helpful. For 16 Kbps delivery, Macromedia recommends completely attenuating all frequencies below 60 Hz and above 6 kHz. (Hint: You can drag the vertical bars left or right to adjust the frequency ranges.)

6.   Normalize the sound. This increases the amplitude of the sound to maximum levels without clipping or distortion. Normalizing audio files that have quiet passages may result in strange effects or distortion, so listen to the sound after you normalize it. Normalize can be found under the Effects menu, or it can be selected from the Toolbar.

7.   Downsample the sound to 22.050 kHz by selecting Sound Format from the Modify menu.

8.   Now you are ready to create the SWA file. Select Export from the File menu. In the Export Type... pulldown menu, select SWA. Name the file using a descriptive name of 8 characters or less, followed by the .SWA suffix. Click OK to save the file.

9.   Upload or transfer the SWA file to your Web server, using the raw data file format option.

Note

The basic conversion process described above requires that you equalize and normalize sounds before compressing them. For more advanced pre-processing, consider using AudioTrack 1.2 from Waves Ltd. (http://www.waves.com), which is a software plug-in for SoundEdit 16 and Deck II. AudioTrack combines a number of audio processors for pre-processing SWA files, including equalization, compression/expansion, and gating, and includes digital signal processing (DSP) algorithms to provide EQ and dynamic limiting. Processing can significantly improve the quality of SWA files before Shockwave compression is applied.

Working with Streaming Audio Files in Director

To implement streaming Shockwave audio files in Director, you must create a special type of cast member that acts as a sort of message center for your streaming audio files. From Director's Insert menu, select Other, and choose SWA Streaming Xtra. Open the Cast window—your new SWA member should be highlighted. Select Cast Properties from the Modify menu and give your SWA member a name. The SWA member in the simpleplayer.dir movie on the *Shocking The Web* CD-ROM is named "SWAholder."

The process of audio playback can be divided into 3 discrete steps: preparation, monitoring, and control. Specific net Lingo commands for each of these processes are explained in detail in Chapter 8, "Shockwave Lingo."

Preparing Director to Stream Audio

First, you have to inform the SWA cast member which audio file to play. You must supply a relative or absolute path to the SWA file from your Shockwave movie, using standard Web conventions.

The `soundConfig` hander is called using the following statement in the `startMovie` handler:

```
soundConfig "SWAholder", ¬
"http://www.dxm.com/Movies/SWA/knodel.SWA"
```

The SWA member and sound file names are supplied to the handler as arguments, facilitating code reuse. The `soundConfig` handler then sets the URL of the SWA file.

```
global gSWAflag
on soundConfig memberName, SWAfile
  set the URL of member memberName to SWAfile
...
```

The `set the URL of member` statement designates the URL of the streaming audio file (`knodel.SWA`) that is played by the SWA cast member (named `"SWAholder"`). The `URL` property of a streaming audio member can be changed at any time using this statement.

When referencing your SWA files in Lingo, you must provide a relative or absolute path to the SWA file from your Shockwave movie. To ensure compatibility with Internet Explorer 3, SWA files placed in the same folder as the Shockwave movies that control them should be referenced using a `"./"` prefix before the filename. For example, if knodel.SWA is in the same directory as simpleplayer.dcr, it would be referred to as `"./knodel.SWA"` in the Lingo scripts within the player movie.

Next, the preload buffer is set to 5 seconds. This configures the audio stream so that the first 5 seconds of the sound are downloaded before playback begins. While setting a preload buffer is not mandatory, it's a good idea because it will protect your streaming audio from dropout should network delays cause file transfer to pause for a second here and there. Such pauses are common on the Internet, and jerkiness in audio playback can make the sound intolerable for the user. So preloading (at least) a few seconds of audio is a good idea.

```
...
  set the preloadTime of member memberName to 5
  preloadBuffer (member memberName)
  set gSWAflag = 1
end
```

Finally, set the global Boolean `gSWAflag` to 1 to indicate that a SWA file is in the process of being used; this global is used to notify the `idle` handler to monitor the SWA playback process.

Monitoring Streaming Audio Status

```
on idle
  global gSWAflag
  if gSWAflag = 1 then controlSWA "SWAholder"
end
```

Once the `gSWAflag` Boolean is set by the `soundConfig` handler, the status of the streaming audio file is monitored constantly during idle time. Barring transfer errors, the `controlSWA` handler plays the streaming sound once, as soon as the preload buffer for the SWA file downloads. The `controlSWA` handler monitors sound playback and updates an indicator that displays how much of the sound has been played, until playback is complete.

```
on controlSWA membername
  global gSWAflag
  set SWAstatus = the state of member membername
  if SWAstatus = 2 then
    -- the SWA is ready to play
    Play (member membername)
  else if SWAstatus = 3 then
    updateTimeBar (the percentPlayed of member membername)
  else if SWAstatus = 5 then
    updateTimeBar 100
    set gSWAflag = 0
  else if SWAstatus = 9 then
    set errorCode = getError(member membername)
    set errorString = getErrorString(member membername)
    debug errorCode,errorString
    set gSWAflag = 0
  end if
end
```

The getError() and getErrorString() functions return information about the error status of a SWA member. Here is a list of possible results returned by these functions:

getError() **returns**	getErrorString() **returns**
0	OK
1	memory
2	network
3	playback device
99	other

The state of member property provides information about the playback state of the sound from the time the file transfer associated with the sound begins until completion of playback. Here are the possible values for this property:

0	Stopped
1	preLoading
2	preLoadDone
3	playing
4	paused
5	done
9	error (This error typically means that the URL specified in the URL of member statement is not valid)

You can use the duration of member and the percentPlayed functions to determine the time status of current playback. For example, if a SWA file is three minutes long, and the percentPlayed function returns a value of 50, the user is currently 1½ minutes into the SWA file. The controlSWA handler uses the percentPlayed function to call another handler that dynamically updates a visual indicator of the current time and the time remaining in the sound.

Note

If you dynamically resize cast members using Lingo, remember to set the stretch property to TRUE. Bitmapped sprites also must be puppeted for sprite resizing to work properly.

Controlling SWA Files

Once the SWA member has been assigned a sound to play, just issue the Play command:

```
Play (member "SWAholder")
```

You also can use the same syntax template to Pause or Stop the sound. Issuing a Play command after a Pause resumes playback at the time in the file at which it was paused; while playback of a stopped file starts at the beginning of the sound. While stopped, you can change the sound to be played by setting the URL of member property to a new value.

The above example is a simple implementation of Shockwave's streaming audio capabilities. You also can use net Lingo to loop sounds (by replaying them once they have stopped), or to create rich visual interfaces for sound playback. Director's soundEnabled and volume of sound commands, along with other audio-related Lingo and net Lingo commands, also can be used to control playback attributes of SWA sounds.

Note

You can use the optional parameters in your <EMBED> or <OBJECT> tag to specify SWA files for playback. Read the location(s) of the sound file(s) using the externalParam(x) function, and then use the same Shockwave movie to play different sounds when posted on different Web pages.

Chapter 7

Assembling the Components
Shockwave Authoring

This chapter addresses some of the authoring issues to consider when you plan and implement Shockwave movies for the Web. Issues include planning your Web server's file and directory structure, determining users' available network bandwidth, and HTML scripting considerations for displaying Shockwave movies within Netscape Navigator and Internet Explorer Web browsers.

Directory Structures and Pathnames

The convention for locating resources on the Web is the URL. A URL is a string of characters that functions as an address for a particular item. The basic format for a URL is:

```
protocol://host[:port]/path
```

At the beginning of the URL, `protocol` designates the protocol for sending and retrieving information, such as HTTP (Hypertext Transfer Protocol) which is the standard for transferring items that are available on the Web, or FTP (File Transfer Protocol) which is the standard for transferring files between computers. `Host` specifies the computer host that contains the item, which is an Internet (or IP) address or a domain name. `Port` is a particular number that identifies the service you are requesting from the host computer, if the service is installed on a port other than the default port. By default, the port for most Web servers is port 80, and it is usually not necessary to include the port number within the URL. The `path` segment of the URL provides the pathname to the location of the HTTP item on the host computer.

URLs should conform to HTTP protocols. Because UNIX is widely considered the operating system of the Internet, the standard URL format is similar to the UNIX filename format. There is no length restriction for UNIX or URL filenames. File and directory names appearing after the domain name in a URL are case-sensitive, and a forward slash (/) separates directories. Eliminate spaces and slashes (backward and forward) from HTTP file names and URLs, and omit all special characters (such as those above the numeric keys on your QWERTY keyboard).

Absolute Pathnames

An absolute path specifies the complete pathname to an HTTP item. This usually means that a URL includes the HTTP header, a full domain name, and all relevant subdirectories for an item's location.

Absolute pathnames provide you with a way to link to other Web servers. There is no way to link to a server other than your own using a relative pathname.

An absolute pathname should not be confused with an absolute URL, which is typically a URL that exists behind a firewall and does not include an HTTP header and domain. For example, the URL http://hrserver.dxm.com/enrollment/form01.html residing on a secure, corporate intranet might be referenced by the following absolute URL: /enrollment/form01.html.

Remember that the pathname Lingo function and other path-related Lingo elements are disabled for Shockwave movie development. You can use absolute pathnames to execute network operations from Shockwave movies, but movies that are displayed within a Web browser cannot use the pathname function to open files on a user's hard disk. Only linked files stored in the Shockwave Support folder are recognized by Shockwave movies.

Relative Pathnames

Relative pathnames specify a location that is relative to the current folder. The advantage of using relative pathnames within your site is that the site can be moved easily from one place to another as long as the file structure is maintained, and it is easy to test Web pages locally and on various computers before transferring files to a Web server. When a relative path is used, the Web browser defaults to the current directory structure.

For Shockwave movie development, you must construct relative paths and execute network operations based on the location of the Shockwave movie—not based on the location of the HTML page that contains the movie.

If you refer to a file in the same directory as your Shockwave movie using a relative pathname, it is important to be aware that Internet Explorer 3.0 handles relative pathnames differently from other browsers. In order to ensure that files will be found by the Internet Explorer browser, put a single period and a forward slash "./" before the filename in your Lingo scripts if the file resides in the same directory as the Shockwave movie. For example, use the syntax GoToNetMovie "./intro.dcr" to branch to a movie in the same folder, instead of using the more common (and Navigator-compatible) GoToNetMovie "intro.dcr" syntax.

Use the same syntax when issuing a GoToNetPage command, or GetNetText command (which retrieves a text file within the same folder as the Shockwave movie). For example:

```
on mouseDown
    GetNetText "./banner.txt"
end
```

Many developers store Shockwave movies within subdirectories on their Web servers (a folder named Movies is used to store Shockwave .dcr files, for example). When referring to a file in a subdirectory using a relative pathname, it is necessary to include only the subdirectory path to the file, separated by forward slashes. For example, the following <OBJECT> tag embeds a movie that is stored in a subdirectory one level below the HTML document:

```
<!-- OBJECT tag for Internet Explorer  -->
<OBJECT CLASSID="clsid:166B1BCA-3F9C-11CF-8075-444553540000"
CODEBASE="http://active.macromedia.com/director/cabs/sw.cab
#version=5,0,1,61" WIDTH="400" HEIGHT="100" NAME="intro"
ID="DXMSW30">
      <PARAM NAME="SRC" VALUE="Movies/intro.dcr">
</OBJECT>
```

When using relative paths in conjunction with the GoToNetPage command, it is often necessary to open a URL for a page that is located one directory level above the Shockwave movie that issues the command.

For example, if you use a relative path to link to an HTML page (URL http://www.myserver.com/mynovel/myfamily/page2.htm) from within a Shockwave movie located in the Movies folder (URL http://www.myserver.com/mynovel/myfamily/Movies/intro.dcr), construct the relative path based on the location of the .dcr file.

To move upward in the server directory levels, use two periods and a forward slash "../" to represent each directory level when constructing relative paths. The following Lingo command could be issued from the intro.dcr movie in the scenario described above:

```
on mouseDown
    GoToNetPage "../page2.htm"
end
```

Accordingly, to reference an HTML page two directory levels above the Shockwave movie, the following Lingo script could be used:

```
on mouseDown
    GoToNetPage "../../familyintro.htm"
end
```

Creating Scaleable Movies for Various Bandwidths

Throughout this book, we have emphasized the importance of designing and creating Shockwave movies to accommodate lowest-commmon-denominator platforms and network connections. But what if you want to provide CD-quality, streaming music for T1-based browsers, while providing lower quality, lower bandwidth music for users with modem connections? Can you serve up megabyte-intensive media for some users, while retaining responsive accessibility for low bandwidth users? Can you accomplish this without having to set up and maintain two separate Web sites?

In a word, yes. Shockwave provides ample features for determining a user's bandwidth, storing the information for future reference, and delivering appropriate media to different users. Using these features can be a fairly complex task, however—especially for media types other than streaming audio. Creating scaleable Shockwave *does* require a fair amount of complex Lingo programming, in addition to the overhead associated with producing multiple sets of equivalent media assets. During the design process, you should consider seriously whether it is necessary to provide high bandwidth versions of Shockwave movies. If your project needs dictate such options, then read on.

Determining User Bitstream

There are essentially two methods for determining the rate of data transfer (or bitstream), supported by individual users:

- User Input Method. Offers bandwidth choices, and asks users to select their connection speed.

- Transparent Detection Method. Script your Shockwave movie to download a file of a specific size. Divide the size of the file by the time consumed by the transfer to determine the amount of bandwidth currently available to the user.

Once the bitstream data is collected, this information can be saved to the user's hard disk and accessed by other Shockwave movies. Both data collection methods can use the same Lingo routine to store the bitstream information to an external file.

Both approaches have a number of associated pitfalls. The first method opens up the possibility that a user may make an incorrect choice—accidentally or intentionally. The second method brings into play all of the typically unpredictable factors that can affect network file transfer: latency, network traffic, other simultaneous downloads, etc. With these factors in mind, you can choose the data collection approach that best suits your needs.

User Input Method

The bitManual.dcr movie on the *Shocking the Web* CD-ROM contains two radio buttons that offer a low or high bandwidth version of the movie. When either button is clicked, the bandwidth value is stored in a variable that is later saved to the user's Shockwave preferences file for the site, using the `setPref` Lingo command. If you choose to use this method, the technical considerations are minimal and your primary concern will be developing an appropriate user interface. The design should prompt the user to make a selection, and the options should be legible and understandable. It is best to use the low bandwidth option as the default selection because most users (at least for Internet, as opposed to intranet, projects) will be accessing the Web via modem.

Transparent Detection Method

The movie named autoDeterminator.dir on the *Shocking the Web* CD-ROM is an example movie that automatically determines the user's bitstream. Shockwave network Lingo commands are used to initiate a file transfer. When the transfer is complete, the time elapsed is used to calculate the effective bandwidth.

Note

Calculating bandwidth based on a single transfer can provide erroneous information at times. If the user is transferring other files at the same time, bandwidth will be divided among the simultaneous connections. Network latency can vary widely, resulting in unpredictable lags between the time the file transfer is requested and the time data actually begins moving. The user also may leave the Web page before the bandwidth test is complete. It is important to note that the bitstream test will use available bandwidth, which may slow down the appearance of graphics and other elements on the Web page while the test is in progress. On a positive note, errors produced by these conditions usually result in a low bandwidth reading; and delivering low bandwidth media to your high bandwidth clients is generally less of a tragedy than delivering high bandwidth data to your low bandwidth clients.

In actuality, a file is *not* used to determine the bitstream in this example; if it was, we would risk the possibility of getting an incorrect bandwidth reading if the requested file already resides in the browser's local disk cache. Instead, Lingo is used to activate a CGI script that transmits a specific amount of data to the browser. By using the CGI script, it is possible to request any amount of data to be sent to the browser, without spending the time to create files and waste disk space by storing them on the server.

The following Lingo script initiates the process of determining bitstream. The script can be found in the autoDeterminator.dir movie on the *Shocking the Web* CD-ROM.

```
global gBitTestData,gBitTestFlag,gKPerSec

on startBitCheck
  set bSize=10000 + random(100)
  getNetText "http://www.dxm.com/cgi/spew.cgi?" &¬
string(bSize)
  set bandID = getLatestNetID()
  set gBitTestData = [#ID:bandID,#start:theticks,¬
#size:integer(bSize),#finish:0]
  set gBitTestFlag = 1
end
```

The local variable bSize determines the quantity of data to be returned by the CGI script. After a bit of experimentation, it was decided to download 10 kilobytes of data. (Ten kilobytes is large enough to mitigate some of the network latency at the head of the transfer—as when the browser is looking up the domain name, etc.—and is not so large as to choke bandwidth for more than a few seconds under normal conditions.) The random(100) value is added to the value of bSize to ensure that each call to spew.cgi is unique, and that the data returned comes from the server and not from the disk cache.

After the CGI script is executed, the relevant data for the transaction is stored in the global property list gBitTestData. In addition to storing the transfer ID (using the getLatestNetID() function) and bSize, the script also stores the time that the transfer is initiated, which will later be used in calculating the bitstream. Finally, gBitTestFlag is set to 1, or TRUE, so that the movie's on idle handler can monitor the bitstream calculation process.

```
on idle
  global gBitTestFlag,gAutoPlayFlag
  if gBitTestFlag = 1 then checkBitstream
...
end
```

We could have stopped the execution of the startBitCheck handler using a repeat loop until the data transfer finished, but that would have stopped all other actions in the Director movie. By monitoring the process using a flag in the idle loop, the movie continues to play and to respond to user actions while the data is transferring from the server.

The checkBitstream handler checks to determine if the spew.cgi program has finished delivering data to the Shockwave movie. If it has, it calculates the bit-stream based on transferred data divided by time, and sets gBitTestFlag to 0, in order to turn off the monitoring process in the idle loop.

```
on checkBitStream
  if netDone(getAprop(gBitTestData,#ID)) then
    if netError() = "OK" then
      setAprop gBitTestData,#finish,the ticks
      set testTime = getAprop(gBitTestData,#finish) - ¬
getAprop(gBitTestData,#start)
      set gKPerSec = float(getAprop(gBitTestData,#size)/1000) / ¬
float(testTime/60)
      debug string(gKPerSec)
      set foo = netTextResult(getAprop(gBitTestData,#ID))
      set foo = 0
      if gKPerSec > 10 then
        set bandwidth = 1
      else set bandwidth = 0
      makePref "bandwidth",bandwidth
    end if
    set gBitTestFlag = 0
  end if
end
```

Note that the parameters previously stored in the `gBitTestData` property list are used to calculate the rate of data transfer. Once `NetDone()` and `NetError()` return satisfactory results, the current time is determined using the `ticks`, and the `#start` property is subtracted. The result is the duration of the data transfer in ticks (or sixtieths of a second). Next, the size of the data transfer is divided by this number (using fractions to convert from bytes to kilobytes and from ticks to seconds) in order to calculate the bitstream in kilobytes per second, which is then stored in the global `gKPerSec`. If bitstream is greater than 10 kilobytes per second, the bandwidth flag is set to `1`. The `makePref` handler is then used to add this value to a table of stored preferences (which is explained below). The `foo` local variable is used to clear the contents of existing variables that may be storing a large amount of unnecessary data.

Note

Single text files—even when created by CGI programs as in this example—will usually transfer at much higher rates than the typical mix of data files found on most Web pages. If you use this method to determine user bandwidth capabilities, keep in mind that text will sometimes move at rates up to 6K per second over a 28.8 Kbps modem.

Working with User Preferences Files

With some relatively simple Lingo scripting, you can use bandwidth data to modify content in a number of ways, including branching along different paths using `GoToNetPage` and `GoToNetMovie` commands, or providing different streaming audio files or external cast libraries. Presumably, if you are using a Shockwave movie to determine bandwidth, it would be advantageous to use this information to alter the delivery of media to the user without having to re-check user bandwidth on each and every Web page, or within every Shockwave movie. The Shockwave preferences file can be used to share this bandwidth data, or other configuration data, between Shockwave movies.

With the release of Shockwave for Director 5, the ability to save text data to the user's hard disk was introduced. For the bitstream test, a preferences file is used to store data about the bandwidth of the user's connection, which can be read by other Shockwave movies. The technique used to save the bandwidth data is a general one, and it can be used in any situation where you would like to save configuration data to share between Shockwave movies. The information that is stored in the preferences file is available to any movie for any Lingo evaluation uses on the client side; the data is not readable by the server, nor can it be transmitted between machines without the use of custom CGI scripting.

There is only one network Lingo command and one function related to user preferences files. The `setPref` command writes a text file in the folder named Prefs inside the Shockwave Support folder. The `getPref()` function reads a text file with a .txt suffix—again, only within the designated Support folder.

The following is a simple example that uses Lingo to write and read a preferences file.

```
on mouseUp
  global gKPerSec
  setPref "myPrefFile.txt", gKPerSec
end
```

The above handler writes a text file named myPrefFile.txt into the Prefs folder, which contains the value stored in the global variable `gKPerSec`. Another movie can read this data as follows:

```
on startMovie
  global gKPerSec
  set prefsData = getPref("myPrefFile.txt")
  if not(voidP(prefsData)) then set gKPerSec = prefsData
end
```

If there is data stored in the preferences file, it is placed into this movie's global `gKPerSec` variable.

This method shows the simplicity of the preferences-related commands. However, it is not very scaleable. There is no internal convention for storing multiple data sets in the preferences file—developers will need to provide such a structure. It's a good idea to use the same structures in all of your Shockwave movies. That way, you can copy and paste the scripts anywhere without writing extra lines of code. If you would like to use our scripts for this purpose, read the next section, which is related to using the sample preferences handlers.

Using the Sample Preferences Handlers

The template used in this example is fairly simple. All Lingo shown below can be viewed in, and copied from the script named "Preferences Script" in the autoDeterminator.dir movie on the *Shocking the Web* CD-ROM.

Here is the sample contents of one of our preferences files:

```
-- DXM Shockwave User Prefs File
bandwidth=0
user=eric
```

Each of the data categories gets its own line in the file. On the left of the equals sign is the name of the preferences category, and on the right is the data value for that category.

Typically, you would read this file on `startMovie`, translate its contents into an appropriate data structure, add or edit values in this data structure, and save the updated information back to the user's hard disk if necessary.

The user preferences file is read by the `readPrefs` handler, which is called using this syntax:

```
readPrefs prefsFileName, [debugArg]
```

Substitute the name of your preferences file for `prefsFileName`, making sure that it has a .txt suffix. If the file does not exist, the `readPrefs` handler will return <void>, but will not cause any runtime errors. You can use `debugArg` to provide mockup versions of the contents of a preferences file while you are debugging your movie in the Director environment.

The user preferences information that was retrieved from the external file is stored in a global property list named `gPrefSettings`. Then, another handler is used to write the data stored in `gPrefSettings` to the user's hard disk. After executing `readPrefs` on the preferences file displayed above, `gPrefSettings` would look like this.

```
gPrefSettings = [bandwidth:0,user:"eric"]
```

Once `gPrefSettings` has been initialized, the values stored in it can be accessed by any Lingo handler using the Lingo `GetAProp` list function, provided that a global declaration is included for `gPrefSettings`.

The following statement sets the global `gBandwidth` equal to the bandwidth value retrieved from the `gPrefSettings` property list, which is `0` in this example:

```
set gBandwidth = getAprop(gPrefSettings,"bandwidth")
```

The `makePref` handler is used to edit values in the `gPrefSettings` property list, or to add properties to the list. It is called using the syntax `makePref category, value`.

```
on mouseUp
  makePref "bandwidth",1
  makePref "color", "blue"
end
```

After executing the handler above, `gPrefSettings` would look like this:

```
gPrefSettings = [bandwidth:1,user:"eric",color:"blue"]
```

To delete a property entirely from the preferences data, call the `deletePref` handler using the syntax `deletePref prefName`. The data will not be erased from the text file on the user's hard disk until you write the file again. To save the data to the user's hard disk, for subsequent use by this or other Shockwave movies, use the `writePrefs` handler.

```
on stopMovie
  writePrefs "myPrefsFile.txt"
end
```

If you include the Preferences Script handlers in your Shockwave movies, you can easily use the `readPrefs`, `writePrefs`, `makePref`, and `deletePref` handlers to manage your user preferences settings and share the data between movies. Remember to call `readPrefs` from your `startMovie` script, and `writePrefs` from your `stopMovie` script. You always can read stored preferences data using `GetAProp`, and create or edit data using `makePref`.

HTML Authoring

The trickiest part of writing HTML to embed Shockwave movies within Web pages is anticipating the behavior of different Web browsers and various Web browser versions. Prior to the release of Internet Explorer 3, the HTML <EMBED> tag was the only tag used to display Shockwave movies. In conjunction with the release from Microsoft of the ActiveX architecture, Internet Explorer 3 supports the HTML <OBJECT> tag for adding ActiveX controls, such as Macromedia's ActiveX Shockwave control, to Web pages.

Like plug-ins, ActiveX controls (formerly known as OLE controls or OCX controls) are reusable software components, or objects that add specialized functionality to Web sites, desktop applications, and development tools.

> **Note**
> ActiveX controls can be viewed in Netscape Navigator using the ActiveX Plug-in for Netscape from Ncompass Labs (available at http://www.ncompasslabs.com).

<EMBED> **and** <OBJECT> **Tags**

A general overview of the <EMBED> and <OBECT> tags was provided in Chapter 3, "Shockwave for Director," as part of the Shockwave production process. The following sections explore the tags and their associated parameters in more detail and offer a few HTML authoring solutions.

When Navigator encounters the <OBECT> tag in an HTML document, it ignores the Shockwave movie in the tag. On the other hand, when Internet Explorer encounters a Shockwave movie in an <EMBED> tag—if the ActiveX Shockwave control is installed—the browser displays the Shockwave movie using the control. If the ActiveX Shockwave control is not installed, the browser ignores the Shockwave movie in the <EMBED> tag.

If the Shockwave control is installed when Internet Explorer encounters a Shockwave movie in an <OBECT> tag, it checks the version number of the user's Shockwave control against the version referenced in the CODEBASE parameter of the <OBECT> tag. If the user's version is the same as, or later than, the version referenced in the CODEBASE parameter, Internet Explorer displays the Shockwave movie. If the user has an older version, Internet Explorer retrieves a new version from the site specified in the CODEBASE parameter, installs it automatically, and displays the Shockwave movie. If the Shockwave control is not installed when

Internet Explorer encounters Shockwave in an `<OBECT>` tag, it retrieves and installs the control from the site specified in the `CODEBASE` parameter, and then displays the movie. Automatic installation of the Shockwave control is a clear advantage of the control over the plug-in.

This table summarizes the browser behavior described above:

Browser Behavior for `<EMBED>` **and** `<OBJECT>` **Tags**

Browser Configuration	Shockwave Movie in `<EMBED>` **Tag**	Shockwave Movie in `<OBJECT>` **Tag**
Navigator 2 or later with Shockwave plug-in	displays movie	ignores tag
Navigator 2 or later without Shockwave plug-in	prompts to get Shockwave	ignores tag
Internet Explorer 3 with Shockwave control	displays movie	checks control version; displays movie
Internet Explorer 3 without Shockwave control	ignores tag	installs control; displays movie

If you are developing a site for compatibility with Web browsers that support JavaScript, consider using the JavaScripts included in Appendix C, "JavaScript Reference for Director Developers," to determine the user's browser and automatically configure either the `<EMBED>` or `<OBJECT>` tag in your HTML document based on the results.

It is also possible to include an `<EMBED>` tag within an `<OBJECT>` tag in order to handle multiple browser scenarios. In browsers that support the `<OBJECT>` tag, the `<EMBED>` tag is ignored if both are present. In browsers that do not support the `<OBJECT>` tag (such as Navigator), the `<OBJECT>` element and `PARAM` attributes are ignored. For example, the following `<OBJECT>` tag contains an `<EMBED>` tag. If the browser does not recognize the `<OBJECT>` tag, the browser is most likely a version of Netscape Navigator. Therefore, the `<OBJECT>` tag is ignored and the `<EMBED>` tag is recognized.

```
<!-- OBJECT tag for Internet Explorer  -->
<OBJECT CLASSID="clsid:166B1BCA-3F9C-11CF-8075-444553540000"
CODEBASE="http://active.macromedia.com/director/cabs/sw.cab
#version=5,0,1,61" WIDTH="200" HEIGHT="100" NAME="menu"
ID="DXMSW33">
     <PARAM NAME="SRC" VALUE="menu.dcr">
     <PARAM NAME="BGCOLOR" VALUE="#FF3333">
     <PARAM NAME="SW1" VALUE="gold,god,glory">
<!-- EMBED tag for Navigator  -->
<EMBED SRC="menu.dcr" WIDTH=200 HEIGHT=100 BGCOLOR=#FF3333
SW1="gold,god,glory">
</OBJECT>
```

In addition to configuring the appropriate tag on-the-fly using JavaScript, or using an <EMBED> within an <OBJECT> tag for cross-browser compatibility, you may choose to use either the <EMBED> or <OBJECT> tag, depending on the target audience for your particular Web site. Consider the advantages and disadvantages of each outlined below.

Using the <EMBED> Tag

Netscape Navigator currently holds the largest share of the Web browser market, so the <EMBED> tag continues to be compatible with the largest number of installed Web browsers and browser versions. However, there are a few issues related to Navigator versions that should be considered when implementing the <EMBED> tag.

While Navigator versions 2 and later recognize the <EMBED> tag for displaying content supported by a plug-in or helper application, the earlier Navigator 1.1N version recognizes the <EMBED> tag as a tag that specifies an OLE link supported by Windows 3.1. As a result, when Netscape Navigator 1.1N comes across an <EMBED> tag that contains a Shockwave movie or any other plug-in data, it displays a broken icon.

You can prevent the broken icon displayed by Navigator 1.1N and other browsers that do not support the <EMBED> tag, by using an HTML <EMBED> tag within a simple JavaScript routine followed by either a <NOEMBED> or a <NOSCRIPT> tag. If the script is encountered by a browser that does not support JavaScript (Navigator versions prior to 2.0, for example), the JavaScript routine is ignored and the <NOEMBED> or <NOSCRIPT> tag is recognized. These tags can be included to display a GIF file in lieu of a Shockwave movie.

Here is a sample script:

```
<SCRIPT LANGUAGE="JavaScript">
<!-- Hide this script from non-Navigator 2.0 browsers.
document.write( '<EMBED WIDTH=175 HEIGHT=135 SRC="movie.dcr">');
<!-- Done hiding from non-Navigator 2.0 browsers. -->
</SCRIPT>
<NOEMBED>
<IMG WIDTH=175 HEIGHT=135 SRC="altimage.gif">
</NOEMBED>
```

<EMBED> **Tag Parameters:** The <EMBED> tag supports a number of pre-defined parameters for embedding Shockwave movies, which are covered in Chapter 3, "Shockwave for Director." Additional parameters can be defined by the user within the <EMBED> tag. These user-defined parameters can then be accessed from Lingo scripts using the external parameter functions externalParamCount(n), externalParamName(n), and externalParamValue(n) within your Shockwave movies.

The user's ability to define parameter names is unique to Navigator and the <EMBED> tag. Internet Explorer 3 and the <OBJECT> tag, on the other hand, support a pre-defined list of parameter attributes for use with the Shockwave ActiveX control. Even though Navigator supports user-defined parameters, consider using the pre-defined <OBJECT> tag parameter names in the <EMBED> tag, and enclose parameter values within quotation marks to ensure compatibility with Internet Explorer.

Using the <OBJECT> Tag

Internet Explorer supports ActiveX controls (or objects) according to the standard object model extension to HTML 3.2. To embed an object within a Web page, such as a Java applet or ActiveX control, Microsoft recommends using the <OBJECT> tag. Properties of an object can be set using the PARAM element.

<OBJECT> **Tag Parameters:** The <OBJECT> tag supports a pre-defined set of parameters for controlling the appearance and attributes of a Shockwave movie that is displayed by the Shockwave ActiveX control.

When writing an <OBJECT> tag to embed Shockwave movies, the tag supports specific parameters that were defined by Macromedia when the Shockwave ActiveX control was developed. (These parameters have names, but they are, in fact, arbitrary—they can be used to store any values.) The following sample <OBJECT> tag includes all available Shockwave PARAM elements. These parameter names and values can be passed to Lingo scripts within the embedded Shockwave movie.

Note

At the present time, parameter data is passed to the Shockwave movie through the <OBJECT> or <EMBED> tag only when the movie first loads. It is not possible to refresh parameter data while a movie plays. The ActiveX architecture (like Netscape's LiveConnect model) is centered around ActiveX controls that are reusable across network, desktop, and development environments. It is probable that future versions of Shockwave will support more dynamic, realtime external parameter access that is not limited to parameters stored in HTML tags.

```
<!-- OBJECT tag for Internet Explorer  -->
<OBJECT CLASSID="clsid:166B1BCA-3F9C-11CF-8075-444553540000"
CODEBASE="http://active.macromedia.com/director/cabs/sw.cab#
version=5,0,1,61" WIDTH="200" HEIGHT="100" NAME="paramov"
ID="DXMSW37">
      <PARAM NAME="SRC" VALUE="paramov.dcr">
      <PARAM NAME="BGCOLOR" VALUE="#336699">
      <PARAM NAME="PALETTE" VALUE="background">
      <PARAM NAME="SW1" VALUE="10,5">
      <PARAM NAME="SW2" VALUE="20,15">
      <PARAM NAME="SW3" VALUE="30,25">
      <PARAM NAME="SW4" VALUE="40,35">
      <PARAM NAME="SW5" VALUE="50,45">
      <PARAM NAME="SW6" VALUE="60,55">
      <PARAM NAME="SW7" VALUE="70,65">
      <PARAM NAME="SW8" VALUE="80,75">
      <PARAM NAME="SW9" VALUE="90,85">
      <PARAM NAME="swURL"
VALUE="http://www.yrserver.com/random.html">
      <PARAM NAME="swText" VALUE="Happy Birthday!">
      <PARAM NAME="swColor" VALUE="3">
      <PARAM NAME="swForeColor" VALUE="39">
      <PARAM NAME="swBackColor" VALUE="25">
      <PARAM NAME="swFrame" VALUE="sideframe">
```

```
            <PARAM NAME="swName" VALUE="userName">
            <PARAM NAME="swPassword" VALUE="userPassword">
            <PARAM NAME="swBanner" VALUE="Now loading...">
            <PARAM NAME="swSound" VALUE="alertSnd">
            <PARAM NAME="swVolume" VALUE="6">
            <PARAM NAME="swPreloadTime" VALUE="5">
            <PARAM NAME="swAudio" VALUE="../SFX/cityamb.SWA">
            <PARAM NAME="swList" VALUE="ny,sf,la">
</OBJECT>
```

Brief explanations of the various parameters follow.

- The CLASSID parameter specifies the universal class identifier for the Shockwave ActiveX control. The code must be entered exactly as above.

- The CODEBASE parameter specifies the URL where the current Shockwave ActiveX control can be obtained by the browser if it is not already installed, or if an earlier version is installed.

- The WIDTH parameter specifies the width of the embed rectangle, in pixels, that the Shockwave movie will play within.

- The HEIGHT parameter specifies the height of the embed rectangle, in pixels, that the Shockwave movie will play within.

- The NAME parameter specifies the name of the Shockwave ActiveX control, which is "Shockwave." This information is provided to the browser for use during FORM processing.

- The ID parameter specifies a unique identifier that can be used to define hyperlink locations within a document. The identifier also can be used by ActiveX objects (or the Web browser) to communicate with other objects within an HTML document.

Additional parameters are specified in the body of the <OBJECT> tag using the PARAM element. The general syntax for the PARAM element is:

```
<PARAM NAME="paramName" VALUE="paramValue">
```

Here are brief explanations of the remaining parameter elements:

- The SRC parameter specifies the URL for the Shockwave movie. This parameter is mandatory.

- There are nine generic parameters (sw1 through sw9) available to developers for passing arbitrary values to Shockwave movies.

- The swURL parameter can be used to pass a URL to Lingo.

- The swText parameter can be used to pass a text string to Lingo.

- The swColor parameter can be used to set the color of a specific object in your Shockwave movie.

- The swForeColor parameter can be used to set the foreground color of an object in your Shockwave movie.

- The swBackColor parameter can be used to set the background color of an object in your Shockwave movie.

- The swFrame parameter can be used to designate an HTML frame or a specific frame in a Shockwave movie.

- The swName parameter can be used to pass a name (or any text) to a Shockwave movie.

- The swPassword parameter can be used to transfer a password to a Shockwave movie.

- The swBanner parameter can be used to display a text banner within a Shockwave movie.

- The swSound parameter passes the name of a specific sound to Lingo.

- The swVolume parameter can specify a volume between 1 and 10 to control the volume of all or part of a Shockwave movie.

- The swPreload parameter specifies the number of seconds to preload a Shockwave audio file before playback begins.

- The swAudio parameter passes the URL of a Shockwave audio file to Lingo.

- The swList parameter passes a list of items, delimited by a comma, to Lingo.

All of the parameter elements listed above can be retrieved, used, and manipulated by Lingo scripts using the external parameter functions `externalParamCount(n)`, `externalParamName(n)`, and `externalParamValue(n)` within your Shockwave movies. In addition, CGI scripts can be used to pass parameter values from a Shockwave movie to the server. JavaScript functions can then be used to pass these new or modified parameter elements back to Shockwave movies. Shockwave's support for external parameters provides developers with added flexibility during authoring and the ability to create easily customizable movies that can be dynamically configured at runtime.

Troubleshooting

A list of Macintosh error codes for Shockwave can be found at the following address on Macromedia's Web site:

http://www.macromedia.com/support/technotes/shockwave/developer/
    troubleshoot/mactrouble.html

Chapter 8

Scripting for the Net
Shockwave Lingo

This chapter includes a Shockwave Lingo dictionary and related
Lingo commands, handlers, and scripts that can be useful during
Shockwave development. The chapter concludes with a list of
restricted and disabled Lingo commands for Shockwave.

Shockwave Lingo Dictionary

This section defines the network Lingo commands currently supported by
Shockwave for Director. Each command is shown with its appropriate syntax and
a brief description of how it can be implemented. Refer to practical examples on
the *Shocking the Web* CD-ROM.

GoToNetMovie URL

Syntax   GoToNetMovie URL

The URL parameter within this command must be a Universal Resource Locator that specifies the HTTP path to a movie, such as:

```
"http://www.yourdomain.com/loopMovie.dcr"
```

Description

This command retrieves a Director movie over the network and displays it in the same area occupied by the calling movie. It is best utilized when playing a sequence of movies of the same height and width within the same HTML page that calls the movie.

The HTML anchor link style—normally used to link to a specific anchor on an HTML page—may be used to specify a marker inside a Shockwave movie. For example, the URL parameter `"http://www.yourdomain.com/demo.dcr #Intro"` would initiate the play of the movie demo.dcr from the marker labeled "Intro."

If you use a relative pathname to retrieve a movie in the same folder as the calling movie, place a single period and a forward slash (./) before the filename to ensure compatibility with Internet Explorer 3.0. This practice also applies to `GoToNetPage`, `PreloadNetThing`, and `GetNetText` commands.

If the destination movie has been preloaded using `PreloadNetThing`, the browser will attempt to load it from the disk cache. If the movie has not been preloaded or has been erased from the disk cache, the browser will download the movie when the `GoToNetMovie` command is executed. If a `GoToNetMovie` command is issued during an active `GoToNetMovie` download, the current download is cancelled and the new command is executed.

Shockwave movies continue to play while the browser downloads data after `GoToNetMovie` is executed. Do not place the `GoToNetMovie` command within a Lingo script that will be called repeatedly, such as an `exitFrame` handler in a looping frame or at the end of a looping movie.

Example

```
GoToNetMovie "http://www.yourdomain.com/demo.dcr"
GoToNetMovie "./demo.dcr"
```

 See the Tutorials folder on the *Shocking the Web* CD-ROM.

GoToNetPage URL[, target]

Syntax   `GoToNetPage URL[, target]`

The URL parameter within this command must be a Universal Resource Locator that specifies an HTTP path, such as:

`"http://www.yourdomain.com/index.html"`

The optional target parameter specifies the name of an HTML frame or window.

Description

This command opens a URL within the Web browser. The URL can refer to an HTML document or any other valid MIME type. The `GoToNetPage` command is the Shockwave equivalent of using the `<A HREF=url></A>` HTML tag.

If the requested URL and/or the files referenced in the URL have been preloaded, the browser will attempt to load these files from the local disk cache instead of transferring them over the network. While it is impossible to predict when pre-loaded files will be erased from the disk cache, using `PreloadNetThing` before issuing the `GoToNetPage` command can improve the user's experience by masking network latency.

Shockwave movies will continue to play while the browser downloads data after a `GoToNetPage` command is issued.

The optional target parameter following the URL in the `GoToNetPage` command can be used to designate a browser frame or window in which to load the requested page. The target can be a specific frame or window name, or one of the "magic" targets beginning with an underscore character, such as `"_blank"`, `"_self"`, `"_parent"`, and `"_top"`.

The `"_blank"` target loads the retrieved page into a new, blank browser window that is not named.

The `"_self"` target causes the retrieved page to load in the same window or frame as the current Shockwave movie.

The `"_parent"` target causes the retrieved page to load in the immediate FRAMESET parent if the Shockwave movie is contained within an HTML page containing frames. The FRAMESET parent is defined within the HTML that establishes the frames. If a FRAMESET parent has not been defined, this target defaults to behaving like the `"_self"` target.

The "_top" target causes the retrieved page to load in the full body of the window containing the Shockwave movie. This is useful for loading a page into the full browser window when you are calling GoToNetPage from a Shockwave movie that is embedded within a frame. It allows you to break out of a nested frame structure in order to fill the browser window with the retrieved page.

Example

This statement opens a URL within the browser window:

```
GoToNetPage "http://www.yrdomain.com/index.html"
```

This statement displays the URL within a window or frame named "menubar":

```
GoToNetPage "http://www.yrdomain.com/index.html","menubar"
```

If "menubar" does not already exist as a frame or window, a new browser window named "menubar" is created.

 See the Tutorials folder on the *Shocking the Web* CD-ROM.

PreloadNetThing URL

Syntax   `PreloadNetThing URL`

The URL parameter within this command must be a Universal Resource Locator that specifies an HTTP path, such as:

`"http://www.yourdomain.com/loopMovie.dcr"`

Description
This command starts the retrieval of an HTTP item to the local file cache. The HTTP item can be anything that the browser can display, such as Director movies, HTML pages, or GIF images. Items are downloaded asynchronously in the background.

In general, once an item has been downloaded, it can be viewed immediately. However, it is impossible to determine when an item has been removed from the disk cache. Cache persistence is dependent on the user's activity and the browser's cache setting.

The status of a file transfer can be monitored using the `NetDone()` and `NetError()` functions. Additional information about the file can be retrieved using the `NetMIME()` and `NetLastModDate()` functions. Preloaded file(s) can be viewed using the `GoToNetPage` or `GoToNetMovie` commands.

If `PreloadNetThing` is used to initiate multiple asynchronous downloads, `GetLatestNetID()` can be used to return a unique identifier for each operation. Most browsers will handle four simultaneous network downloads. The number of simultaneous connections can be specified in the browser's preferences file. However, you can only assume that visitors to your site will have the default browser settings.

If requests exceeding the limit are issued using any of the `Get` commands, which include `PreloadNetThing`, `GoToNetPage`, `GoToNetMovie`, `GetNetText`, or `getPrefs`, the browser will not process the additional requests. By monitoring the status of each request using the `GetLatestNetID()` and `netDone()` functions, you can control preloading within the four-connection limit.

Example
This statement begins preloading a GIF file named dog.gif that resides in the same directory as the current movie:

```
PreloadNetThing "dog.gif"
```

This handler preloads a file and adds its network identifier to the list
gXferIDlist:

```
on preloadItem theURL
  global gXferIDlist
  preloadNetThing theURL
  append(gXferIDlist,getLatestNetID())
end
```

 See the Tutorials folder on the *Shocking the Web* CD-ROM.

Syntax   `GetNetText URL`

The URL parameter within this command must be a Universal Resource Locator that specifies an HTTP path, such as:

       `"http://www.yourdomain.com/index.html"`

Description

This command initiates the retrieval of an HTTP item, which will be read by Lingo as text. The item is downloaded in the background.

`GetNetText` may be used to dynamically alter the content of Shockwave movies based on data stored in text files on the Internet.

The status of the file transfer can be monitored using the `NetDone()` and `NetError()` functions. Once the transfer is complete, the text information can be read into Lingo using the `NetTextResult()` function.

If `GetNetText` is used to initiate multiple asynchronous downloads, `GetLatestNetID()` can be used to return a unique identifier for each operation.

Example

This command starts downloading a text file named jokes.txt from the top level directory of the www.funnystuff.com server:

`GetNetText "http://www.funnystuff.com/jokes.txt"`

See the Tutorials folder on the *Shocking the Web* CD-ROM.

GetLatestNetID()

Syntax   `GetLatestNetID()`

Description
This function returns a unique identifier for the last asynchronous download operation initiated using `PreloadNetThing` or `GetNetText`. The identifier may be passed to other functions to determine the status of the file transfer and to retrieve text data related to the transfer.

Using the function `GetLatestNetID()` enables the Lingo script to monitor several simultaneous downloads. If you are downloading multiple items simultaneously, you must call `GetLatestNetID()` before you start each new download. You then can use the returned value to track the download operation using the `NetError()` and `NetDone()` functions.

Example
This handler begins downloading the image myDog.gif from myserver.com and stores the network identifier for this operation in the global variable `gCurrID`.

```
on preloadPictures
  global gCurrID
  PreloadNetThing "http://myserver.com/myDog.gif"
  put GetLatestNetID() into gCurrID
end
```

See the Tutorials folder on the *Shocking the Web* CD-ROM.

NetDone()
NetDone(NetID)

Syntax   `NetDone()`
              `NetDone(NetID)`

Description

This function returns TRUE when the asynchronous transfer specified by `NetID` is finished. Until that time, this function returns FALSE.

- The optional `NetID` parameter is an identifier returned by `GetLatestNetID()` after an asynchronous transfer is initiated.

- If the `NetID` parameter is omitted, `NetDone()` will return the status of the most recently initiated file transfer.

Example

This statement plays a bell sound if the last requested transfer is complete:

```
if NetDone() = TRUE then puppetSound "Bell.aif"
```

This statement records the status of a transfer by assigning the value of `NetDone()` to a variable.

```
put NetDone(lastTransferID) into isDone
```

In this case, `lastTransferID` is an identifier returned by `GetLatestNetID()`. If the file transfer is complete, `isDone` is set to TRUE. If the transfer is incomplete, `isDone` is set to FALSE.

See the Tutorials folder on the *Shocking the Web* CD-ROM.

NetError()
NetError(NetID)

Syntax   `NetError()`
                     `NetError(NetID)`

Description
This function returns `"OK"` when an asynchronous transfer is completed successfully. If the operation fails, `NetError()` returns a string describing the error. If the operation is not yet complete, `NetError()` returns an empty string.

- The optional `NetID` parameter is an identifier returned by `GetLatestNetID()` after an asynchronous transfer is initiated.

- If the `NetID` parameter is omitted, `NetError()` will return the error status of the most recently initiated file transfer.

In most cases, `NetError()` will not return an error if the requested file does not exist. Most Web servers respond to invalid requests by returning a valid HTML page containing the words "File Not Found." You can parse the results of `GetNetText()` to guard against this type of unreported error.

Example
This script will display an alert containing the relevant error message if the most recently attempted transfer returns an error:

```
if NetError() contains "Error" then
    alert "Network Error:" && NetError()
end if
```

The following `on idle` handler monitors a download. The network identifier for the item being downloaded is stored in the global variable `gCurrID`. When `NetDone()` returns `TRUE`, the handler checks for possible error conditions. If the file was downloaded successfully, the global variable `gNextMovieReady` will be set to `TRUE`.

```
on idle
  global gCurrID, gNextMovieReady
  if NetDone(gCurrID) = TRUE then
    if netError(gCurrID) = "OK" then
       if NetTextResult(gCurrID) contains "not found" then
          alert "File Not Found"
       else
          set gNextMovieReady = TRUE
       end if
    else if NetError() contains "Error" then
       alert "Network Error:" && NetError()
    end if
  end if
end
```

See the Tutorials folder on the *Shocking the Web* CD-ROM.

NetLastModDate()
NetLastModDate(NetID)

Syntax   `NetLastModDate()`
　　　　　 `NetLastModDate(NetID)`

Description
This function returns the date last modified string from the HTTP header for an item that was downloaded using `GetNetText` or `PreloadNetThing`.

- The optional `NetID` parameter is an identifier returned by `GetLatestNetID()` after an asynchronous transfer is initiated.

- If the `NetID` parameter is omitted, `NetLastModDate()` will return the last modified date of the most recently initiated file transfer.

Example
This statement will place the date for the most recently transferred file into the variable called `docDate`.

```
put NetLastModDate() into docDate
```

See the Tutorials folder on the *Shocking the Web* CD-ROM.

NetMIME()
NetMIME(NetID)

Syntax   NetMIME()
              NetMIME(NetID)

Description

This function returns the MIME type of an HTTP item that was transferred using
GetNetText or PreloadNetThing.

- The optional NetID parameter is an identifier returned by
  GetLatestNetID() after an asynchronous transfer is initiated.

- If the NetID parameter is omitted, NetTextResult() will return the error
  status of the most recently initiated file transfer.

Example

This statement will place the MIME type of the transfer, identified by NetID,
into the variable called gMimeType.

```
put NetMIME(NetID) into gMimeType
```

The following handler will evaluate the MIME type of a downloaded item. If the
MIME type is "application/x-director" it will display the file using the
GoToNetMovie command. If the downloaded item is something other than a
Shockwave movie, it will be handled by the browser using the GoToNetPage
command. The transferComplete handler requires two arguments: theURL
argument which contains the Universal Resource Locator for the file, and netID
which is the identifier returned by the NetMIME function.

```
on transferComplete theURL, netID
   if NetMIME(NetID) contains ¬
"application/x-director" then
     GoToNetMovie theURL
   else
     GoToNetPage theURL
   end if
end
```

 See the Tutorials folder on the *Shocking the Web* CD-ROM.

NetTextResult()
NetTextResult(NetID)

Syntax   `NetTextResult()`
               `NetTextResult(NetID)`

Description

This function returns the text result of an asynchronous transfer operation.

- The optional `NetID` parameter is an identifier returned by `GetLatestNetID()` after an asynchronous transfer is initiated.

- If the `NetID` parameter is omitted, `NetTextResult()` will return the text of the most recently initiated file transfer.

Typically, `NetTextResult()` is used to retrieve the text of a `GetNetText` operation after the operation is completed. It also may be used to retrieve the text contents of a completed `PreloadNetThing` operation. `NetTextResult()` is useful only if the preloaded item is a text document.

Example

This statement will place the text contents of the transfer identified by the `NetID` parameter into the variable called `netDocumentText`.

`put NetTextResult(netID) into netDocumentText`

See `NetError()` for information on using `NetTextResult()` to filter out seemingly successful downloads of non-existent HTTP items.

 See the Tutorials folder on the *Shocking the Web* CD-ROM.

NetAbort

Syntax   NetAbort

Description
This command cancels the current network operation. NetAbort may be used to cancel a preloading operation if the preloading file becomes unnecessary.

Example
This handler—when placed inside a cast member acting as a button—will cancel the current file download before going to the movie "vacation.dcr." The global variable gBaseURL is used to store the path to the HTTP items.

```
on mouseDown
    global gBaseURL
    if NetDone() = FALSE then NetAbort
    GoToNetMovie gBaseURL & "vacation.dcr"
end
```

See the Tutorials folder on the *Shocking the Web* CD-ROM.

setPref prefName, prefValue

Syntax   `setPref prefName, prefValue`

Description
This command writes a string to a file stored on the user's local disk. The filename is specified in the `prefName` parameter and the string is defined in the `prefValue` parameter. When the `setPref` command is executed, a folder named Prefs is automatically created inside of the Shockwave Support folder. Any file created by the `setPref` command is stored within the Prefs folder.

The `SetPref` command is used to write an entire file to the local disk. It cannot be used to append text to an existing file.

Macromedia recommends limiting the filenames stored in `prefName` to 8 or less alphanumeric characters.

Example
This handler—when placed inside a cast member acting as a button—will record the current value stored in a field named `Score` in a preferences file named XYZgame.txt.

```
on mouseDown
    setPref "XYZgame.txt", the text of field "Score"
end
```

In the following example, multiple preferences are stored in a property list named `gPrefSettings` using the `makePref` handler. The `writePrefs` handler is called to write the contents of the list to an external preferences file (named DXM.txt in this example). Generic `movie` script handlers are shown below. You can customize this code by simply changing the name of `gPrefsFile` in the `writePrefs` handler.

```
global gPrefsFile, gPrefSettings


on makePref prefName, prefData
    if voidP(gPrefSettings) then ¬
set gPrefSettings = [:]
    setAProp gPrefSettings, prefName, prefData
    debug string (gPrefSettings)
end
```

```
on writePrefs
   if the movieName contains ".dcr" ¬
and listP(gPrefSettings) then
      if not(gPrefsFile) then ¬
set gPrefsFile = "DXM.txt"
      set prefData = ""
      repeat with i = 1 to count(gPrefSettings)
      set prefName = getPropAt(gPrefSettings,i)
      set prefSetting = ¬ getProp(gPrefSettings,prefName)
      set prefData = ¬
prefData & prefName & "=" & prefSetting & RETURN
      end repeat
      setPref gPrefsFile, prefData
      debug "writing prefs: " & prefData
   end if
      end
```

See the Tutorials folder on the *Shocking the Web* CD-ROM.

getPref(prefName)

Syntax   `getPref(prefName)`

Description

This function returns the text of the file named `prefName` that was created using the `setPref` command. The function returns `<VOID>` if there is no such file located in the Prefs folder.

Example

The following `startMovie` script returns the text stored in the file named XYZgame.txt and stores it in a global variable named `gLastScore` when the Shockwave movie is first loaded:

```
on startMovie
    global gLastScore
    set gLastScore = getPref("XYZgame.txt")
    put gLastScore into field "Score"
end
```

This handler retrieves a single item from the external preferences file. In the event that multiple preferences are stored, it is necessary to parse the data retrieved from the file in order to use it. See "Determining Bitstream" in Chapter 7, "Shockwave Authoring," for a detailed example.

> **Note**
>
> *A number of Shockwave developers are working to develop standards for inter-movie communication and external preference files. If you are interested in these issues, you can follow the discussions on the ShockeR listserv (visit http://www.shocker.com/shocker to subscribe).*

 See the Tutorials folder on the *Shocking the Web* CD-ROM.

externalParamCount([integer])

Syntax   `externalParamCount([integer])`

Description

This function returns the number of arguments (as an integer) that are passed to a Shockwave movie from the parameter elements in the HTML `<EMBED>` or `<OBJECT>` tag.

Example

```
on startMovie
    global gParamNum
    set gParamNum = externalParamCount()
end
```

See the Tutorials folder on the *Shocking the Web* CD-ROM.

externalParamName([integer])

Syntax   externalParamName([integer])

Description

This function returns the name(s) of external arguments that are passed to the Shockwave movie from the parameter elements in the HTML <EMBED> or <OBJECT> tag. The externalParamName() function returns a string.

For example, an <OBJECT> tag used to embed a Shockwave movie could contain the following Shockwave PARAM element that passes a URL to Lingo:

<PARAM NAME="swURL" VALUE="http://www.yrserver.com/random.html">

The externalParamName() function is used below to index the number of external parameters to the external parameter name(s), and then store the names in a list.

Example

```
on startMovie
    global gParamNum, gParamNameList
    set gParamNum = externalParamCount()
    if gParamNum then
        if voidP(gParamNameList) then set gParamNameList = [:]
        repeat with n = 1 to gParamNum
            set parName = externalParamName(n)
            setAProp gParamNameList, n, parName
        end repeat
    end if
end
```

See the Tutorials folder on the *Shocking the Web* CD-ROM.

externalParamValue([parameter])

Syntax   `externalParamValue([parameter])`

Description

This function returns the value of external arguments that are passed to the Shockwave movie from the parameter elements in the HTML <EMBED> or <OBJECT> tag. The `externalParamValue()` function returns the number of the external parameter value if (`[parameter]`) is an integer. If (`[parameter]`) is a string, such as the parameter name, the function returns the value of the parameter that matches the string. If a matching parameter string or integer does not exist, Lingo returns <VOID>.

Examples

In this example, (`[parameter]`) is an integer:

```
on startMovie
    global gParamNum, gParamNameList
    set gParamNum = externalParamCount()
    if gParamNum then
        if voidP(gParamNameList) then set gParamNameList = [:]
        repeat with n = 1 to gParamNum
            set parName = externalParamName(n)
            set parValue = externalParamValue(n)
            setAProp gParamNameList, parName, parValue
        end repeat
    end if
end
```

In this example, (`[parameter]`) is a string:

```
on exitframe
    global gRandomPage, gUrlFlag
    if gUrlFlag then set gRandomPage = externalParamValue("swURL")
    if gRandomPage contains "http" then ¬
        preLoadNetThing gRandomPage
end
```

 See the Tutorials folder on the *Shocking the Web* CD-ROM.

Syntax   `the URL of member`

The URL property of a Shockwave audio (SWA) cast member designates the streaming audio file played by that cast member. The command syntax is as follows:

```
set the URL of member [SWA member] = [HTTP path]
```

The HTTP address of the URL property may contain a relative or absolute path to the SWA file. For example:

```
set the URL of member "SWAHolder" = "./dieknodel.SWA"
```

Description

URL is a special property available only to cast members created using the Shockwave Streaming Audio Xtra. Once the URL of a SWA member is set, all subsequent messages to that SWA member will be used to control, or get information about, the SWA file specified in [HTTP path]. Relative paths may be used, but remember to add "./" before the names of SWA files that are located in the same folder as your Shockwave movie to ensure compatibility with Internet Explorer 3.

The URL property of a streaming audio cast member may be changed at any time (except during playback).

Example

```
on mouseDown
    global gSWAHolder
    set the URL of member gSWAHolder = ¬
    "http://www.peltzman.com/leefeldman/living.SWA"
    prepForPlayback(gSWAHolder)
end
```

See the Tutorials folder on the *Shocking the Web* CD-ROM.

the PreloadTime of member

Syntax   the PreloadTime of member

This property of a SWA cast member designates the number of seconds that a SWA file is preloaded into memory before playback of the sound begins. Example command syntax:

set the PreloadTime of member [SWA member] = [seconds]

Description

The PreloadTime of member property is set to the number of seconds that a SWA will transfer to the client computer before playback begins. The PreLoadBuffer command, described below, is then issued to initiate the transfer. Preloading a few seconds of audio protects the audio stream from glitches caused by unpredictable network behavior. Preloading at least 3 to 5 seconds of audio before playback is highly recommended. The PreloadTime property can be changed at anytime.

Note that the designated number of seconds defines how many seconds of audio should be preloaded, and not the amount of time the browser should spend executing the preload operation. The length of time required to preload x seconds of audio can vary widely based on the bit rate of the SWA file, the speed of the user's connection, and overall network throughput.

Example

```
on prepForPlayback(SWAcast)
    set the preloadTime of member SWACast = 5
    ...
end
```

See the Tutorials folder on the *Shocking the Web* CD-ROM.

PreloadBuffer ([SWA member])

Syntax   PreloadBuffer ([SWA member])

Description
The PreloadBuffer command initiates preloading of the SWA file controlled by [SWA member], based on the PreloadTime of member property.

For more information, see the description of the PreloadTime of member above.

Example
```
on prepForPlayback(SWAcast)
    set the preloadTime of member SWACast = 5
    preloadBuffer (member SWACast)
end
```

 See the Tutorials folder on the *Shocking the Web* CD-ROM.

Play ([SWA member])

Syntax   Play ([SWA member])

Description

The Play command starts the playback of a streaming audio file controlled by [SWA member]. The URL of member property must be set before the Play command is issued. Preload operations are not mandatory for the execution of the Play command.

Example

```
on mouseDown
    Play (member "SWAHolder")
end
```

See the Tutorials folder on the *Shocking the Web* CD-ROM.

Pause ([SWA member])

Syntax   `Pause ([SWA member])`

Description

The `Pause` command halts playback of a streaming audio file controlled by
`[SWA member]`. If playback is resumed using the `Play` command, the sound file
will resume playing from the point at which it was paused.

The `Pause` command's function is analogous to pressing the pause button on an
audio CD player. In many software CD players, the Play button becomes a Pause
button while the sound is playing, and reverts back to a Play button when the
sound is paused.

Example

```
on mouseDown
    set SWAStatus = the state of ¬
        member "SWAHolder"
    if (SWAstatus <= 2) or (SWAstatus = 4) then
        play (member "SWAHolder")
    else if SWAstatus = 3 then
        pause (member "SWAHolder")
    end if
end
```

See the Tutorials folder on the *Shocking the Web* CD-ROM.

Stop ([SWA member])

Syntax   Stop ([SWA member])

Description

The Stop command halts playback of a SWA file referenced by [SWA member]. If playback is resumed using the Play command, the sound begins to play from the head of the sound file.

Example

```
on mouseDown
    Stop (member "SWAHolder")
end
```

 See the Tutorials folder on the *Shocking the Web* CD-ROM.

the state of member [SWA member]

Syntax   `the state of member [SWA member]`

This property determines the current status of the streaming audio file that is controlled by `[SWA member]`.

Description

The `state of member` property is essential for monitoring the progress of SWA files. For example, while a file is preloading you can `monitor the state of member` in an `idle` loop to determine when the sound is ready for smooth playback.

These are the possible codes that can be returned for the `state of member` property:

0   stopped
1   preLoading
2   preLoadDone
3   playing
4   paused
5   done
9   error

Example

```
on idle
global gSWAflag
    if gSWAflag = 1 then
        set SWAStatus = the state of member ¬
            "SWAHolder"
        if SWAStatus = 2 then
            set gSWAFlag = 0
            Play (member "SWAHolder")
        end if
    end if
end
```

 See the Tutorials folder on the *Shocking the Web* CD-ROM.

the duration of member [SWA member]

Syntax   `the duration of member [SWA member]`

Description

This property returns the length, in seconds, of the streaming audio file refer-enced by the URL property of `[SWA member]`.

Information about specific SWA files is not available until after transfer of the SWA file from the server to the browser begins. `The duration of member` property will return a value of `(0)` until streaming has started (or preloading is finished).

Example

```
on displaySWAData
    if the state of member "SWAHolder" >= 2 then
        put the duration of member "SWAHolder" ¬
            into field "duration"
    end if
end
```

See the Tutorials folder on the *Shocking the Web* CD-ROM.

the percentStreamed of member [SWA member]

Syntax   `the percentStreamed of member [SWA member]`

Description

This property of SWA cast members returns the percentage of the SWA file controlled by `[SWA member]` that has already been streamed to the client.

`The percentStreamed of member` is not tied directly to playback. For information about the amount of a SWA file that has actually been played on the client
computer, use `the precentPlayed of member` property.

Example
```
on idle
    if the state of member "SWAHolder" = 1 then
        showLoading(the percentStreamed of ¬
            member "SWAHolder")
    end if
end
```

See the Tutorials folder on the *Shocking the Web* CD-ROM.

the percentPlayed of member [SWA member]

Syntax   `the percentPlayed of member [SWA member]`

Description

This property of SWA cast members returns the percentage of a SWA file controlled by `[SWA member]` that has already been played on the client computer.

The `percentPlayed of member` property returns an integer between `0` and `100`. This function is useful for making graphical status bars to display how much of the sound has been played and how much of the sound is left to play.

Example

```
on idle
    if the state of member "SWAHolder" = 3 then
        updateStatusBar(the percentPlayed of ¬
            member "SWAHolder")
    end if
end
```

See the Tutorials folder on the *Shocking the Web* CD-ROM.

the bitRate of member [SWA member]

Syntax   `the bitRate of member [SWA member]`

This property returns the bit rate of a SWA file referenced by `[SWA member]`, after the file has been preloaded.

Description

The `bitRate of member` property returns `(0)` until preloading is complete. To expedite the acquisition of information about SWA files (at the possible expense of sound quality) set `the preLoadTime of member` equal to `1`.

Example

```
if the state of member "SWAHolder" = 2 then
    set bRate = the bitRate of member "SWAHolder"
end if
```

See the Tutorials folder on the *Shocking the Web* CD-ROM.

getError(member [SWA member])
getErrorString(member [SWA member])

Syntax   getError(member [SWA member])

getErrorString(member [SWA member])

Description

These functions return information about streaming audio errors. The getError()
function returns an integer, and the getErrorString() function returns a text
string that describes the error.

Here is a list of the codes returned by the getError() and getErrorString()
functions. The getErrorString() text corresponds directly to the getError()
code on the same line.

getError()		getErrorString()
0	=	OK
1	=	memory
2	=	network
3	=	playback device
99	=	other

Example

```
on idle
    if getError(member "SWAHolder) <> 0 then
        alert "SWA Error" && ¬
            getErrorString(member "SWAHolder")
    end if
end
```

See the Tutorials folder on the *Shocking the Web* CD-ROM.

Restricted Lingo for Shockwave Development

Some Lingo commands and functions work differently, or not at all, in Shockwave movies. Lingo capabilities are usually restricted in cases where use of a particular command or function can violate certain security protocols adhered to by all Web browsers. For example, you cannot use Lingo to read files from the client computer unless they reside in the Shockwave Support folder. The Shockwave engineering team at Macromedia is reportedly working on a solution which bundles linked media with the Shockwave movie. In the meantime, linked media is limited to files that are accessible through the Support folder. The Support folder resides inside the browser's folder, but has a different name depending on the user's platform and operating system. Use the following chart to determine the proper default name and path for the Support folder.

Netscape Navigator 2.0 or later

Windows 95 C:\ProgramFiles\Netscape\Navigator\Program\Plugins\NP32DSW

Windows 3.1 C:\NETSCAPE\PLUGINS\NP16DSW

MacOS PowerPC ...:Plug-ins:NP-PPC-Dir-Shockwave folder

Macintosh 68k   ...:Plug-ins:NP-Mac68k-Dir-Shockwave folder

Microsoft Internet Explorer 2.0 or later

Windows 95 C:\Program Files\Microsoft Internet\Plugins\NP32DSW

Windows 3.1 C:\WINDOWS\SYSTEM\NP16DSW

MacOS PowerPC ...:Plug-ins:NP-PPC-Dir-Shockwave folder

Macintosh 68k   ...:Plug-ins:NP-Mac68k-Dir-Shockwave folder

The following is a directory of Lingo elements that have restrictions or limitations when used in Shockwave movies.

OpenXLib fileName
CloseXLib fileName

Syntax   OpenXLib fileName
             CloseXLib fileName

Description

These commands are invoked by Director to open external library files—Xtras, Xobjects, DLLs, and XCMD files. Any external file your movie uses must be present on the user's machine inside the Support folder. Transition Xtras, Sprite Xtras, Lingo Xtras, Xobjects, and DLLs may all be used by Shockwave movies, but they must reside in the proper folder. Shockwave cannot automatically download files into the Support folder at this time. Director will ignore all path information included in the fileName parameter of the OpenXLib and CloseXLib commands.

Note

The process described above also may be used to provide XCMD and XFCN access to Shockwave movies on Macintosh computers. However, all XCMDs and XFCNs, as well as XObjects, must be contained in a file outside the Shockwave movie, as Shockwave movies do not have a resource fork.

Example

This line of Lingo will open the PrintOMatic Xtra.

```
OpenXLib "PrintOMatic"
```

Remember to dispose of any objects created by a Lingo Xtra or XObject/DLL, and close external libraries after you have finished using them.

Open Castlib fileName
ImportFileInto

Syntax
```
Open Castlib fileName
ImportFileInto member whichCastMember, theFileName
    ImportFileInto member whichMember of castLib ¬
    whichCastLib, fileName
```

Description

These commands are used to import new content into your Director projects. Open Castlib may be used to make any cast library available to the current movie. External cast libraries can be used to expand and change your Director or Shockwave project; new or occasionally accessed cast members may be stored in external casts, while universal assets and Lingo scripts are best kept in your central movie.

ImportFileInto will import linked media into Director movies. You can use this command to play digital video files from your Shockwave movies. (Shockwave does not support direct playback of linked QuickTime or Video for Windows cast members.) Shockwave movies will not overwrite an existing cast member when importing linked media; you must import these files into empty cast member positions.

Any external cast libraries or linked files your movie uses, or aliases/shortcuts to these files, must be present on the client inside the Support folder. Shockwave cannot automatically download files into the Support folder at this time. If you use external casts you must provide a means (via FTP, floppy, or CD-ROM, for example) for the user to obtain these files and transfer them into the proper folder.

Example

The following function will import files specified by theFile into the cast of an active Shockwave movie, starting at the first empty cast member position greater than 500.

```
on importIt theFile
  global gImportIndex
  if not(gImportIndex) then
    set gImportIndex = findEmpty(member   500)
  else
    set gImportIndex = (gImportIndex + 1)
  end if
  importFileInto member gImportIndex, theFile
  updateStage
  return gImportIndex
end
```

Movie
MovieName

Syntax   Movie

               MovieName

Description

These functionally-equivalent Lingo terms are used to get the name of the current movie. They operate normally in shocked movies—however, since browsers change the names of inline files when downloading to the local disk cache, the movieName of the Shockwave movie on the client machine will not match the name of the Shockwave movie on the server.

For example, a movie named shocktest.dcr may be named cache123456.dcr after it has been downloaded for inline display by the Web browser.

Load to cache operations will not change the suffix of the Shockwave movie, so you can still test for the .dcr suffix in your Lingo scripts. This technique can be useful for avoiding net Lingo while you are working in the offline Director authoring environment.

Example

The following handler will execute a GoToNetPage operation only if the current movie has a .dcr suffix.

```
on goPage thePage
   if the movieName contains ".dcr" then
      GoToNetPage thePage
   else
      put thePage
   end if
end
```

Delay numberOfTicks

Syntax   `Delay numberOfTicks`

Description

The `delay` command is used to pause playback of a Director movie for a specific length of time, measured in ticks. One tick equals one sixtieth of a second.

Delay commands and Wait settings in the Score's Tempo channel do not work in movies created using Shockwave for Director 4. You can replace delay commands and Wait settings with a handler that remains in a repeat loop for a specified period of time.

Example

The following handler can be used to replace the `delay` command, or to simulate Wait settings in the Tempo channel.

```
on waitFor ticksToWait
    set startTime = the ticks
    repeat while the ticks < startTime + ticksToWait
     nothing
    end repeat
end
```

An alternative handler, which does not use a repeat loop, can be used to keep the playback head on the current frame until the specified number of ticks has elapsed. (Repeat loops lock out system events and prevent the user from interacting with the Shockwave movie and the browser. They should be avoided when possible.)

```
on waitFor ticksToWait
  if the timer > ticksToWait then
    startTimer
  else
    go the frame
  end if
end
```

The following handler can be used to replace the Wait for Sound setting in the Tempo channel. The playback head will remain in the current frame until the sound in the specified channel is finished playing.

```
on waitForSnd SoundChannel
    if soundBusy(SoundChannel) then go the frame
end
```

pause

Syntax   pause

Description

The pause command is used to pause playback of a Director movie. This command is not functional in movies created using Shockwave for Director 4.

Replace pause commands by causing the playback head to loop on a frame—which is most often accomplished within an on exitframe handler.

Example

A basic frame script can be used in place of a pause command.

```
on exitFrame
    go the frame
end
```

Lingo Disabled for Shockwave Development

The following Lingo terms are disabled for Shockwave development—primarily for security reasons. All of the commands and functions are used to manipulate external files, pathnames, and system events.

`quit`

> This command exits the Director application or a Director projector.
>
> *Existing Shockwave behavior: Lingo ignored.*

`restart`

> This command restarts the computer when issued under the MacOS. The command is not cross-platform; it has no effect when issued under the Windows OS.
>
> *Existing Shockwave behavior: unsupported Lingo error.*

`shutdown`

> This command shuts the computer down when issued under the MacOS or Windows 95. Under Windows 3.1, the command exits Director or a Director projector and then exits Windows.
>
> *Existing Shockwave behavior: unsupported Lingo error.*

`open [filename with] whichApplication`

> This command is invoked to launch an application. The optional filename parameter can be included to open a particular file when the specified application is launched.
>
> *Existing Shockwave behavior: unsupported Lingo error.*

`openResFile filename`
`closeResFile filename`

> Under the MacOS, these commands are used to open and close resource files that reside outside of a Director movie. Custom fonts, cursors, and icons, for example, can be stored in resource files. These commands are not cross-platform; they have no effect when issued under the Windows OS.
>
> *Existing Shockwave behavior: unsupported Lingo error.*

`saveMovie [filename]`

This command saves a movie to a file. The movie is saved under the current name unless the optional `filename` parameter is specified.

Existing Shockwave behavior: unsupported Lingo error.

`the colordepth`

Setting `the colordepth` property lets you change the color depth of the user's display under the MacOS, and has no effect when issued under the Windows OS. Setting `the colordepth` property has been disabled for Shockwave. (However, it is possible to test the color depth of both Macintosh and Windows displays using this property within Shockwave movies.)

Existing Shockwave behavior: unsupported Lingo error.

`printFrom startframe[,stopFrame][,reduction%]`

This command prints the Director Stage within a frame or range of frames. The reduction parameter can be used to reduce the output size of the printed frames to 50 or 25 percent.

Existing Shockwave behavior: unsupported Lingo error.

`the pathName`
`the moviePath`

These functions return a string containing the full pathname to the current Director movie. They are functionally equivalent.

Existing Shockwave behavior: unsupported Lingo error.

`the searchCurrentFolder`

This function contains a Boolean value that determines whether Director searches the current folder when searching filenames.

Existing Shockwave behavior: unsupported Lingo error.

`the searchPath`
`the searchPaths`

The `searchPath` function gets or sets a list containing the pathname that Director searches when a file does not exist in the current folder or directory. The `searchPaths` is a global property that gets or sets a list of full pathnames to search.

Existing Shockwave behavior: unsupported Lingo error.

the fileName of castLib whichCast

>This property gets or sets the full pathname and filename of an external cast library. The property can be tested and set from within Director movies and projectors. (If an internal cast is specified, the property displays the current movie name.)
>
>*Existing Shockwave behavior: unsupported Lingo error.*

fileName of window whichWindow

>This window property gets or sets the filename of the movie in a window (MIAW) assigned to the window specified by the whichWindow parameter.
>
>*Existing Shockwave behavior: unsupported Lingo error.*

getNthFileNameInFolder (folderPath, fileNumber)

>This function returns the name of a file at a specified path and location within a folder.
>
>*Existing Shockwave behavior: unsupported Lingo error.*

pasteClipboardInto member whichMember

>This command pastes the contents of the Clipboard into the specified member.
>
>*Existing Shockwave behavior: unsupported Lingo error.*

mci "string"

>The mci command sends specified strings to the Windows media control interface in order to communicate with the multimedia system extensions. These commands are not cross-platform; they have no effect when issued under the MacOS.
>
>*Existing Shockwave behavior: unsupported Lingo error.*

```
FileIO
SerialIO
Ortho Protocol
```

These code libraries (written prior to the development of Macromedia's Xtras architecture) extend Director's functionality. The `FileIO` Xobject/DLL is used to read and write text files, while `SerialIO` is used to transfer data through the computer's serial port. The `Ortho Protocol` is a set of standards established by Macromedia that permits Director to communicate with third party hardware devices, such as videodisc and videotape players.

Existing Shockwave behavior: Xobjects and DLLs are functional within Shockwave movies if they are stored in the Shockwave Support folder. However, it is strongly recommended that developers behave responsibly and do not implement FileIO in Shockwave movies because movies created by others could unintentionally, or intentionally, exploit its features to write or delete files on the user's local disk.

Lingo Potentially Available for Shockwave Development

At the present time, the Lingo terms related to displaying a movie in a window and building custom menus are disabled. However, these may become enabled in a future Shockwave release—but we offer no guarantees.

Movie In A Window (MIAW)

The following Lingo commands, functions, event handlers, and properties are used to open, close, and manipulate a movie in a window from within a Director movie.

```
window windowName
open window windowName
on openWindow
close window windowName
on closeWindow
drawRect of window windowName
fileName of window windowName
forget window windowName
modal of window windowName
moveToBack window windowName
moveToFront window windowName
the rect of window windowName
the title of window windowName
the visible of window windowName
the windowList
```

Existing Shockwave behavior: unsupported Lingo error, or Lingo is ignored.

Custom Menus

Shocked Director movies cannot take advantage of custom menus defined by a field cast member at the present time. The following Lingo terms are used to create and modify custom menus.

```
menu
installMenu whichMember
the name of menu whichMenu
the name of menuItem whichItem of menu whichMenu
the script of menuItem whichItem of menu whichMenu
the checkMark of menuItem whichItem of menu whichMenu
the number of menuItems of menu whichMenu
the number of menus
the enabled of menuItem whichItem of menu whichMenu
```

Existing Shockwave behavior: unsupported Lingo error, or Lingo is ignored.

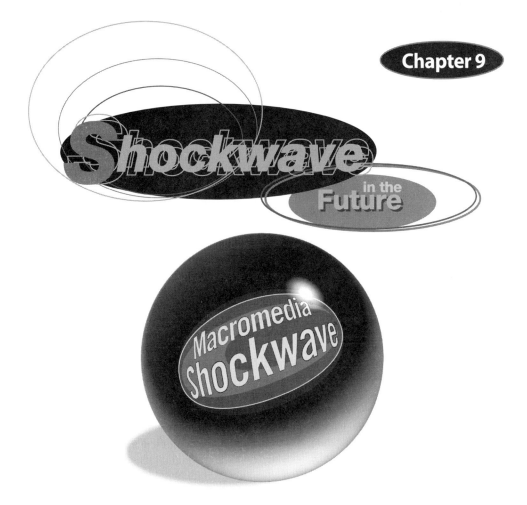

Online Opportunities
Shockwave in the Future

Shockwave is at the forefront of multimedia technology on the Internet. Macromedia has moved quickly over the past year to position the company's entire product line to take advantage of the new opportunities afforded by the Internet. Let's examine some of the challenges facing multimedia on the Internet and explore potential future directions for Shockwave.

Bandwidth, Bandwidth, Bandwidth!

Currently, anyone who has used the Internet, and Shockwave in particular, will tell you that the greatest impediment to broad-based consumer acceptance is time—specifically, time required to download files. No matter how fresh and exhilarating the content, if a file takes half an hour to download its appeal is limited to hard core enthusiasts and people with too much time on their hands. Although some Shockwave developers have created some amazingly small movies of very high quality, it is unlikely that any of them would turn down the opportunity to deliver larger files with more graphics and sounds if they could be downloaded just as quickly.

The source of the time problem is bandwidth. Bandwidth determines the amount of data that a user may access in a given period of time. In older communications media, such as radio and television, bandwidth is a fixed commodity. These older media were established in an era of strict government regulation. Because television and radio signals travel through the public airwaves, the government allocated portions of the electromagnetic spectrum to licensees and regulated how the spectrum was divided. Hence, the portion of the spectrum the licensee was granted—their bandwidth allocation—was fixed, and the signals broadcasted through the bandwidth had (and still have) to conform to strict standards. This system of allocation and regulation has been spectacularly successful for all parties concerned: the broadcasters, the radio and television equipment manufacturers, and the listeners and viewers. However, the electromagnetic spectrum is a finite commodity, which can be divided into only a discrete number of channels. To increase bandwidth, the broadcasters and others have turned to cable, a medium that also plays into the future of the Internet.

How does digital communication in general, and the Internet in particular, relate to older communications media? In one sense, digital communications are the exact opposite of broadcast analog communications: the size of the communication "channel" is scaleable to fit the size of the content offered, the source of the information is distributed (as opposed to the centralized source of the broadcast media), the content can be any data which can be digitized, and for the most part, the information is not time-based—that is, the receiver can conceivably download the information at any time. However, digital communications and broadcast analog communications are both dependent upon bandwidth.

Broadcasters have filled the fixed bandwidth allotted to them by the government while conforming to standards and regulations which mandate that a uniform product be delivered to the consumer. In the deregulatory times in which we live, it is highly improbable that Internet content providers can expect a similar set of standards by which to guide their development, and most do not want them. The wide variations in bandwidth accessed by Internet consumers—from T1 access by many business users to 14.4 and 28.8 kbps access by most home users—is the determining factor in the creation of content. Text-only Web sites accommodate the lowest common denominator, while high-bandwidth sites containing content such as streaming video virtually exclude the low-bandwidth consumer. This is a choice broadcasters never have to make. However, this very same scaleability of content means that Internet content providers can change the nature of their offerings as bandwidth increases; for example, a site can evolve from a combination of text and static images to Shockwave movies and virtual environments. Broadcasters, hemmed in by standards and regulations, must always deliver content in the same form.

It is highly unlikely that television broadcasters will change the format of their content even given higher bandwidth. The original proposal for high-definition television (HDTV) called for the allotment of more bandwidth in the electromagnetic spectrum to the broadcasters in order to handle the increased data requirements of HDTV. Broadcasters, instead, have seized upon this opportunity to air more channels of content in the same format that they currently employ.

Internet content providers on the other hand—as befitting an unregulated new medium—are creating their own standards and constantly changing them. The version of Shockwave we will be using five years from now (if it has not become an entirely new product!) will no doubt be substantially different from the current version. The driving force in the change will be increased bandwidth. As more and more people are connected to higher bandwidth networks, technologies like Shockwave will adapt to take advantage of greater capacity.

Who will provide this increased bandwidth? For the past several years, the telephone companies have appeared to be the most likely candidates. Most people currently access the Internet via modems using the twisted pair analog network of the companies that comprised AT&T before its breakup in the early 1980s. These Regional Bell Operating Companies (RBOCs) have frequently been in the news with stories of online trials of higher bandwidth services. However, bringing high-bandwidth services to consumers will require a major infrastructure investment for these companies as they switch from twisted pair wiring to the necessary high-capacity fiber optic lines. As telephone companies define and redefine their online ventures, their erstwhile partners in online development, the cable companies, are developing their own strategies.

The cable companies have a unique advantage in that they have spent the last 30 years building a high-speed communications infrastructure. Trials in Sunnyvale, California, by @Home, and in Jacksonville, Florida, by Continental Cablevision, point to a future of high-speed digital access by way of cable modems over the existing cable TV network. How much faster? For the round of cable modems expected to be released by the end of 1996, the cable providers tout an initial delivery speed of approximately 10 megabits (or 1.25 megabytes) downstream—which is to the end user's computer, and 1 megabit (or 125 kilobytes) upstream—which is from the end user's computer. Potential delivery speeds of approximately 30 megabits (or 3.75 megabytes) downstream and 2.5 megabits (or 312 kilobytes) upstream are expected.

Content Evolution

If, as it is becoming apparent, bandwidth limitations are satisfactorily addressed by cable access (or any other solution), how will increased capacity affect the content delivered over the Internet?

Although 10 megabits per second may sound like a vast pipeline, other "super" conduits of the past (like the Interstate highway system) have demonstrated the human capacity for maximum utilization of a finite resource. Let's assume a future in which everyone is connected to the Internet at full cable-modem speed. As data transfer rates over the Internet surpass the speed of CD-ROM, the type of content available on the Web will evolve. Shockwave and other emerging multimedia technologies discussed below are currently like seeds waiting to germinate in this coming golden age.

Digital Video and Audio

Digital video and audio are the most likely benefactors of the coming increase in bandwidth. Desktop digital video and audio production has been a reality for some time now, and these media types are now being transmitted over the Internet. Radio stations that broadcast solely over the Internet are cropping up almost daily, thanks to technology being utilized in products such as Shockwave with Streaming Audio from Macromedia. Other players will no doubt enter this market with new products and standards. Likewise, digital video transmission is becoming a reality thanks to the efforts of Apple Computer with its QuickTime technology and the recent agreement between Intel and Microsoft to release a joint standard.

Director's capability to coordinate and control these data types in the realm of CD-ROM make it a natural for a similar role on the Internet. So it's very likely that Shockwave will continue to serve as a nexus for these two types of data. With the release of Shockwave for Director 5 and its support for linked media, we see the beginnings of this role.

Virtual Reality

Virtual Reality Modeling Language (VRML) is a standard for transmission of 3D data over the Internet. Although it is currently not possible to view a VRML scene from within Shockwave, it's not out of the question in the future. Macromedia is already supporting QuickDraw 3D, which is a similar technology, from within Director, and Extreme3D (Macromedia's 3D software) exports VRML2 files. With greater computational power in the hands of users in the future and the advances made in 3D display technology, it's likely that more content providers will use virtual reality as a means of presentation. Whether virtual reality is incorporated into Shockwave, or Shockwave is accessed from within a VRML scene, we can expect to see these two leading technologies together on the Net.

Java

Java from Sun Microsystems is a complex, object-oriented programming language that provides a unique architecture for online application and applet creation across multiple platforms and operating systems. The Java language is quickly becoming a standard and is supported by a growing number of Java-enabled Web browsers, such as Navigator and Internet Explorer. Java applets, like Shockwave movies, display seamlessly within Web pages and are downloaded to a user's local system before being executed by the browser.

Java's object-oriented programming environment is based on the C++ language. At the present time, creating Java applets requires programming skills. Some Java authoring tools are available, but they do not as yet offer the degree of control over media elements that Director provides. The majority of existing Java examples are technically impressive, but often lack smooth animation, sophisticated graphics, and tight synchronization of media elements.

At the same time, the Java language can perform many network and system-level tasks that Director cannot. Java's object-oriented language makes it possible to easily create reusable code modules. Java class libraries provide system input and output capabilities and other portable cross-platform utility functions that could extend the power and functionality of Shockwave movies. For example, the integration of Shockwave with Java could provide developers with the ability to build complex simulations and teaching tools to filter data input by multiple users. These applications would be comparable to those created in other programming languages such as C or C++. Considering that Java is already an integral part of the Navigator and Internet Explorer browsers, Shockwave developers should plan to leverage Java in the future.

LiveConnect

In the area of interoperability, Netscape has developed its LiveConnect communications layer, which enables HTML elements, Java applets, Netscape plug-ins such as Shockwave, and JavaScript scripts to communicate and control one another within Netscape's Open Network Environment (ONE).

It is currently possible for Shockwave movies to call JavaScript functions and to pass parameters between JavaScript and Shockwave in order to alter the performance of a Shockwave movie on the fly, or to store and change values between Shockwave movies. It is easy to imagine additional benefits of the LiveConnect model. For example, the ability to communicate between plug-ins could enable a Shockwave animation to trigger and control playback of an embedded QuickTime video, or a Shockwave movie could provide a navigation controller for a VRML scene.

ActiveX

Along the same lines as Netscape's LiveConnect communications layer, Microsoft has developed ActiveX. ActiveX is the new incarnation of what was OLE (Object Linking and Embedding). The ActiveX architecture allows developers to create small programs, or ActiveX controls, which run much like Java applets. (Java applets are supported as ActiveX controls.) In both Java/LiveConnect and ActiveX models, larger programs can be formed by linking smaller components together, with an emphasis on facilitating communication between the smaller components.

Shockwave Integration

How does Shockwave technology relate to the Java and ActiveX development environments? Regardless of whether the Java strategy from Sun and Netscape or Microsoft's ActiveX strategy becomes the industry standard, Shockwave developers appear to be in a good position. Macromedia has announced that future versions of Shockwave will be integrated with Java, and the company is currently developing Java Media APIs (Application Programming Interfaces). At the same time, Shockwave is the first ActiveX control to be distributed by Microsoft with Internet Explorer and the Windows 95 operating system. Using ActiveX controls, Shockwave can communicate with the entire Internet Explorer environment and any other ActiveX controls on the user's desktop.

As Shockwave continues to be a multimedia standard on the Web, it will be further integrated with other network technologies. Features on the horizon from Macromedia are reported to include:

- Progressive Play, or streaming animation. If the Progressive Play feature is implemented in future versions of Shockwave, it will support streaming of animation from the Web server. The Shockwave movie will be interactive while the streaming is in progress, thereby reducing user frustration during long downloads.

- Macromedia Common Scripting (MCS). MCS will provide a common scripting language across all Macromedia Studios applications. Developers will be able to write scripts using Lingo or Java, and MCS (an enhanced Lingo-like scripting language) will provide compilation, bytecode interpretation, and cross-platform portability. In effect, it will be possible for Lingo scripts to be compiled into Java bytecode. In turn, it will be possible to use Java (and Lingo) to write Xtras which call Macromedia Open Architecture (MOA) APIs.

- Macromedia Network. The Macromedia network architecture will provide MOA and Xtra access to Internet protocols and services such as TCP/IP, HTTP, FTP, and SMTP. This will make it possible to create stand-alone Director applications that access the Internet to send and retrieve data.

- Plug-in and ActiveX Adapter Xtras. In conjunction with Macromedia Network services, Adapter Xtras will enable developers to integrate any ActiveX control or Netscape plug-in within a Director or Shockwave for Director movie.

It is evident that developers can look forward to an integrated set of authoring tools from Macromedia that includes integration of Shockwave throughout all Macromedia products and across prominent network technologies. Macromedia is building its core technologies in a way that will prepare developers to take advantage of future Internet multimedia standards such as Java.

Related Web Sites

Following are related Web sites for easy reference. Bookmarks to these sites are included on the *Shocking the Web* CD-ROM.

Java

http://java.sun.com

The official Java site from Sun Microsystems.

http://www.gamelan.com

A large collection of Java resources and applets for developers. Shockwave & JavaScript

http://www.magic.ca/~qwi/ShockDev.html

Developer site featuring a JavaScript function that puts parameters into HTML, and then has Shockwave retrieve the results. Source code available for download.

LiveConnect

http://home.netscape.com/comprod/products/navigator/version_3.0

Netscape's page describing LiveConnect, with links to a Showcase page featuring LiveConnect implementation for various plug-ins.

http://home.netscape.com/comprod/mirror/navcomponents_download.html

Netscape plug-ins directory.

ActiveX

http://www.microsoft.com/activex/activex-contents1.htm

Microsoft's overview of ActiveX.

http://www.activextra.com

http://ebola.science.org/ActiveX

Third party sites featuring ActiveX resources and links.

http://www.intel.com/intel/internet/

Intel's Internet strategy, with links to press releases and related information.

Part 2:
Case Studies

CASE STUDY

enhancing an existing web site

http://www.macromedia.com

Macromedia selected DXM Productions to shock its Web site in preparation for the introduction of Shockwave at the Macromedia International Users Conference. Using Shockwave, we enhanced existing graphics from the Macromedia site and created some original animations. We shocked banner grapics by adding small, random animations and interactivity; and we added rollover highlights and sounds to clickable graphics, or "hot spots," to provide users with feedback. In some cases, the Shockwave movies we created were as small as the original GIF files they replaced.

The Hot Contents Movie
Enhancing an existing graphic

One way you can use Shockwave is to add an interactive capability to an existing graphic. When Macromedia decided to shock its Web site, they wanted to retain the existing look and header graphics, while adding Shockwave interactivity. This made the task of shocking the site easier, as the graphic design and production were already done. The challenge, however, was finding ways to animate what had been designed originally as a static image.

MOVIE SPECS

Movie Name:
hotcon.dir

Original File Size:
148K

Audio: 76K

Afterburned
File Size: 70K

Net Lingo Used:
GoToNetPage URL

Stage Size:
464w x 136h

LINGO
SCRIPTING
LEVEL
intermediate

The Hot Contents graphic mainly served as a clickable index of the content found on Macromedia's site. We needed to maintain this functionality, while making it interesting and fun. We managed to do this by adding sound, some new graphics for animation, and by employing *algorithmic animation*—that is, writing routines in Lingo that produce animation without the overhead of additional graphic elements.

We concentrated our efforts on three areas of the Hot Contents graphic: the navigation icons displayed along the bottom of the graphic, the Hot Contents "bullseye," and the "M" in the red rectangle to the left of the graphic. This chapter examines each of these areas separately and explains each area's function in the context of the completed movie.

The Navigation Icons

In the original GIF file, the navigation icons were the "hot" areas in an imagemap. When the user clicked one of the icons in the imagemap, a CGI script was triggered which sent the user to a new page on Macromedia's site. We needed to duplicate this functionality in our movie using Director's Shockwave Lingo commands, as well as add animation to provide user feedback and make these icons more interesting.

1. Because we did not have access to the original source file for the GIF, we converted the GIF image from Macromedia's Web page into a PICT file. After conversion, we imported the PICT into Director's Cast. We made a duplicate cast member to save as a reference before altering the original image.

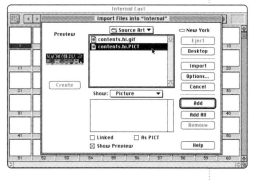

2. Next, we set the Stage size (by choosing Movie Properties from the Modify menu) to approximately the size of the graphic; 470 pixels wide by 136 pixels tall.

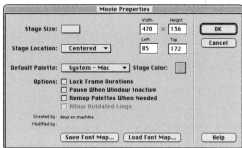

Note

Director rounded down the Stage width to 464; this was OK, because we were able to specify the exact stage size when we wrote the HTML `<EMBED>` tag to create the shocked Macromedia page.

3. Before we could do any animating or scripting, we needed to isolate the seven navigation icons as separate cast members. We used the selection tool in the Paint window to cut the icons off of the graphic and paste them into new cast members.

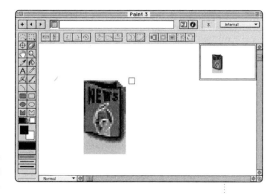

Note

We could have chosen an alternative approach for isolating the seven icons from the background. In the Cast window, we can duplicate the entire graphic seven times and then edit each duplicate in the Paint window to delete all but the single icon. By deleting the backgrounds surrounding each icon, the registration points for all icons would remain the same as the original background graphic. In this case, however, cutting and pasting the icons into new cast members gave each bitmap the default centerpoint registration.

4. The colored squares within the background graphic that contained the icons were filled with a flat color. Using the Control Panel window, we also changed the stage color to the same gray as the color at the bottom of the original graphic.

5. After separating the icons from the background, we were now ready to place them on the Stage. We placed the unaltered background graphic on Stage in channel 1 of the Score and aligned the upper left corner of the graphic with the upper left corner of the Stage. We then put the new background and icons on Stage one at a time in sequential order and set their ink mode to Reverse. By moving the reversed graphics over

the original graphics and tweaking them with the arrow keys, we were able to place the graphics in their original location. When all the graphics were aligned, we set their inks to Matte and deleted the original from channel 1.

6. With the background, button icons, and other graphic elements in place, we began scripting. In the `startMovie` handler of the movie script, we typed this command:

```
set gAddressList = ["http://www.macromedia.com/Brain", ¬
        "http://www.macromedia.com/Industry", ¬
        "http://www.macromedia.com/Tools", ¬
        "http://www.macromedia.com/AYS", ¬
        "http://www.macromedia.com/Gallery", ¬
        "http://www.macromedia.com/Toys", ¬
        "http://www.macromedia.com/Search",¬
        "http://www.macromedia.com/Industry/Macro"]
```

This handler instantiates the variable list `gAddressList` with a list of the URLs which are used by the icon buttons.

7. The on `startMovie` handler instantiates variables used within the movie—such as those representing the sprite channels—and then puppets these same channels. Puppeting transfers control of the sprite channel from the Score to Lingo.

8. The animations we created were for the most part triggered by rolling the mouse over various sprites on the Stage. The entire movie runs in a single frame which serves as a main event loop. The script for this one frame is as follows:

```
on exitFrame
  checkRoll
  go to the frame
end
```

9. The `checkRoll` handler is the key to most of the animations that occur in the movie. It determines which icon sprite the mouse is currently over and then animates the icon accordingly. The goal was to make the icons animate without adding file size. The solution was to make them jiggle whenever the mouse passed over one of them. The following Lingo code fragment taken from the `checkRoll` handler explains how:

```
-- Make the sprites wiggle on rollover...
repeat with spriteCounter = 11 to 17
  put the loc of sprite spriteCounter into holdLoc
  repeat while rollover(spriteCounter)
    -- If the user mouses down, then make a graceful exit.
    if the mouseDown then
      set the loc of sprite spriteCounter = holdLoc
      updateStage
      exit
    end if
    set the loc of sprite spriteCounter = holdLoc + point(2, 0)
    updateStage
    set the loc of sprite spriteCounter = holdLoc + point(2, 2)
    updateStage
```

```
    set the loc of sprite spriteCounter = holdLoc + point(0, 2)
    updateStage
    set the loc of sprite spriteCounter = holdLoc
    updateStage
  end repeat
  set the loc of sprite spriteCounter = holdLoc
  updatestage
end repeat
```

When the mouse passes over a particular navigation icon, several things occur. First, the location of the sprite is stored in the temporary variable holdLoc. Next, the handler enters a repeat loop where the animation occurs. The handler then checks to see if the mouse is down, indicating that the user has clicked on one of the icons. If the mouse is not down, the icon animation occurs. It moves two pixels to the right, then two pixels down, then two pixels back to the left, and finally moves to its initial position. The screen is updated after each move, giving the effect that the icon is moving in small circles as long as the mouse remains over the sprite. If the mouse moves off the sprite, the handler exits the repeat loop and resets the icon to its original location.

10. If the user does click the mouse on the icon while the animation is occurring, the handler sets the icon back to its original position, exits checkRoll, and then executes the sprite script. The script for all icons is the same:

```
global gAddressList
on mouseUp
 set myAddress = getAt(gAddressList, (the clickOn - 10))
 goToNetPage myAddress
end
```

Note

Here is where the gAddressList list variable comes into play. We could have given each icon its own script indicating a discrete destination. However, a much "cleaner" way to script this is to capture the number of the sprite channel which has been clicked and subtract an offset amount of channels (10, in this case, because our first icon appears in channel 11). This number is used to look up the appropriate destination from gAddressList.

This method only works if the order of destinations in gAddressList corresponds to the order in which the sprites appear in the Score. Once the appropriate destination has been determined, it is passed as an argument to the goToNetPage() command, sending the user to a new page on the site.

The Hot Contents Bullseye

The Hot Contents icon in the upper right of the graphic was a non-interactive design element in the original GIF image. We decided to use this icon to add a bit of non-essential fun to our Shockwave movie.

Because the graphic looked somewhat like a hard disk viewed from above (and because we had a very good sound sample of a hard disk spinning up and down), we decided to create a simple click animation that would seem to spin this image. Unlike the animating icons described in the previous section, it was necessary to create new artwork in order to simulate the spinning effect.

1.   We began by bringing the original GIF image into Adobe Photoshop in order to manipulate it. The Hot Contents icon was 62 pixels by 62 pixels. We converted the image to RGB mode and duplicated it three times.

2.   The first image was the default; no image processing was applied. To give the appearance of a spinning disk, the remaining three duplicated images required image processing which would result in a three-frame animation that appeared to have many more frames. The three images were rotated by a set increment; the first image was rotated 120 degrees, the second image was rotated 240 degrees, and the third image remained unchanged.

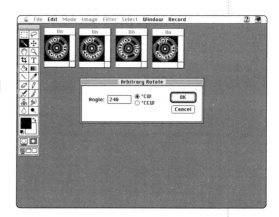

3.   Next, we applied the Motion Blur filter to each image. The settings were: Spin, Good, and 30 degrees. Each image was then converted to 8-bit and imported into Director.

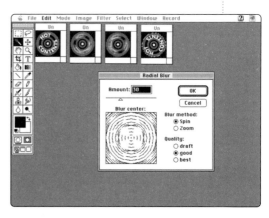

4. It was important that we import the default image into the Cast first, followed by the three blurred images in consecutive order, because our Lingo code would be written to reference offset cast positions.

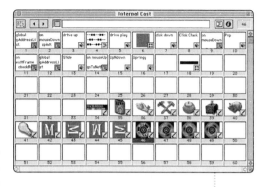

Note

If you have enough RAM in your computer, keep the Photoshop and Director applications open simultaneously so you can copy from Photoshop to the Clipboard, and paste directly into the Director cast. This is particularly useful for small Shockwave animations, which may consist of only a few frames. Remember to save the Photoshop layer file in case you need to edit the original art.

5. The original Hot Contents image was placed in its correct position on the Stage using the reverse ink method described for the navigation icons. We used channel 18 for this sprite. In the `on startMovie` handler in the Movie script, we added these two lines of Lingo to set two important global constants:

```
global cSpinSprite, cSpinCast

set cSpinSprite = 18
set cSpinCast = the castNum of sprite cSpinSprite
```

These constants come into play when the user clicks the Hot Contents icon.

6. In the Score, we attached the following sprite script to the Hot Contents icon in sprite channel 18:

```
on mouseDown
 spinIt
end

on mouseUp
 slowItAndStopIt
end
```

7. Let's examine the Lingo script to see how it accomplishes what we wanted. When the user clicks the Hot Contents icon, the spinIt handler (located in the Movie script) is invoked:

```
on spinIt
 if the castNum of sprite cSpinSprite <> cSpinCast then
  exit
 else
  startTimer
  puppetsound "drive up"
  set delayRepeats = 1000
  repeat with i = 1 to 4
   set delayRepeats = delayRepeats/2
   repeat with x = 1 to 3
    set the castNum of sprite cSpinSprite = cSpinCast + x
    updateStage
    repeat with yy = 1 to delayRepeats
    end repeat
   end repeat
  end repeat

  puppetsound "drive play"
  set delayRepeats = 12
  repeat while the mouseDown
   repeat with x = 1 to 3
    set the castNum of sprite cSpinSprite = cSpinCast + x
    updateStage
```

```
      repeat with y = 1 to delayRepeats
      end repeat

   end repeat
  end repeat
 end if
end
```

The handler first verifies that the graphic clicked is the original still graphic:

```
if the castNum of sprite cSpinSprite <> cSpinCast then
 exit
else
```

This was done by design because the graphic would continue to "spin" while the user holds the mouse down. We only wanted the animation to kick in if the still graphic was clicked.

After it is determined that the user is clicking the correct graphic, we wanted the disk to gradually spin up, accompanied by a spin-up sound:

```
startTimer
puppetsound "drive up"
set delayRepeats = 1000
repeat with i = 1 to 4
 set delayRepeats = delayRepeats/2
 repeat with x = 1 to 3
  set the castNum of sprite cSpinSprite = cSpinCast + x
  updateStage
  repeat with yy = 1 to delayRepeats
  end repeat
 end repeat
end repeat
```

This portion of the handler is dependent upon two repeat loops. The first loop is responsible for switching the blurred graphics incrementally. The second nested repeat loop, within the first, is designed to allow some control over how quickly the disk spins up. Director is very efficient at executing repeat loops (it ignores all other events while the loop is executing), so it is often necessary to slow the execution down. This is the purpose of the delayRepeats variable. After delayRepeats is instantiated with a value (in this case 1000), it is divided by 2 each iteration through the major repeat loop. This makes each succeeding blurred graphic appear on stage only half as long as its predecessor, giving the impression that the disk is increasing its rotational speed.

After the disk begins spinning, the next repeat loop will continue to execute as long as the user is holding the mouse down:

```
puppetsound "drive play"
set delayRepeats = 12
repeat while the mouseDown
  repeat with x = 1 to 3
    set the castNum of sprite cSpinSprite = cSpinCast + x
    updateStage

    repeat with y = 1 to delayRepeats
    end repeat

  end repeat
end repeat
```

This repeat loop executes in much the same manner as the spin up loop, except that it does not use a decreasing value to change the speed. It continues to make the disk appear to spin until the user releases the mouse button. Likewise, the slowItAndStopIt handler uses on mouseUp in the same way just described, except in reverse and with different sounds.

Plan Ahead

Checking Processor Speed

One inherent problem with designing animation to be played on personal computers is the wide range of processor speeds that must be accounted for (unless the animation is destined for a controlled environment such as a kiosk). Creating Shockwave movies is no different, and is potentially even more problematic than multimedia designed for CD-ROM. This is because any PC or Macintosh connected to the Net may access a Shockwave animation. Consequently, it may be helpful to add a method for checking the processor speed before an animation is run. The following handler could be used to assign a value to the speed of the host processor:

```
global gMySpeedVar

on checkspeed
 set howMany = 0
 startTimer
 repeat while the timer < 60
  set howMany = howMany + 1
 end repeat
 set gMySpeedVar = howMany
end
```

The global variable gMySpeedVar could be used to determine the number of iterations of a repeat loop in order to control the speed of an animation.

The Stretchy "M"

The final animation on the Hot Contents page also was created for fun and contains an example of the algorithmic animation mentioned previously. The Macromedia "M" performs four discrete animations, but we'll only examine one of them: The Stretchy "M." This animation causes the "M" in the lower-left corner to stretch upward, and then back down, while playing a rubber-band-like, stretching sound effect.

1. We began by separating the "M" graphic from the original GIF, just as we did the other two animations. However, after placing our cut-out "M" in sprite 19 (the topmost channel in this movie), we placed a QuickDraw rectangle of equal size, and colored the same red as the background of the "M," in sprite channel 10. Sprite 10 would be our key rollover sprite instead of the "M" sprite in channel 19. We did this so that even if the sprite were to animate away from the cursor, the rollover animation would continue to execute.

2. The "M" sprite is puppeted in the on startMovie handler, so that it's available for animation any time the movie is playing. The on startMovie handler also contains other calls which are pertinent to the stretchy "M." The first is:

```
set cMList = ["MrStretchUp", "MrStretchDown", "MrWalkAround",
"MrRotater"]
```

This call instantiates a list that contains the names of the potential actions for the "M" sprite, which are invoked by the do command. The action we are concerned with is MrStretchUp.

3. The second relevant call in the on startMovie handler is:

```
set cHoldRect = the rect of sprite cMSprite
```

This call sets a global variable which saves the left, top, right, and bottom screen coordinates for the "M" sprite in a special Lingo container, known as a rect data type. We need to store these numbers up front as a global so that we can reset the "M" to its original size when our animation ends.

4. If we return to the checkRoll handler we find this code fragment:

```
if rollover(10) then
  set whichOne = getAt(cMList, random(count(cMList)))
  do whichOne
end if
```

This rollOver command picks a random action from the list of potential actions and uses the do command to execute it. This randomness adds to the unpredictability of the animation, and to the liveliness of the movie as well.

5. Now let's get down to the nitty-gritty of how MrStretchUp does his business. Here's the entire handler:

```
on MrStretchUp
  set cHoldRect = the rect of sprite cMSprite
  set MLeft = getAt(cHoldRect,1)
  set MTop = getAt(cHoldRect,2)
  set MRight = getAt(cHoldRect,3)
  set MBottom = getAt(cHoldRect,4)
  set MDirection = #up
  puppetsound "UpNdown"

  repeat while rollover(10)
    if the mouseDown then
      set MTop = getAt(cHoldRect, 2)
      spriteBox cMSprite, MLeft, MTop, MRight, MBottom
      puppetsound 0
      updateStage
      exit repeat
    end if
```

```
 if MDirection = #up then
   set MTop = MTop - 2
   if MTop = 0 then
     set MTop = MTop + 2
     set MDirection = #down
   end if
 else
   set MTop = MTop + 2
   if MTop > getAt(cHoldRect,2) then
     set MTop = MTop - 2
     set MDirection = #up
   end if
 end if
 spriteBox cMSprite, MLeft, MTop, MRight, MBottom
 updateStage
end repeat
set MTop = getAt(cHoldRect, 2)
spriteBox cMSprite, MLeft, MTop, MRight, MBottom
puppetsound 0
updateStage
startTimer
end
```

6. The beginning of the handler contains this code:

```
set MLeft = getAt(cHoldRect,1)
set MTop = getAt(cHoldRect,2)
set MRight = getAt(cHoldRect,3)
set MBottom = getAt(cHoldRect,4)
set MDirection = #up
puppetsound "UpNdown"
```

The first four lines set local variables that are used later in the handler. They are
the left, top, right, and bottom coordinates of the "M" derived from the rect we
saved upon starting the movie. The next local variable MDirection, sets the
initial direction of the stretch. We want the animation to begin by stretching
upward, so we set MDirection to #up. Finally, we start our rubber band sound.
(The Loop option was selected for this sound in the Cast Info window.)

7. Next, `MrStretchUp` launches into a repeat loop that continues as long as the mouse is rolling over sprite 10 (the QuickDraw rectangle). The first action item in the repeat loop is to check whether the user has pressed the mouse button. For the moment, let's assume the user is holding the cursor over sprite 10 and watching the animation. Here's what happens:

```
if MDirection = #up then
 set MTop = MTop - 2
 if MTop <= 0 then
  set MTop = MTop + 2
  set MDirection = #down
 end if
else
 set MTop = MTop + 2
 if MTop => getAt(cHoldRect,2) then
  set MTop = MTop - 2
  set MDirection = #up
 end if
end if
spriteBox cMSprite, MLeft, MTop, MRight, MBottom
updateStage
```

The first element above is an `if...then-else` statement to determine in which direction the sprite is stretching. Since we just instantiated `MDirection` to #up, the upper portion of the statement will execute. In this case, it decrements to variable `MTop` by 2 pixels.

Next, we find an `if...then` statement that tests whether the top of the sprite has equaled or exceeded the top of the Stage window. If it has, two pixels are added to `MTop` and the direction is changed to #down (remember that the pixel numbering on the Stage increases from top to bottom). On the next iteration through the repeat loop, because the direction is now #down, the second half of the `if...then` statement is executed. It continues to execute downward until the original top coordinate of the sprite is equaled or exceeded. Then the process is once again reversed.

The next line is the key to this example of algorithmic animation. After we've changed the top coordinate of the "M" sprite, we invoke the `spriteBox` command to change the vertical shape of the sprite, immediately followed by an `updateStage` command. By repeatedly stretching the sprite we have created an animation which only uses one small cast member. This represents a tremendous savings in file size and download time—both important factors in Shockwave development. The one caveat to this method of animation is that the bitmaps tend to look pixelated if stretched too far. This can be circumvented if the cast member to be stretched or squashed is a DRAW-type PICT cast member. (However, a DRAW-type PICT cast member would not animate as quickly as a bitmap.)

8. Two of the other animation handlers for the "M" graphic also use algorithmic animation; `MrStretchDown` and `MrWalkAround`. The third, `MrRotater`, relies on 3 additional bitmap cast members to form its animation. These handlers can be examined in the Movie script of the Hot Contents movie on the *Shocking the Web* CD-ROM.

9. One testament to the compression capabilities of AfterBurner is that before the addition of sound effects this file was only 9K larger than the original GIF. Had we opted to forgo the sounds, this file would have delivered animation on the Internet for essentially the download cost of a still graphic. Not bad! As it happened, the sound effects, which really make the movie come alive, add less than 40K and a few additional seconds of download time.

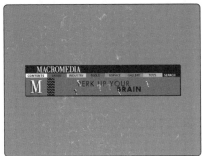

The Perk Up Your Brain Movie
Creating Lingo-controlled, single-frame animations

You can create an animation in Director to use as a Shockwave movie two ways: the entire animation can be "hard-wired" into the Score window; or the animation can be generated via Lingo. Both methods have valid and distinct purposes. Animations constructed in the Score play exactly the same every time the movie runs. Likewise, Lingo-based animations can play back the same each time, or the animation can play back in a random fashion if necessary. Usually, code-based animation can be accomplished in a single Score frame, with Lingo controlling all sprite movement.

For Macromedia, DXM created a single-frame Shockwave animation for the purpose of adding eye-catching random movement to an otherwise static Web page. This kind of movement is in contrast to looping animations which constantly repeat a series of images, such as a rotating logo. DXM chose a Lingo-controlled, single-frame animation to avoid this type of repetition.

Let's examine the script of this relatively simple animation. The movie uses parent/child scripting to randomly animate images of a rotating 3D question mark in multiple instances across a subset of the Stage.

MOVIE SPECS

Movie Name:
brain.dir

Original File Size:
66K

Audio: 25K

Afterburned
File Size: 11K

Net Lingo Used:
GoToNetPage

Stage Size:
480w x 90h

LINGO
SCRIPTING
LEVEL

challenging

When the movie begins, an on `startMovie` handler sets up the initial conditions for the animation:

```
global cQMOffset, cBound, gQMObjList, gAddressList, cStageH, ¬
  cStageW
global gReleaseTime, gReleaseAtTime, gTrackingList

on startMovie
  set the randomSeed = the ticks
  preLoadCast 25, 51
  setConstants
  setGlobals
  liberateQM getAt(gQMObjList, 1)
end startMovie
```

Let's go through this handler to see what each line is doing and why.

1. First, because we are going to use the `random()` function frequently in this movie, we set the `randomSeed` property to something that is truly random: the amount of time that has passed since the user turned on the computer. Next, the bitmaps for the rotating question marks are preloaded into memory. We then call two handlers, `setConstants` and `setGlobals`, to assign values to constants and global variables used throughout the movie.

2. Before we finish with the `startMovie handler`, let's examine the constants and variables set at this point by these two handlers:

```
on setConstants
  set cStageH = the stageBottom - the stageTop
  set cStageW = the stageRight - the stageLeft
  set cLeftEdge = 91
  set cTopEdge = 36
  set baseCastNum = the number of cast ("QM1")
  set baseWidth = (the width of cast baseCastNum)/2
  set baseHeight = (the height of cast baseCastNum)/2
  set cBound = rect((cLeftEdge + baseWidth),(cTopEdge + ¬
    baseHeight), (cStageW - baseWidth), (cStageH - baseHeight))
  set cQMOffset = 20
end
```

We confined animation to a portion of the Stage so that it does not interfere with the user's access to navigation buttons. The first four lines of the setConstants handler determine the boundaries in which the animation will occur. However, because the registration point for the question mark sprites is in the center of each bitmap, we then subtracted half the height and half the width of a representative question mark bitmap from each of the four boundaries. If we had used the animation boundaries rather than the constant cBound, the question marks would go halfway off the screen before rebounding back into view. Accordingly, we stored the value of the screen subset rectangle in a rect data type–which is, in essence, a list of the boundary's values. The final line of the handler sets the sprite offset constant, cQMOffset, for the question mark sprites.

3. The next handler, setGlobals, initializes the variables:

```
on setGlobals
  set gQMObjList = []
  repeat with x = 1 to 10
    add(gQMObjList, new(script "QMs Parent Script", x))
    puppetSprite (x + cQMOffset), TRUE
  end repeat
  set gReleaseTime = the ticks
  set gTrackingList = [0,0,0,0,0,0,0,0,0,0]
  set gReleaseAtTime = 500
end
```

The setGlobals handler initializes the two lists that will be used throughout the movie for tracking and updating the floating question marks: gQMObjList and gTrackingList. We created the gQMObjList and then filled it with ten objects within a repeat loop. A script named Question Mark Parent Script gives birth to the objects. (We will examine this script momentarily.) With each pass through the repeat loop, a sprite channel is puppeted for use. In this instance, we used sprite channels 21 through 30 to allow the question marks to animate over the background image.

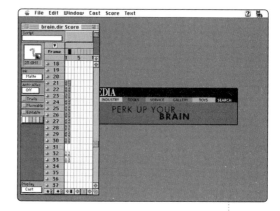

Finally, two variables are set that will affect how many question marks are on screen at any particular time. The first is gReleaseTime, which is set at this time (and whenever it is called) to the current time in ticks. This variable acts as half of a timer mechanism. The other half of the mechanism, gReleaseAtTime, is used to control how often the movie will check gTrackingList to determine if the movie should release another question mark. A lower value causes the movie to release question marks more frequently. We could check the screen dimensions of the host platform and—if we determined that the movie was running on a large screen—decrease the value of this variable to release more question marks onto the Stage at any given time.

4. Now, at long last, we return to the final call of our `startMovie` handler: `liberateQM getAt(gQMObjList,1)`, which is a handler in the Question Mark Parent Script. Before we look at `liberateQM`, we will first examine the `new` handler for this script that was used in the `setGlobals` repeat loop.

```
global gTrackingList, cBound, cQMOffset, gReleaseTime

property pState, pFloatTime
property pVelocityH, pVelocityV, pMySprite, pMyListPosition,
pLifeTime, pMySize
property p1stCastNum, pLastCastNum, pDirection

on new me, listPosition
 set pMyListPosition to listPosition
 set pMySprite = pMyListPosition + cQMOffset
 set pState = FALSE
 set pVelocityH = random(7)
 set pVelocityV = random(7)
 return me
end
```

5. In the repeat loop within the `setGlobals` handler, we instantiated ten objects and appended them incrementally into the `gQMObjList`. We assigned each object a unique position in the list—a value that also happens to correspond to its sprite channel.

6. We pass the `listPosition` argument to the `new` handler and assign it to the `pMyListPosition` property variable for each object. We then assigned another property variable, `pMySprite`, the same value *plus* the sprite offset value, `cQMOffset`. The property variable `pMyListPosition` corresponds to the object's place in `gTrackingList` and `gQMObjList`. The property variable `pMySprite` represents each object's assigned sprite channel.

7.   The next line of the new handler sets the Boolean property variable pState to FALSE. The initial location for all the sprites is significantly offstage to the left of the screen. We used the pState variable to track whether the sprite is onstage (TRUE) or offstage (FALSE). The value of each was set initially to FALSE, so the question marks would come onto the screen sequentially.

8.   The next two lines set up the initial velocity in the horizontal and vertical directions for each question mark. The two property variables pVelocityH and pVelocityV were set to a random number between 1 and 7, inclusively. Because these values will almost certainly be different for each object, the question marks will each have a unique velocity and initial direction.

9.   Now we are ready to see what the last line of the startMovie handler, liberateQM getAt(gQMObjList, 1), actually accomplishes when it acts upon the first object in gQMObjList. You can examine the liberateQM handler in the Question Mark Parent Movie script to see what happens when we liberate a question mark:

```
on liberateQM me
  setAt(gTrackingList, pMyListPosition , 1)
  set startH = randomInRange(getAt(cBound, 1), getAt(cBound, 3))
  set startV = randomInRange(getAt(cBound, 2), getAt(cBound, 4))
  set the loc of sprite pMySprite to point(startH, startV)
  set gReleaseTime = the ticks
  set pState = TRUE
  set randNum = random(2) - 1
  if randNum then
    set p1stCastNum = 25
    set pLastCastNum = 51
    set pDirection = (-1)
  else
    set p1stCastNum = 51
    set pLastCastNum = 25
    set pDirection = 1
  end if
  set pFloatTime = the ticks
  set pLifeTime = randomInRange(1800, 3600)
end
```

10. The first action `liberateQM` performs is to "check out" a question mark from the `gTrackingList`. It changes the Boolean value of the list item that corresponds to the sprite in question from 0 to 1. We'll see momentarily how the movie constantly scans `gTrackingList` to determine which question marks are floating.

Note

Did you notice how the last Boolean was set to TRUE or FALSE and this one is set to 0 or 1? Logical constants (TRUE or FALSE) and values (0 or 1) are interchangeable in Lingo.

The next four lines in our current handler place the question mark sprite at a random location within the bounding rectangle that was established earlier. It uses a function called `randomInRange()`, which Macromedia included in the original Apartment movie that was released with Director version 2.0, and which you still may find on the latest Director CD-ROM.

11. The next line sets `gReleaseTime` to the ticks (as described earlier). We then set the value for the property variable `pState` to TRUE because the sprite has now moved onto the stage. The next ten lines will set three important property variables: `p1stCastNum`, `pLastCastNum`, and `pDirection`. These three variables determine the direction in which the question mark will spin once it is on Stage. If `pDirection` is -1, then the question marks will increment through the cast members positively. If `pDirection` is 1 however, the question marks will increment through the cast members in reverse order and appear to spin in the opposite direction.

12. The final two lines of `liberateQM` set property variables that will determine how long a question mark will stay on the Stage—that is, for our purposes, its lifetime. The `pFloatTime` variable establishes a beginning time for the question mark and `pLifeTime` uses `randomInRange()` to give the question mark a random time on Stage between 1800 and 3600 ticks (30 to 60 seconds).

Note

In this movie, we never dispose of the object. Remember that the animating question mark is only a visible manifestation of the object. When a question mark is no longer needed, its position is moved offstage and its sprite is turned off in gTrackingList. We will examine the Parent Script function that controls this activity below.

13. It may seem odd that you have yet to see the script of the frame in which all the animation occurs. Here it is:

```
on exitFrame
  animateQMs
  go to the frame
end
```

That's it! One of the beauties of single-frame scripting is the simplicity of the frame scripts. Clearly, animateQMs is an important handler, as it has the responsibility of controlling the entire movie.

14. Here is the animateQMs handler which is found in the Movie script:

```
on animateQMs
 repeat with t = 1 to 10
  QMAction getAt(gQMObjList, t)
 end repeat

 if the ticks - gReleaseTime > gReleaseAtTime then
  repeat with x = 1 to count(gTrackingList)
   set spriteToTry = x
   set whichOne = getAt(gTrackingList, spriteToTry)
   if NOT whichOne then
    liberateQM getAt(gQMObjList, spriteToTry)
    exit repeat
   end if
  end repeat
  set gReleaseTime = the ticks
 end if

end
```

At every update to a frame in the movie, the score script calls animateQMs. Every call to animateQMs results in a repeat loop in which every object in the gQMObjList calls the parent script handler QMAction. QMAction acts on each object in the gQMObjList in turn. Later, we will bounce over to the Question Mark Parent Script one final time to see what QMAction does. Let's first determine what else occurs at every frame within our current handler.

15. After the objects for this frame have been updated, the next order of business is to check the time. Take the current time in ticks and subtract the current value of gReleaseTime, then compare the result with the constant value gReleaseAtTime. If the result of the subtraction is not greater than gReleaseAtTime, then nothing will need to be done for this frame and we can exit the handler. However, if the result is greater, it means that we may need to release another question mark. First, a check must be performed to determine if any question mark objects are available for release. To do this, we set up a loop that checks the value of every item in gTrackingList. Each value is retrieved and checked as to whether it is 1 or 0.

Note

Remember that we stored the tracking values as Booleans. We can therefore check without writing an equation, which is faster. This is one of the main reasons to use Booleans in your scripting, particularly if you are using them in a repeat loop while an animation is running. The processor spends less time calculating; therefore, it has more time to devote to your animation.

16. When the repeat loop first encounters a 0 during the search, it calls for the liberateQM handler from the Question Mark Parent Script. Since we have accomplished what we wanted to do in the repeat loop, there is no need to continue, so we use the exit repeat command to terminate the search. Regardless of whether a question mark was released (all ten conceivably could be on screen already), we wanted to reset the value of gReleaseTime to the current time in ticks so the repeat loop wouldn't have to execute again until the value of gReleaseAtTime had been passed.

17. Lastly, we return to the Question Mark Parent Script to explore the QMAction handler, with its corresponding checkFloatTime handler, that was skipped in our explanation of the animateQMs handler above:

```
on QMAction me

 if pState then
  set currentPositionH to the locH of sprite pMySprite + ¬
    pVelocityH
  set currentPositionV to the locV of sprite pMySprite + ¬
    pVelocityV

  if currentPositionH < getAt(cBound, 1) then
   set pVelocityH to -1 * pVelocityH
   set currentPositionH to getAt(cBound, 1)
  end if

  if currentPositionV < getAt(cBound, 2) then
   set pVelocityV to -1 * pVelocityV
   set currentPositionV to getAt(cBound, 2)
  end if

  if currentPositionH > getAt(cBound, 3) then
   set pVelocityH to -1 * pVelocityH
   set currentPositionH to getAt(cBound, 3)
  end if

  if currentPositionV > getAt(cBound, 4) then
   set pVelocityV to -1 * pVelocityV
   set currentPositionV to getAt(cBound, 4)
  end if

  if the castNum of sprite pMySprite = p1stCastNum then
   set the castNum of sprite pMySprite = pLastCastNum
  else
   set the castNum of sprite pMySprite = (the castNum of sprite ¬
     pMySprite) + pDirection
  end if
```

```
  set the loc of sprite pMySprite to point(currentPositionH, ¬
    currentPositionV)
  checkFloatTime
 end if
 updateStage
end


on checkFloatTime me
 set howLong = the ticks - pFloatTime
 if howLong > pLifeTime then -- Get rid of the Question Marks...
  set pState = FALSE
  -- Note the state of the sprite.
  setAt(gTrackingList, pMyListPosition, 0)
  set the loc of sprite pMySprite = point(-1000, -1000)
 end if
end
```

The QMAction handler's only concern is the objects represented on Stage by the animating question marks. Consequently, the first determination we need to make is whether the object is active. If the pState property of the object is FALSE, then its sprite is offstage and does not need updating. However, if pState is TRUE for this object, its sprite channel needs to be updated.

18. The first task is to move the sprite, at its predetermined velocity value, along the horizontal and vertical axes. However, we don't want the sprite to violate our bounding rectangle, so before we can move the sprite, we must perform a check to ensure that we are still in bounds. We created two local variables for the task: currentPositionH and currentPositionV. We assigned them values based upon the current position of the sprite, plus the value of the velocity property variables. Using the resulting values, we tested them with a series of four if-then statements, one for each side of the bounding rectangle. They all work in the same manner, so examining the first one will indicate how all four work.

19.   If our new `currentPositionH` variable is less than the first stored value of the bounding rectangle, we know that we will move too far to the left. To remedy this, we turned our sprite around and sent it back in the opposite direction. This gives the appearance of the question mark bouncing off the left side of the screen. We do this by multiplying the horizontal velocity property variable by -1 (negative 1). For example, if the question mark was moving six pixels per frame on the horizontal axis, it would now be moving at negative six pixels per frame. Once the velocity has been changed, we then change the value of `currentPositionH` to the value of the left boundary. We continue checking the position against the other three boundaries, as it is possible that the question mark could be beyond both the left and top boundaries at once.

20.   Once the sprite is back in bounds, it's time to update its cast member to make the question mark appear to rotate one increment per frame. We checked to see if the current cast member for this object was the first of the series. Remember that when we called `liberateQM` for this object, the question mark sprite representation could be spinning in either one direction or the other, depending upon which cast members we selected as first and last. So for this particular

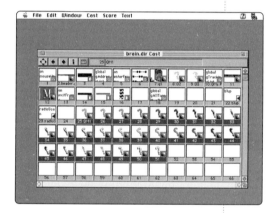

object, the first cast number may be 25, or it may be 47. Regardless, if it's at the end of the series, it needs to be reset to the beginning. If it is somewhere in the middle of its cycle of cast members, increment it by 1, in whichever direction it is spinning.

21. Before we call updateStage to complete the work for this frame of the animation, we need to perform one final housekeeping task using the checkFloatTime handler. As you recall, we initialized each object with a variable, pLifeTime, which represents the time the object's question mark would animate on Stage during any particular cycle. (The name pLifeTime is something of a misnomer because, at the end of any particular cycle, we do not dispose of the object; we act only upon the sprite representation of the object.) We needed to determine if the object had exceeded its time on Stage. As we have done in other instances, we created a new local variable, howLong, by subtracting the pFloatTime property variable (initialized by the liberateQM handler earlier) from the current time in ticks. We compare this resulting value with the pLifeTime property variable to determine if the time has expired. If it has not, the handler is exited. If the value is greater than pLifeTime, the question mark is moved offstage until it is needed again.

22. We perform three actions to move the question mark offstage. First, the object's pState is set to FALSE. Next, we set the item in the gTrackingList that represents this object to 0. Finally, we physically pick up the sprite using Lingo and plunk it down at point(-1000, -1000)—significantly off stage. These actions ensure that the sprite will not use any processor cycles until we again call upon it to spin across the Stage.

23. At the end of the QMAction handler, we finally call updateStage to show the results to the viewer. We set the tempo in the Score to 36 so that the movie executes all of these actions 36 times every second. Although the playback head in the Score never moves off frame 2, a complete random animation occurs constantly on the Stage.

The two Shockwave movies created for Macromedia's site are examples of how static Web graphics can be made dynamic and entertaining using Director's Lingo scripting language. By adding a minimal amount of additional graphic overhead, existing images can be transformed into multimedia applets.

CASE STUDY

creating a shockwave web site

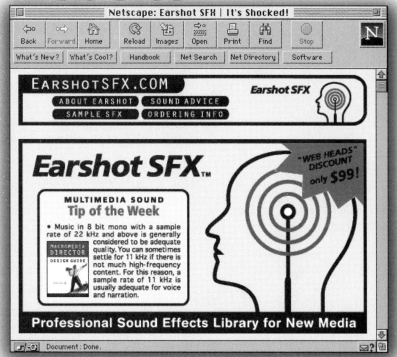

http://www.EarshotSFX.com

EarshotSFX is the aural equivalent of a stock photo library: a CD-ROM product that contains over 2,000 studio sound effects. It is intended to fulfill both the mundane and extravagant sound design needs of multimedia designers. DXM decided to focus promotional efforts for EarshotSFX on the World Wide Web due to its popularity among new media creators and because the Web provided an opportunity to demonstrate the product using new media. In addition to promoting the sound library, the EarshotSFX site aims to show other new media producers how sound design can radically improve the usability and entertainment value of presented materials, even in a medium as bandwidth-constricted as the Internet.

The Navigation Bar Movie
Beyond Imagemaps

In developing the EarshotSFX.com site, DXM wanted to provide a richer inter-action paradigm and a livelier user experience using Shockwave. CGI scripting and server-push animation do not support real-time interaction very well, and this kind of Unix-based development would require more time and a larger budget than was originally intended. At the same time, we needed to leverage some of the Director-based materials that had already been created for the EarshotSFX CD-ROM.

MOVIE SPECS

Movie Name:
esNavBar.dir

Original File Size:
83K

Audio: 2.5K

Afterburned
File Size: 16.4K

Net Lingo Used:
GoToNetPage URL

Stage Size:
480w x 74h

LINGO
SCRIPTING
LEVEL

intermediate

From a design and production standpoint, Director was already our primary authoring tool and we were comfortable using Shockwave to build content for the Internet. From a technical perspective, there were several attractive Shockwave features. Afterburner compression for Shockwave movies worked as well as advertised, providing file compres-sion ratios from 4:1 up to 10:1. Shockwave's network command set allowed preloading of movies, images, and HTML pages in the back-ground, before an explicit network request was received. This greatly improved the performance and responsiveness of the shocked site over the non-shocked site.

This case study focuses on three Shockwave movies within the EarshotSFX Web site: the Navigation Bar movie, which contains navigation buttons with rollover text balloons; the EarshotSFX Cover movie, which was used to disguise network latency; and the sample browser movie, which provides sample audio clips from the EarshotSFX product. Preloading routines that appear throughout all movies also are explained.

The Navigation Buttons

The usability of simple interface elements, such as a navigation bar, can be greatly enhanced with Shockwave at little to no cost in file size. In designing the navigation bar for the EarshotSFX site, the main goal was to develop a navigational paradigm that would give more natural feedback to users than common Web navigation schemes. Prior to the release of Shockwave, there was simply no way to attach highlight states, confirmation tones, or help balloons to buttons using HTML scripting. Using Shockwave, we were able to accomplish these things quickly, in a file that was smaller than 20K.

The navigation bar contains four rounded buttons that highlight when clicked, and then update a frame below the menu. This is accomplished using a `GoToNetPage` command that contains the optional target parameter. When the user makes a selection, the target HTML page loads in the nearby frame.

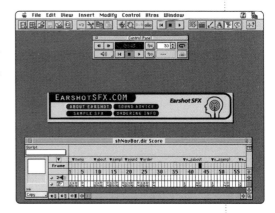

1. First, we established a convention for naming the HTML pages within the site. All Shockwave pages begin with e_s (for earshot shockwave) followed by the first 5 letters of the page topic, and ending with the obligatory .html extension. For example, the About Earshot page is named e_sabout.html.

2. The four button graphics were created in FreeHand, rasterized, imported into Photoshop, and saved as 24-bit PICT files.

3. The buttons were imported into Director and mapped to the Netscape color palette. The Netscape palette is included in the Palettes cast under the Xtras menu.

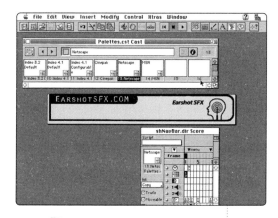

4. Cast members were named according to the topic of the HTML page they linked to; about, sampl, sound, and order. The button cast members were placed on the Stage over the menu background. We used the name of cast Lingo property to obtain the unique filename data for each page, and one simple sprite script was written to cover all of the navigation buttons:

```
on mouseDown
   ...
   if not(gReadyToGo) then
      --for absolute pathname:
      --set gNextPage = gBaseURL & "e_s" & the name of cast ¬
(gRealCast) & ".htm"
      set gNextPage = "../e_s" & the name of cast (gRealCast) &¬
".htm"
      goPage gNextPage,"earMain"
      go label(the name of cast (gRealCast))
   end if
end
```

Note

This handler does not call the GoToNetPage command when a button is clicked and does not immediately advance the current movie to the next page. Instead, the playback head advances to a frame that contains a highlighted version of the selected button. The GoToNetPage command is then issued by a frame script. This method provides feedback to the user and prevents multiple GoToNetPage requests for the same HTML page.

5. To prevent net requests from executing repeatedly, we developed a standard structure for calling the GoToNetPage command.

6. Markers corresponding to the truncated names of the HTML pages were created in the Score, such as e_sabout, which is formed by the concatenation "e_s" & the name of cast (the mouseCast). The segment following each marker contains the "radiohead" animation (our equivalent of a wait cursor), and other state information pertaining to the HTML page that the user is heading towards.

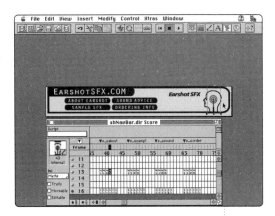

7. Each marker frame contains the same script:

```
on enterFrame
  global gReadyToGo
  set gReadyToGo = TRUE
  -- trap enterFrame so rollovers are not available
end

on exitFrame
  global gNextPage
  goPage gNextPage
end
```

The global variable gReadyToGo contains a Boolean value indicating whether or not a new page is about to be accessed. This variable is used by other handlers to stop any preload caching and prevent the movie from initiating multiple simultaneous downloads. The enterFrame handler is used locally to prevent the movie level enterFrame script from receiving the on enterFrame message. The exitframe handler then passes a goPage command to the movie script handler that contains the name of the destination page as its only argument.

8. Since `GoToNetPage` should be called only once, it is important to place this command in a non-looping frame. The last frame of the e_sabout sequence contains the following script that loops playback without repeating the command:

```
on exitFrame
  go marker(0) + 1
end
```

9. The `goPage` handler in the movie script contains the `GoToNetPage` command, and several lines of Lingo:

```
on goPage thePage
  global gBaseURL,gLoadStatus,gCurrLoading,¬
gPreloadingOn,gReadyToGo
  -- if thePage is not a full path, then add the default path:
  if not(thePage starts "http://") then ¬
set thePage = gBaseURL & thePage
  if not (thePage contains ".html") then ¬
set thePage = thePage & ".html"
  -- check if page is now preloading; if not, then cancel preload:
  if (not(thePage contains ¬
getAprop(getAt(gLoadStatus,gCurrLoading),#name))) ¬
AND (not(net Done())) then NetAbort
-- various operations use these 2 globals to determine behavior:
  set gPreloadingOn = FALSE
  set gReadyToGo = TRUE
  GoToNetPage thePage
  -- the following will fade out sounds currently playing
  set fadeDuration = 200
  if sound Busy(1) or sound Busy(2) then set lPlaying = true
  if sound Busy(1)then sound FadeOut 1, fadeDuration
  if sound Busy(2)then sound FadeOut 2, fadeDuration
  if lPlaying = true then waitForTicks fadeDuration
end
```

10. The goPage handler processes any requests for navigation to a new Web page. It uses several global variables:

gBaseURL contains the pathname to the top level directory for the site, in this case http://www.EarshotSFX.com.

gLoadStatus contains a list of files contained in the current movie's preload queue. This list, which also contains the various attributes of each file, is created by the AddToPreloadList handler described later.

gCurrLoading contains the index to the most recently downloaded file in the gLoadStatus list.

gPreloadingOn and gReadyToGo are Boolean values used by various handlers to determine behavior.

11. The goPage handler takes one argument, thePage. It specifies the name of the HTML document that the user is attempting to access. After the goPage handler verifies that thePage contains a full path to the new Web page along with the proper .html suffix, the following line determines if there is a file other than thePage currently preloading.

```
if (not(thePage contains ¬
getAprop(getAt(gLoadStatus,gCurrLoading),#name))) ¬
AND (not(net Done())) then NetAbort
```

12. Two conditions must be satisfied for the NetAbort command to be invoked.

First, the most recently attempted preload must be a file other than thePage. This is derived from the #name property contained in the property list gLoadStatus at index gCurrLoading.

Second, there must be a preload in progress. If NetDone(), without any arguments, returns FALSE, there is a preload in progress.

13. Next, the GoToNetPage command is called. The handler then determines if there are any sounds currently playing. If there are, a sound FadeOut command is used to fade sounds over a time period specified in ticks by the fadeDuration variable. If a fadeout is necessary, a delay is added to ensure that subsequent sounds accompanying the radiohead animation will play properly.

14. To accomplish this task, the goPage handler calls the following waitForTicks handler:

```
on waitForTicks theTicks
  set startTime = the timer
  repeat while startTime + theTicks > the timer
    nothing
  end repeat
end
```

This simple handler causes the playback head to wait in a repeat loop for the amount of time specified in ticks by theTicks. This handler is useful for replacing the Wait commands in the Score's Tempo channel—which are not recommended for use in Shockwave movies.

Rollover Balloons

We wanted to keep the navigation bar
as clean and simple as possible, but we
also wanted it to provide information
about the other pages and attractions
within the EarshotSFX site. We chose
a scheme similar to Balloon Help,
which is built into the MacOS. When
a user passes the cursor over one of the
navigation buttons, a bubble containing relevant information about that
page appears.

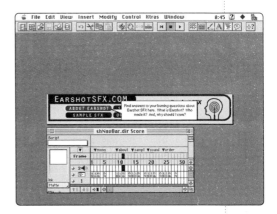

1. We used Director's `rollover` function to simulate the Balloon Help effect.
However, during testing, the feature became a little bit annoying, so we altered
the behavior of the bubbles. They only appear if the user holds the cursor over a
button for more than one second.

2. The `checkRollovers` handler, found in the movie script, monitors rollovers
and displays information bubbles. The `checkRollovers` handler is called by an
`enterFrame` script within the same movie script.

```
on enterFrame
  global gReadyToGo
  if not(gReadyToGo) then checkRollovers
end
```

3. This technique provides two criteria for averting the `checkRollovers`
handler. The `checkRollovers` handler will not be called if the `gReadyToGo` variable is set to `TRUE`, or if the current frame contains an `enterFrame` handler in the
Score that overrides the `enterframe` handler in the movie script.

4. If the criteria in step 3 are not met, the checkRollovers handler is called:

```
on checkRollovers
  global gLastRollTime,gLastRollover
  repeat with i = 6 to 9
-- if the buttons are turned off, do not show the balloons
    if rollover(i) AND (the visible of sprite i) then
-- if user is still over same sprite,check how long it's been
      if (i = gLastRollover) then
        if (the mouseup) AND (gLastRollTime +60 < the timer)¬
then
          --if user has been over button for 60 ticks, show bubble
          set gLastRollTime = 0
          puppetSound "switches1"
          go label(the name of cast(the castNum of sprite i))
        end if
        exit
      else --if rollover is different from last rollover
      -- reset the timer because user is over a new button
        set gLastRollTime = the timer
      end if
      set gLastRollover = i
      exit
    end if
  end repeat
  --if no rollovers, reset global to avoid inadvertent matches
  set gLastRollover = 0
end
```

Note

The checkRollovers *handler uses two global variables:* gLastRollTime *and* gLastRollover. gLastRollTime *contains the value of the timer when the user last placed the cursor over one of the active rollover sprites.* gLastRollover *contains the sprite number of the last active rollover.*

5. The checkRollovers handler checks each navigation button sprite, 6 through 9, represented by i. If it encounters rollover(i) = TRUE, and the rollover sprite is visible, the handler determines whether the cursor has been over sprite channel i for more than 60 ticks. If this is the case, a sound is triggered and the playback head advances to a marker in the Score that contains the appropriate information bubble.

6. If the current rollover channel is within the appropriate range, but is not the same as the value stored in gLastRollover, the handler updates gLastRollTime with the current time and stores the current rollover sprite in gLastRollover.

Note

As in the previous navigation bar example, the name of cast *property is used to advance the playback head to a label in the Score. In this case, labels have the same names as the corresponding navigation buttons.*

7. The following script appears in all frames that contain information bubbles:

```
on enterFrame
  nothing
end

on exitFrame
  global gLastRollover
  if rollover(gLastRollover) and the mouseup then
    if the frame = marker(0) + 3 then
      go marker(0)
    end if
  else
    go label("menu")
  end if
end
```

The enterFrame handler is used solely to trap the enterFrame message so that it does not try to display the bubble when it is already on screen. The exitFrame handler causes the playback head to loop in the frame containing the bubble until the user moves the cursor or clicks the mouse. Any user activity returns the movie to the menu frame, in which none of the bubbles are displayed.

The EarshotSFX Cover Movie
Minimizing Download Times

Using a cover screen is a simple way to minimize the amount of time that Web surfers need to spend staring at blank pages while waiting for files to download. Shockwave cover screens are very small movies that load quickly and use the `GoToNetMovie` command to open a new movie in the same window.

The EarshotSFX cover screen contains one graphic: a simple version of the EarshotSFX logo. We eliminated as much visual information as possible to maximize the benefits of Afterburner's image compression, which works best on images with large areas of flat color.

1. The cover movie, named shHomeCover, was set to the same stage size as the main shHome movie. It compressed down to 9k, versus 50k for the shHome movie. Accessing the net with a 14.4 modem, this reduces load-to-first-image time by about 40 seconds.

2. The shHomeCover movie contains one important script in the first frame.

```
on exitFrame
  GoToNetMovie ¬
"http://www.EarshotSFX.com/Movies/shHome.dcr"
end
```

MOVIE SPECS

Movie Name:
shHomeCover.dir

Original File Size:
24.7K

Audio: 0K

Afterburned
File Size: 9.3K

Net Lingo Used:
GoToNetPage URL

Stage Size:
480w x 260h

**LINGO
SCRIPTING
LEVEL**
easy

Note
Remember not to place network commands in the Script channel of looping frames, or Shockwave will attempt multiple downloads of the same document.

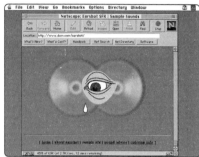

The Sample Browser Movie
Branching to Multiple Movies

DXM created a promotional demo version of the EarshotSFX product using Director for inclusion in the CD-ROM version of Macromedia's SoundEdit 16 software. The full-screen demo version was repurposed into a Shockwave movie for the EarshotSFX Web site by reducing the movie's Stage size and breaking up the demo into 37 discrete, linked movies.

MOVIE SPECS

Movie Name:
earMenu.dir

Original File Size:
236K

Audio: 3K

Afterburned
File Size: 83K

Net Lingo Used:
GoToNetPage URL

Stage Size:
320w x 240h

**LINGO
SCRIPTING
LEVEL**
intermediate

The purpose of the Web sample browser is to demonstrate the effectiveness of EarshotSFX sound effects when they are used in conjunction with simple animations. The sample browser's main screen contains two overlapping CD graphics that function as a menu to randomly access 36 short animation sequences. By breaking the browser into smaller units the download time for each segment is kept to a minimum.

The Mini Browser Movie

The EarshotSFX sample browser was originally created as a 640 x 480 pixel Director movie. At this size, the movie was not a small enough Shockwave file for playback on the Web, so we resized the entire movie to 320 x 240 pixels.

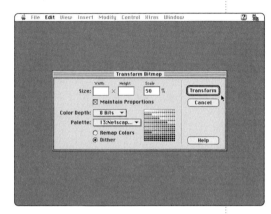

The idea had merit, but the thought of using a graphics program to resize every cast member, along with all of the concomitant export and import tasks, seemed daunting. So we took a gamble on resizing everything in one fell swoop using Director, and it worked pretty well. Here's how it was accomplished:

1. Set the monitor's color depth to 24 bit.
2. Open the Cast Window and Select All.
3. Select Transform Bitmap from the Modify menu.
4. Select 32 bits and Remap Colors. Click Transform.
5. Select Transform Bitmap from the Modify menu.
6. Scale 50% and click Transform.
7. Select Transform Bitmap from the Modify menu.
8. Select 8 bits (experiment with Dither vs. Remap Colors options) and click Transform.
9. Open the Score window and Select All.
10. Click and drag all selected sprites to the upper left corner of the Stage.
11. Choose Modify, Movie, Properties to resize the stage.
12. Set the Stage Size to 320 x 240 and click OK.

When resizing bitmaps, registration points may change: Check the placement of all artwork to make sure it is positioned correctly. Also, antialiasing artifacts may become apparent after resizing, so touching up some of the artwork may be necessary.

This technique is not foolproof or guaranteed, but we were able to resize the sample browser movie in 15 minutes, and it's almost as entertaining at quarter screen as it was at full screen.

The Sound Preview Buttons

Even at one-quarter screen size, the file size of the EarshotSFX sample browser was still too large to even consider embedding it in an HTML page. Luckily, this movie was inherently structured to facilitate segmenting it into smaller pieces.

Splitting up the sample browser into 37 separate movies was fairly simple, due to the common behavior of the 36 sampler animations (i.e., play segment, then return to the main earMenu movie). It was important to keep as much of the Lingo scripts as possible in the earMenu movie to avoid making changes in all the movies if script changes were necessary.

1. Our first priority was to create a template movie into which each of the short animation sequences could be pasted. The template movie contains four Lingo scripts which are used by all animations. These scripts include the `waitForTicks` handler which was used previously in the Navigation Bar movie, the frame script for returning to the earMenu movie, and the following simple scripts that maintain audio and animation synchronization:

```
on exitFrame
    if soundBusy(2) then go the frame
end
```

2. We knew that the local pathname used during authoring would change when Shockwave files were uploaded to the Web. Since global variables persist between movies opened with the GoToNetMovie command, we initialized a global variable, gBaseURL, in the earMenu movie to store the pathname to the site's top level directory. gBaseURL remains the same from movie to movie. In this case, it stores "http://www.earshotSFX.com/Movies/" so that the same script, in the second to last frame of each animation movie, can be used for returning to the earMenu movie:

```
on exitFrame
  global gMenuMovie,gBaseURL,gLeftGoToList,gRightGoToList
  -- determine where to return to in the earMenu movie
  if getOne(gLeftGoToList,line 1 of the labelList) then
    set returnAnchor = "#LeftChoice"
  else if getOne(gRightGoToList,line 1 of the labelList) then
    set returnAnchor = "#RightChoice"
  else
    set returnAnchor = ""
  end if
  -- gBaseURL must be valid
  if not(gMenuMovie) then set gMenuMovie = "earMenu.dcr"
  goToNetMovie gBaseURL & gMenuMovie & returnAnchor
end
```

Note

This script is intentionally placed in a frame other than the last frame of the movie, to prevent GoToNetMovie from executing multiple times on the last frame.

3. All of the global variables referenced in this handler are set in the earMenu movie. gLeftGoToList and gRightGoToList contain the names of all animation movies (without the .dcr suffix) called by clicking the right and left CD graphics in the browser. As part of our template structure, the first label in each animation movie also contains this name. We used line 1 of the labelList to determine which marker in the earMenu movie in which to return. Shockwave uses HTML's Anchor format to advance to specific markers in movies. The following command starts the earMenu movie from the marker labeled RightChoice, instead of starting the movie from the first frame:

```
GoToNetMovie gBaseURL & "earMenu.dcr#RightChoice"
```

Note

The anchor format is, as of this writing, case sensitive.

4. The gMenuMovie variable was included as a safety net in case the name of the calling movie changed or if, for some reason, we decided to play an animation movie from somewhere other than the earMenu movie. If gMenuMovie is set to a new value, the subsequent line of code will use it to form the argument for the GoToNetMovie command. Otherwise, the default name of earMenu.dcr is used.

Note

Once the template format was finalized, the template was saved as TailTemplate.dir and the file was converted to a Stationery pad. To convert a file to a Stationery pad, select the file in the Finder and choose Get Info from the File menu. Select the Stationery pad option in the Get Info window. Converting your template to a Stationery pad can prevent accidentally saving the template file with specific data.

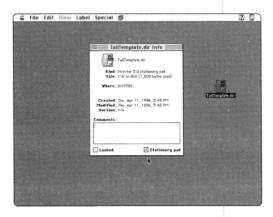

5. Once the template movie was built, we copied each animation segment into a separate movie. We accomplished this by opening the original movie's Score window, highlighting all relevant channels in all relevant frames, and copying to the Clipboard. By pasting into the Score of each destination movie, all movie assets were also pasted into the destination movie's internal Cast.

Downsampling Audio

Prior to the release of Shockwave Audio (SWA) for Director, Shockwave did not support audio compression during Afterburner processing. Audio file size optimization was accomplished by downsampling high-quality original audio for downloading over the Web. All EarshotSFX sound effects were produced at CD-quality using a 48kHz sampling rate with 16-bit resolution. At this quality level, a five second sound consumes about 470K of disk space. The EarshotSFX Shockwave files were created prior to the release of SWA, so downsampling was necessary. Most sounds, especially those containing less information at the high end of the audible spectrum, were acceptably downsampled to 11kHz with 8-bit resolution for direct playback over the Web. We used WaveConvert software from KS Waves to downsample the sound effects prior to importing them into the Director Cast. WaveConvert supports batch processing and maintains excellent sound quality for downsampled audio files.

With the release of SWA, it is beneficial to use compressed audio in your Shockwave movies. The SWA Compression Xtra and SWA Settings Xtra are used to compress internal sounds, such as short sound effects, that are embedded in your Director movies.

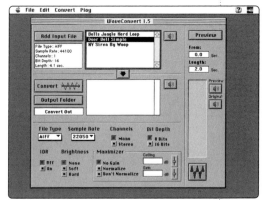

Downsample internal sounds to 22kHz/16-bit before compressing.

For sounds of longer duration, use Shockwave streaming audio. Streaming audio eliminates large downloads for end users, and does not increase the size of your shocked Director movies. The SWA Export (Mac) or Converter (Windows) Xtra compresses audio for streaming over the Web. For streaming audio, it is best to begin with CD-quality source files, or 22kHz/16-bit files if a higher resolution is not available. See Chapter 6, "Shockwave Media Creation," for more information about using Shockwave Audio compression.

The EarshotSFX Preloading Routines
Managing Asset Preloading

One of the most promising features of Shockwave is the capability to load items into the disk cache before they are explicitly requested by the Web browser. To use Shockwave's preloading capabilities to their full potential, preloading routines must:

- load files one at a time, so as not to diffuse bandwidth
- operate in the background with little or no effect on playback performance
- halt preloading operations immediately, when necessary

Ideally, they should also:

- provide notification if specified files do not exist, or cannot be downloaded
- prevent the same data from being accidentally downloaded multiple times, whenever possible

All of the EarshotSFX movies that manage asset preloading contain the same preload routines. You can copy and paste them into your own movies and call the addToLoadQueue handler to load files into the disk cache. These routines work best when opening sequential Director movies on the same page using the GoToNetMovie command, as they take advantage of the persistence of global variables across movies. They also work well for loading HTML pages and related files. However, since the persistence of preloaded documents depends on a combination of user activity and the size of the user's preload cache, you can never be certain that a document that has been registered as preloaded still exists on the user's hard disk.

To use the EarshotSFX preload routines in your own movie, just copy the following handlers from the movie named earMenu.dir on the *Shocking the Web* CD-ROM:

```
initPreloadStuff
addToLoadQueue
checkQueue
getLoadID
on idle  [You can, of course, add the contents of this on idle handler
         to your own on idle handler.]
clearPreloadList
```

To add a file to the list of files to be preloaded, use the following format:

```
addToLoadQueue fullFilePath
```

Note
fullFilePath *should contain the full path to the file, including the "http://" prefix.*

To temporarily stop all preloading, set the global Boolean gPreloadingOn to FALSE. To clear a list of items to be preloaded, call clearPreloadList without any arguments.

In the following section, we will review the inner workings of the EarshotSFX preload routines. You can refer to the scripts themselves, which contain their own documentation in the form of comments, for help in dissecting these handlers.

1. The global property list gLoadStatus is the data structure at the heart of the EarshotSFX preload routines. Each entry in the list contains the relevant data for each file in the preload queue: the file's name, including the full path; the transfer ID, which is derived from Shockwave's GetLatestNetID function; the #loaded property, a Boolean indicating whether the file has been successfully preloaded; and error messages, if any, resulting from the file's download operation.

2. The `addToLoadQueue` handler adds files to `gLoadStatus`, which is the list of
items to be preloaded.

```
on addToLoadQueue theFile
   global gLoadStatus, gPreloadList
   -- make sure the request is not already on the list:
   if gLoadStatus <> "[]" then
     repeat with i = 1 to count(gLoadStatus)
       if getPos(getAt(gLoadStatus,i),theFile) = 1 then exit
       -- the name is always the first position in the list
     end repeat
   end if
   set PropTemplate =[#name:theFile,#ID:0,#loaded:0,#error:""]
   append gPreloadList,theFile
   append gLoadStatus,PropTemplate
end
```

`addToLoadQueue` accepts one argument: the full path to the file to be preloaded.
After checking that this file is not already in `gLoadStatus`, it sets up
`PropTemplate`, which creates a property list entry for filename and default
values for the `#ID`, `#loaded`, and `#error` properties. It then adds this template
to the `gLoadStatus` list.

3. File transfer management is provided by the `checkQueue` handler, which is
called by the `on idle` handler:

```
on idle
   global gPreloadingOn
   if gPreloadingOn = true then checkQueue
   pass
end
```

`gPreloadingOn` is a global Boolean used to turn preloading on and off. File
transfers happen in the background, and should not significantly affect the
performance of Shockwave movies. However, since idle-based scripts can use
a significant amount of processor time, preloading is generally not started
(set to `FALSE`) at a movie's start (in the `startMovie` script) in the interest of
optimizing internal asset load time.

4. The `checkQueue` handler initiates all download operations, monitors the results, and sets the properties in `gLoadStatus` accordingly.

```
-- this handler should be called on idle, or when convenient
on checkQueue
  global gCurrLoading,gLoadStatus,gBaseURL,gRetries,gMaxRetries
  if gLoadStatus <> [] then
    -- if no files, then do nothing; gCurrLoading is current index
    if gCurrLoading = "" then set gCurrLoading = 0
    if not(gCurrLoading > count(gLoadStatus)) and ¬
(gCurrLoading <>0) then
        set currLoaded = ¬
getAprop(getAt(gLoadStatus,gCurrLoading),#loaded)
        -- find out the loaded status of the top of the queue
        if currLoaded = 1 and (count(gLoadStatus) > gCurrLoading) ¬ then
          -- there is a new file in gPreloadList
          set gCurrLoading = (gCurrLoading + 1)
          put "checkQueue:wake up"
          -- the following line starts the actual download
          put ¬
getLoadID(getAprop(getAt(gLoadStatus,gCurrLoading),#name))into currID
          -- now set the ID property
          setAprop getAt(gLoadStatus,gCurrLoading),#ID,currID
        end if
        -- get the ID for the xfer happening now and check status
        set currID = getAprop(getAt(gLoadStatus,gCurrLoading),#ID)
        if netDone(currID) = true and ¬
getAprop(getAt(gLoadStatus,gCurrLoading),#loaded) = 0 then
          -- the transfer has been done since the last time we checked
          if netError(currID) = "OK" then
          -- this conditional checks to make sure the xfer hasn't
          -- returned "OK" because server returned a 'not found' message
            if not(NetTextResult(gCurrID) contains "not found") then
                put "checkQueue:recv OK, updating"
                setAprop getAt(gLoadStatus,gCurrLoading),#loaded,1
              else
                setAprop getAt(gLoadStatus,gCurrLoading),#loaded,0
                setAprop getAt(gLoadStatus,gCurrLoading),#error,"not found"
```

```
        end if
        -- if xfer is done & there's more waiting, start another xfer
        if count(gLoadStatus) > gCurrLoading then
          put "checkQueue:get new"
          set gCurrLoading = (gCurrLoading + 1)
          put getLoadID ¬
          (getAprop(getAt(gLoadStatus,gCurrLoading),#name)) ¬
          into currID
          setAprop getAt(gLoadStatus,gCurrLoading),#ID,currID
          set gRetries = 0
        end if
      else if netError(currID) = "" then
        nothing
      else if netError(currID) contains "error" then
        put "checkQueue:transfer error"
        -- if an explicit xfer error, retry gMaxRetries times before
        -- giving up & going on to the next file
        if gRetries > gMaxRetries then
          if count(gLoadStatus) > gCurrLoading then
            set gCurrLoading = (gCurrLoading + 1)
          else
            set gRetries = gRetries + 1
            exit
          end if
        end if
        put getLoadID(getAprop(getAt(gLoadStatus,gCurrLoading),#name)¬
into currID
        setAprop getAt(gLoadStatus,gCurrLoading),#ID,currID
      end if
    end if
  else
    -- this part runs after the first file is added to gPreloadList
    set gCurrLoading = (gCurrLoading + 1)
    put "checkQueue:starting up"
    put getLoadID(getAprop(getAt(gLoadStatus,gCurrLoading),#name)) ¬
into currID
    setAprop getAt(gLoadStatus,gCurrLoading),#ID,currID
  end if
else
  if gCurrLoading <> "" then set gCurrLoading = ""
end if
end
```

The checkQueue handler downloads files one at a time. This behavior maximizes the efficiency of the routine, especially on modem-based connections. The global integer gCurrLoading contains an index to the current download process in the gLoadStatus list. While files are downloading, checkQueue uses getAprop(getAt(gLoadStatus,gCurrLoading),#ID) to retrieve Shockwave's transfer ID for the current download. When NetDone() for the current transfer returns OK, NetError() is used to determine the final status of the transfer. If NetError() returns an explicit error, checkQueue will attempt to restart the transfer up to gMaxRetries times. If NetError() returns OK and the file has transferred, checkQueue will set the #loaded property accordingly and move on to the next transfer.

If the file requested is not available on the server, or the filename or path in the #name property is incorrect or misspelled, most servers will send back an HTML page informing the user that the file was not found. Consequently, a positive result for NetError() may not necessarily indicate that the requested file was actually transferred. If the words "not found" are detected in the GetNetTextResult() for the transfer, checkQueue marks the file with a "not found" error.

5. Since global variables persist across movies that are opened using GoToNetMovie, gLoadStatus is monitored throughout the 37 movies that make up the EarshotSFX sample browser. The following lines in the on startMovie handler ensure that preloading-related variables will not be initialized if they contain data carried over from another movie.

```
on startMovie
...
  if not(gLoadStatus) then set gLoadStatus = []
  if not(gCurrLoading) then set gCurrLoading = ""
...
end
```

The variables will not reset to their default states if they contain data.

Creating Arbitrarily Shaped Hot Regions

The pie-shaped regions in the EarshotSFX sample browser are irregularly-shaped hotspots that perform with speed and precision. Steve Gerber, a Lingo programmer, discovered this useful technique.

1. Set your display to 8-bit, 256 colors.

2. Generate an outline image containing the cursor-sensitive areas you'd like to place on the screen.

   ### Note

   Use a graphics editing tool, like Adobe Photoshop, that supports layers to easily create the overlay outline on top of the original image.

3. Fill each of the areas in the outline with a different color. Make sure that colored areas are solid, not dithered. For the EarshotSFX sample browser, there are two such images. This is the one for the left CD:

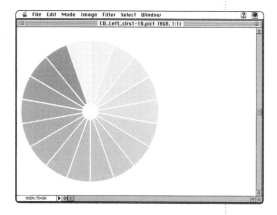

4. Export the image in Raw file format. Raw files are actually text files that use ASCII codes to represent any of the 256 possible color values for any pixel.

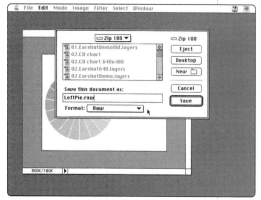

5. Open the Raw image in a text editor and copy its contents to the Clipboard.

6. Create a new text cast member in Director and paste the contents of the file into it.

7. Your new text cast member can now be used as a lookup table to determine the proper area to highlight on a rollover. In the earMenu.dir movie, this task is accomplished by the FindColorOfPixelUnderCursorL function.

```
on FindColorOfPixelUnderCursorL
    set x = (the mouseH)/2
    set y = (the mouseV)/2
    set locOfPixelInString = (y*160) + x + 1
    return charToNum(char locOfPixelInString of
    gPictInAStringL)
end
```

This function returns the numerical value of the ASCII character in gPictInAStringL that corresponds to the screen pixel at the current mouse location. Since the original image was scaled by 50% before exporting the Raw version, we multiply by 160, instead of 320, to determine the proper index for the current cursor location. In our experiments, we found that this loss of resolution was unnoticeable and improved the performance of the movie.

CASE STUDY

http://www.isn.com

Internet Shopping Network (ISN) contracted DXM Productions to create a series of Shockwave movies that would enhance the ISN Web site. The attraction of Shockwave for an online retailer such as ISN is a natural. Shockwave movies would contribute to a dynamic, animated presence on the Web, which would certainly catch the attention of prospective customers. In developing online marketing and sales promotions, a primary development goal was to create Shockwave applications that would serve as templates and could be easily updated with new content by the creative services staff at ISN.

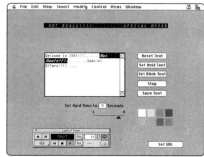

The LED Banner Movie
Retrieving text from the network

This case study examines the LED Banner movie, which was designed to display text messages.

The goal was to create a movie containing animated text, analogous to an LED "ticker" display, that continuously presented a scrolling message. Additionally, the design specification called for a movie that ISN could easily update, so that the text message could change daily if necessary. To accomplish this goal, we used the network Lingo command getNetText(). This command enables Shockwave developers to access text files over the Internet and incorporate them into their productions.

At the start of this project, several design decisions were made based upon the multi-platform nature of the Web, as well as the requirements of the client. The first major decision was to use bitmapped text to display the message, rather than using ASCII text. Bitmaps were created for each alphanumeric character. We chose to do this because ASCII text within a Director movie can have a distinctly different appearance on a computer running Windows than it does on a Macintosh. Not only is font shape different from one platform to the other, but the spacing between words and letters, or kerning, also may vary. By using bitmapped letters, we were able to maintain a consistent appearance across platforms.

However, the use of bitmapped lettering presented its own set of challenges. ISN stipulated that the message displayed by the movie be easily updatable. Had we used ASCII text to display the messages, we simply would have retrieved text using the `getNetText()` command, and displayed the imported text in a field on the Stage. By using bitmapped text, we had to devise a method to animate the individual characters in a fluid and convincing manner. Additionally, ISN requested the ability to color the text, and they wanted the animation to have the capability to pause and blink on designated words.

To develop a solution, we broke the problem into two parts: input and output. Using Director, we would create a program that would allow ISN to enter text, specify color, and choose pause locations as needed. Then, ISN would use this file to output an ASCII text file (through Director's built-in FileIO Xtra) that contained all the necessary information to update a Shockwave movie over the Internet. The Shockwave movie, along with the ASCII text file, would reside on the ISN server.

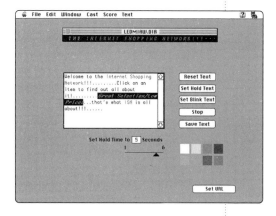

It is not necessary to deconstruct the Director input movie to understand how the Shockwave movie operates. In summary, the input movie translates the user's ASCII text into the cast member numbers that correspond to each alphanumeric character. It also records the point at which the moving letters are to pause and blink, and the colors of the individual alphanumeric characters. This case study examines the method by which the text is made to scroll across the Stage, how the text is colored, and how `getNetText()` is used in the context of the Shockwave file.

If you wish to further explore the Director input movie, the source file is included on the *Shocking the Web* CD-ROM.

Scrolling the Bitmapped Text

The first and most important aspect of the Shockwave movie is the bit-mapped type that occupies members 1 through 48. These members possess two qualities needed to make the LED display work. One, the members are 1–bit graphics; and two, the name of each member corresponds to the alphanumeric character that the member represents. The members must be 1–bit in order to be colored on the fly using Lingo. The names

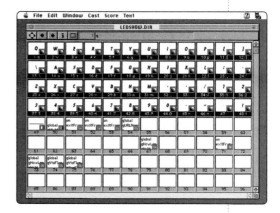

of the members need to be the same as the bitmapped characters in order to use the ASCII text file created by the input movie.

To simulate the scrolling letters of an LED screen, the positions of the sprites are not moved across the Stage, as might be expected. Instead, sprite channels 12 through 47 remain in fixed locations on the Stage and the individual members are sequentially updated to the next character in the string of characters that make up the message. This method gives a more LED-style appearance to the ani-mating characters. The following graphic illustrates this principle by showing the movie in the process of writing the word "WELCOME" on a frame-by-frame basis.

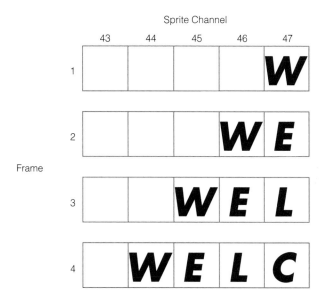

The graphic depicts the last five sprite channels over the first four frames of the movie. Initially, all of the sprites are occupied by a member containing a blank space that has the name " ". In turn, each sprite is changed to the successive letter of the message. The sprites are evenly spaced 12 pixels apart which is the minimum width that will accommodate the letter W, the widest character. At the end of the message, the movie enters a loop by repeating the process.

Reading Text from the Network

The best place to begin an investigation of the LED movie is with the
`on startMovie` handler in the main Movie script.

```
on startMovie
  puppetTempo 10
  . . .
  repeat with x = 12 to 47
    puppetSprite x, 1
  end repeat
  getNetText("./LEDText.txt")
end
```

First, the tempo is set to a speed compatible with reading the text as it moves
across the Stage. Next, the sprites where the letters will be drawn are puppeted.
Finally, the `getNetText()` command is initiated to read the text file named
"LEDText.txt" from the server.

Because of the asynchronous nature of the Internet, we cannot determine how
long it will take to conclude the text reading process. Before the text can be used,
it is necessary to confirm that the `getNetText()` command has been completed
successfully. The Lingo `netDone()` function is used to accomplish this. The next
code segment, taken from the frame script found in frame 2 of the movie, illustrates how `netDone()` can be used.

```
global gStopPoint, gHowLongHold, gStopFlag, gBlinkFlag,
gBlinkOffset, gNumCharsToBlink
global gStopOffset, gCharToNumList, gCharColorList, gURLName

on exitFrame
  go to the frame
end

on idle
  if netDone() = TRUE   then

    set newLEDValues = NetTextResult()

    if NOT listP(value(line 8 of newLEDValues)) then
      alert "Not a valid LED Player text file!"
      go "Set Up"
    else
      set gStopPoint = value(line 1 of newLEDValues)
      set gHowLongHold = value(line 2 of newLEDValues)
      set gStopFlag = value(line 3 of newLEDValues)
      set gBlinkFlag = value(line 4 of newLEDValues)
      set gBlinkOffset = value(line 5 of newLEDValues)
      set gNumCharsToBlink = value(line 6 of newLEDValues)
      set gStopOffset = value(line 7 of newLEDValues)
      set gCharToNumList = value(line 8 of newLEDValues)
      set gCharColorList = value(line 9 of newLEDValues)
      set gURLName = line 10 of newLEDValues
    end if

    if gStopFlag then
      go "WriteNStop"
    else
      go "Write Message"
    end if

  end if
end
```

After making the perfunctory global declarations, an on exitFrame handler instructs the movie to go to the frame. The on idle handler that follows contains the netDone() function. The netDone() function needs to be placed within an on idle handler in order to work properly. In Lingo programming other than for Shockwave, this type of procedure checking would normally be placed within a repeat loop, rather than within an on idle handler. Because the text file is relatively small, checking within a repeat loop on a local drive makes sense. However, on the Internet, you never know when a network operation will conclude. If the checking were done in a repeat loop, the host application (such as Netscape Navigator or Microsoft Internet Explorer) and other running applications would "lock up" during the period of the open-ended download. This is unacceptable. Performing network retrievals from within an on idle handler allows the system to continually update all running applications and avoid system lock-up.

After the text file is completely read in, it is parsed line by line to set the global variables that are necessary for the movie's operation. The variables determine whether or not the LED text pauses, where the LED text pauses, for how long it pauses, which words will blink, the color of each individual LED character, and which bitmap to use for each LED character. Finally, the handler checks the newly set gStopFlag Boolean variable to see if the message will pause and blink at any point. If so, the movie proceeds to the frame labeled WriteNStop; otherwise it goes to the frame labeled Write Message.

1-Bit Colored Text

The final technique that the LED movie employs is the use of 1-bit members of type #bitmap that are colored on the Stage via Lingo. When viewed in the Paint window, these bitmaps appear as solid black. If members are placed on the Stage, they may be colored via the pop-up color palette in the Tool Palette window, or via Lingo if the sprite is puppeted. (Members of type #shape can also be colored this way.) The main advantage of this method is that the size of a 1-bit graphic is one eighth the number of bytes of an identical 8-bit bitmap. The disadvantage is that the graphics are of a solid color—no antialiasing or gradients are available. In this instance, the text need only be a flat color to be effective.

In the LED movie file, the members that contain the text are found in sprite channels 12 through 47. The ink property for these sprites is set to Transparent, and the foreground color is set to 113 (bright green in the Netscape palette) as a default.

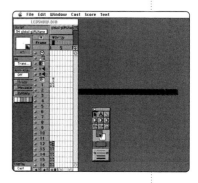

If we examine the text file created by the Director input movie, we see that the final two lines are composed of lists in the form:

[47, 47, 47... 27, 22, 8, 27, 21, 47 ... 47, 47, 47]

These values are stored in the gCharToNumList list.

[113, 113 113, 113... 186, 186, 186... 113, 113, 113]

These values are stored in the gCharColorList list.

The first list is a list of member numbers and the second list is a list of the corresponding color numbers. Each time a sprite is updated, it is drawn using the next member in the first list. The forecolor property is set to the corresponding number in the second list. You also may notice that the first and last 35 numbers of the gCharToNumList correspond to the "null" bitmap member. This was intentional. We wanted the LED display to initially display a blank screen before the text scrolled on. The gCharColorList list determines the color of any sprite at a given point in the sequence.

Note

The LED Banner movie was created using the Netscape color palette. Text color options available to the user in the Director input movie are limited to eight bright colors from the palette which display well on a black background (colors 0, 5, 16, 35, 48, 113, 186, and 194). However, the characters could easily be assigned any of the available colors in the active color palette; changing the color would amount to assigning the sprite a new forecolor as chosen from the color list.

The net effect of sequentially switching the stationary sprite's bitmap member and the forecolor property is to give the appearance of text moving from right to left across the Stage, with various words and characters colored differently. If the global variable gBlinkFlag has been set to TRUE, the motion will cease momentarily and the selected words will flash. This is accomplished by having the playback head in the Score jump to the frame labeled HoldNBlink.

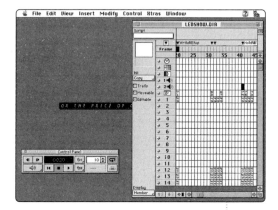

In this frame, the sprite channels for the blinking characters are repeatedly made invisible, and then visible again, by setting the visibility property. The playback head then returns to the frame labeled WriteNStop and continues scrolling the text.

Using a combination of the net Lingo command getNetText(), switching bitmap members sequentially, and coloring 1-bit members via Lingo, we were able to make a size-efficient Shockwave movie that can be updated easily by swapping an external text file whenever the message changes. The same Shockwave movie can be used to display an infinite number of messages without reprogramming for each new message.

CASE STUDY

http://www.levi.com

For Levi Strauss & Company, DXM created a Web-distributed advertisement to the theme of Levi's current 501 advertising campaign. The Internet ad mimicked a popular billboard in the San Francisco area which features a small 501 logo centered within a large, circular moiré pattern. Using Shockwave and an often-ignored Director technique, color cycling, we animated a gradient pattern to create a "brain-twisting" optical effect.

Creating the gradient animation using in-between frames in Director would have been extremely difficult and impractical, given the bandwidth limitations of Web-based multimedia. Therefore, we decided to use color cycling to create the illusion of motion within the 501 gradient.

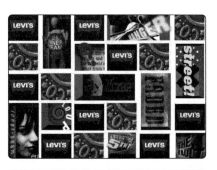

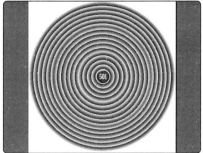

The 501 Movie
Optical illusion: using color cycling

Color cycling animates an image by cycling through a range of colors in a palette. The palette and range of colors to be cycled are specified using Director's Set Palette dialog box. (You can access the Set Palette dialog box by double-clicking in the Palette channel of the Score.) Palette effects display properly when the user's display is set to a color depth that matches the number of colors in the palette used for cycling. In this case, we used an 8-bit, 256-color palette.

Therefore, the user's display must be set to display 8-bit color in order for the technique to work properly.

The Levi's 501 Shockwave movie animates a single image. To make this image, we used image-editing software (Adobe Photoshop) to experiment with various gradients. Using these gradients in Director was tricky because we had to ensure that the colors to be cycled were not used in any portion of the Netscape browser window. Color cycling will affect anything on the computer screen that uses the palette colors being cycled. The rule of thumb is to avoid cycling any colors with RGB values that are identical (or very close to) to the RGB values of buttons and other elements in the browser window.

MOVIE SPECS

Movie Name:
501.dir

Original File Size:
220K

Audio: 35K

Afterburned
File Size: 69K

Net Lingo Used:
GoToNetPage URL

Stage Size:
480w x 480h

LINGO
SCRIPTING
LEVEL

intermediate

By making our gradients 16-color images, we were able to avoid conflicts by isolating the color tables of our gradient images. At 4 bits per pixel, the image still contains enough detail to create interesting cycling effects, and the cycling looks smooth because it plays back quickly. Director can cycle the entire, 16-color sequence in about half a second. Cycling speed is controlled using the frames per second slider bar in Director's Set Palette dialog box.

Note

Shockwave movies are non-interactive during color cycling operations. Be sure to design your color cycling segments with this constraint in mind.

To prepare images for Shockwave color cycling, follow these steps:

1. Create an image and index it to 16 colors.

2. Add a tint to the 16-color image to avoid color table conflicts with the browser. We applied a light, green tint to the image.

3. Copy the image's 16-color palette into a copy of the default system palette for the platform you are using. Make sure you keep the colors in the same order, and do not overwrite colors that are used by the browser. Using a Macintosh, the 16 colors from the gradient image were pasted into palette positions 192 to 207.

Note

On a Windows system that is set to display 8-bit, 256 colors, Netscape uses a 6-bit color cube to draw 216 colors. All colors use one of the following values for their red, green, and blue intensity: 0, 51, 102, 153, 204, or 255. To ensure that your graphics appear properly on Windows computers, use these RGB values in composing your images and custom palettes.

4. Remap the image to your new, 8-bit palette.

5. Import the image into Director. Make sure your display is set to 256 colors. When Director prompts you to select a palette option for the new cast member, select Install Palette In Cast. Then, enter a name for the palette.

6. After placing the imported image on the Stage, double-click on the Palette channel in the Score. Select the imported palette using the pop-up menu. Then, highlight the colors to cycle on the displayed palette.

7. When you have achieved the desired color cycling effect, use Afterburner to create a Shockwave movie.

8. Embed the Shockwave movie within a Web page. If toolbars within the browser window are color cycling unintentionally, it may indicate that one or more, of the 16 colors that were edited into the custom palette is being used by the browser. Open the Palette window in Director, find the offending color(s) in the palette, and tweak them manually. After you have made the adjustment, use Afterburner to create a new Shockwave movie.

9. Once the image, palette, and color cycling range have been established, you should have a color cycling movie that functions properly on any computer running in 8-bit display mode. Color cycling effects do not appear properly on displays set to more or less than 256 colors. To handle these situations, Lingo provides control over the `colordepth` property. Under the MacOS and Windows, the `colordepth` property of the current display can be tested. For Shockwave movies, the `colordepth` property cannot be set.

10. The `initForScreenDepth` handler, which is called by the `startmovie` script, determines if the current display is in 8-bit mode. If it is not, the script executes different routines based on the operating system.

```
on initForScreenDepth type
  set gOldDepth = the colorDepth
  if not(type = "dcr") and  gPlatform = "Mac" then
    if the colorDepth <> 8 then
      set the colorDepth to 8
    else
      set the switchColorDepth to false
    end if
  else
    if the colorDepth <> 8 then
      alert "Your screen must be set to 256 colors to view ¬
this file properly. The movie will pause until your monitor ¬
is set to 8-bit mode."
      set gSuspend = true
      set gBeenHere = 0
    end if
  end if
end
```

The `type` parameter that is passed to the `initForScreenDepth` handler is defined by the `star movie` handler. This parameter specifies whether the current file is a compressed Shockwave file (`"dcr"`) that is playing via the Shockwave plug-in or control, or whether it is a Director projector or movie (`"dir"`) that is not playing within a Web browser.

In addition to creating the Shockwave version of the 501 movie, we built a downloadable version as a Director projector for the client. If the movie plays as a projector on a Macintosh, we use the `colorDepth` property to set the display mode to 8-bit. If the movie plays within a Web browser, setting the `colorDepth` property has no effect. In this case, we use an `alert` command that prompts the user to change the display's color depth. The playback head then pauses, but the movie continuously checks the status of the color depth in an `idle` handler.

```
on idle
  if gSuspend then
    if the colorDepth = 8 then
      set gSuspend = 0
      continue
    end if
  end if
end
```

If the `colorDepth` becomes equal to 8, then the gSuspend flag is set to 0 (or `FALSE`), and the `continue` command restarts playback of the movie. Another script calls `GoToNetPage` to reload the page. If the page is not reloaded after the color depth changes, undesirable palette artifacts display on the screen.

The global gOldDepth stores the original display setting. On a Macintosh computer, the projector version of the movie uses this variable within the `stopMovie` handler to reset the state of the display when the user exits the movie.

```
on stopMovie
  global gOldDepth
  ...
  if (gOldDepth) then set the colorDepth to gOldDepth
  ...
end
```

Since the `stopMovie` handler is called only when the user exits the Web page or projector (there are no `GoToNetMovie` commands within this movie), there is no need to force a palette refresh by reloading the Web page, as we did earlier.

Note

Changing the `colorDepth` *property of a Macintosh display causes a momentary white flash.*

Multi-purpose Delivery Issues

Color cycling in the Levi's 501 movie performs differently on Windows and Macintosh computers, and each playback platform requires different tempo settings and a different layout in the Score window. The Macintosh version of the projector uses an Xtra to hide the Finder behind the Director Stage, which is not required for the Windows projector version. The Shockwave version of the movie uses a GoToNetPage command to refresh the display, which is not needed (or even recognized) by the projector. Instead of making four separate movies, we used a series of conditionals at the beginning of the startMovie handler to determine the playback environment.

```
on startMovie
  if the machineType <> 256 then
    set gPlatform = "Mac"
  else
    set gPlatform = "Win"
  end if
  if string(version) contains "net" then
    initForScreenDepth "dcr"
    initForShock
  else
    initForScreenDepth "dir"
    initForLocal
  end if
  ...
end startMovie
```

These conditional statements establish criteria for determining delivery method and platform, and the results are used to configure the movie properly. The following script occurs in the frame before color cycling begins. It uses the global variable gPlatform, which was set by the first conditional in the startMovie handler, to branch to the appropriate frame based on the current platform.

```
on exitFrame
  global gPlatform
  go label("cycle" & gPlatform)
end
```

The "cycleMac" section of the Score contains a single-frame animation that cycles at a rate of 28 fps (frames per second). The "cycleWin" section is spread over 16 frames, with a tempo setting of 26 fps.

The `if string(version)`... conditional is used to trap NetLingo that is contained within a single handler (`initForShockHandler`). The Shockwave plug-in/control currently returns the Director version number appended with the word "net." The `version` system variable can be used to determine whether a Director movie is running locally or via Shockwave within a Web browser.

Director users can employ color cycling to create many different optical effects. Experiment with various images and palettes. Color cycling animations can mesmerize users while only slightly affecting file size. Color cycling animations usually play smoothly—even on slower computers—so they are handy for creating low-bandwidth Shockwave movies.

CASE STUDY

Chapter 14

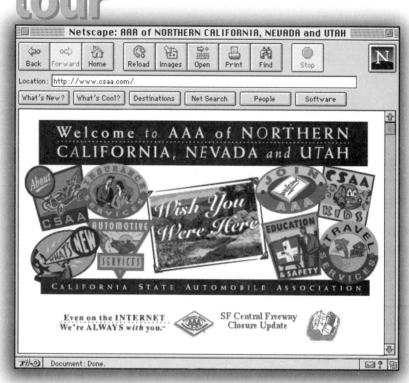

http://www.csaa.com

The California State Automobile Association (CSAA) wanted one central location where members could get a glimpse of the content and structure of the entire CSAA Web site. DXM Productions was contracted by Organic Online, the developers of the CSAA site, to design the CSAA site tour using an automobile trip metaphor. Original illustrations were created by Tim Carroll.

Within the tour, the viewer drives down a road, reading billboards that describe each area of the site. The Shockwave tour movie synchronously updates textual information in a nearby frame while the user drives from one billboard to the next. A tour map provides random access to each of the billboards and tracks the user's actions for his or her own reference.

The Interactive Site Tour
Recording User Actions

When a user clicks on the tour map icon on the lower right corner of the car's dashboard, the tour map screen fills the browser frame. As the cursor rolls over different site tour destinations (represented by numerals 1–9), corresponding thumbnail graphics display the names of each section to provide user feedback.

When a destination is selected from the map, it is recorded by the Shockwave movie. Then, an animation that simulates driving on a road is played for the user to extend the driving metaphor as the car travels to the selected destination. The tour map screen records the site tour segments the user has visited and marks them with a check mark each time the map is revisited.

MOVIE SPECS

Movie Name:
csaaDriveZ.dir

Original File Size:
409K

Audio: 30K

Afterburned
File Size: 200K

Net Lingo Used:
goToNetPage

Stage Size:
396w x 310h

**LINGO
SCRIPTING
LEVEL**

intermediate

1. When the user selects a tour destination, the entry is logged chronologically in a list, and duplicate viewings are removed from the list to reduce maintenance of extraneous data. The following script records the user's actions when the map is clicked.

The goPage handler is used to manage GoToNetPage commands.

```
on goPage thePage,target
  recordHistory thePage
  if the movieName contains ".dcr" then
    if not(stringP(target)) then
      GoToNetPage thePage
      set gReadyToGo = true
      fadeAllSounds 200
    else
      goToNetPage thePage,target
    end if
  end if
end
```

2. The first line in the goPage handler adds the next URL to be visited to the history list by invoking the recordHistory handler.

```
on recordHistory theURL
  if voidP(gHistory) then set gHistory = []
  set index = getPos(gHistory,theURL)
  if index then deleteAt gHistory,index
  append gHistory theURL
end
```

This handler continues to add the next URL visited to the end of the global gHistory list. (The list is declared a global at the beginning of the movie script so it can be used by other scripts.) Before the URL is added to the list, recordHistory checks to determine if the URL is already in the list; if it is, the last occurrence of the URL is removed from the list and replaced by the new occurrence at the end of the list.

3. Here's a simple example of how the gHistory list may appear in practice. After a user visits four of the tour destinations, the list might look like this:

```
["education.html", "about.html", "join.html", ¬
"auto_services.html"]
```

If they next visited the URL about.html, the list would look like this:

```
["education.html", "join.html", ¬
"auto_services.html", "about.html"]
```

In summary, a URL is never duplicated on the list. The list maintains a log of the total number of destinations a user has visited, along with the chronological order in which the destinations have been visited. When the map activates, the gHistory list is checked against the contents of gTargetList, which contains the names of all the pages referenced by the map. The CSAA movie does not take advantage of all the features inherent in the structure of the gHistory list, but you can use these features in your own movies by copying the handlers from the source file found on the *Shocking the Web* CD-ROM.

Plan Ahead   Offline Authoring Tip

The goPage handler includes a trap for GoToNetPage calls in a local development environment. Traps are useful for working with Shockwave Lingo commands within .dir files during offline development. Until the Director application (in addition to the Shockwave plug-in) recognizes and supports Lingo Network extensions, creating scripts to trap the commands saves time and eliminates frustration caused by repeated Lingo error messages.

```
if the movieName contains ".dcr" then
    if not(stringP(target)) then
      GoToNetPage thePage
      set gReadyToGo = true
      fadeAllSounds 200
    else
      goToNetPage thePage,target
    end if
  end if
```

If the name of the movie does not contain the .dcr file extension, all GoToNetPage commands are bypassed. The movieName function only can be used in this limited manner inside Shockwave movies, and cannot be used to test for full file names. This is because the browser renames the file upon download, but does retain the three-character (.dcr) suffix.

An alternative method is to test for the version string using Lingo. The version system variable contains the version string for the Director application. For Shockwave, the version contains "net." In the local Director environment, it does not.

Reusing Small Elements

While the csaaDrive.dcr movie is rather large at 200K, it adapts several strategies for file size reduction. The terrain elements (such as the clouds, mountains, and trees) are reused from scene to scene, and sometimes resized on the Stage. The most efficient example of file size conservation, however, is in the horn sound.

When you click on the steering wheel, the "BellTone" sound plays. This sound file contains a single triangle wave that is only 226 bytes, even though it is sampled at 22kHz! The sound is set to loop in the Properties dialog box, so the horn will continue to honk as long as you press on the steering wheel.

To make the sound a bit more interesting, the honkHorn handler adds a fade in and fade out:

```
on honkHorn arg
  global gOldVol
  if arg then
    put the volume of sound 1 into gOldVol
    sound fadeIn 1,6
    set the volume of sound 1 = 50
    puppetSound "BellTone"
    updateStage
  else
    sound FadeOut 1,2
    updateStage
  end if
end
```

The existence of the gOldVol global variable enables other handlers to know that the sound volume has been altered; gOldVol can be used to reset the level of the sound channel back to its default after it has been manipulated for the purpose of this movie.

Note

The BellTone sound is one of a number of low-bandwidth sounds tailored for Web use that is available from the Earshot SFX library. All of the sounds in csaaDrive.dcr movie come from this sound effects library, a sampler of which is included on the Shocking the Web *CD-ROM.*

Object-Oriented Eyeballs

The two eyes in the rear-view mirror constantly follow the position of the mouse as the user moves the cursor around the screen. These eyes are the progeny of a parent script that creates sprites which appear to rotate and track other objects on the screen.

The FollowObject Parent Script

Parent-child scripting provides a convenient method for creating objects that share certain behaviors. Since the eyeballs both utilize the `getFollowAngle` calculation in similar ways, their movement is generated by the FollowObject Parent Script, which configures sprites to follow other sprite movements on the Stage.

1. The following lines in the `initSprites` handler create objects for both eyeballs.

```
repeat with i = gEyeBallChan to gEyeBallChan + 1

append(gFollowList,new(script "FollowObject Script", ¬
    i,"mouse","newH","newT"))

end repeat
```

Each object created by this script is stored in the global list `gFollowList`. This list is later used to display the objects in response to movements on the screen.

2. A new `FollowObject` is created using the following Lingo template, which supplies the basic configuration information needed to set up a sprite with the desired behavior.

```
new(script "FollowObject Script", channel, objectToWatch, ¬
    startCast, stopCast)
```

The four arguments required by the script to create a new object are:

channel—the sprite channel to be used for the object.

objectToWatch—either an integer for another sprite channel, or the mouse cursor.

startCast—the cast member that looks up (toward the 12 o'clock position).

stopCast—the last cast member in the rotational sequence. If there were 12 members in your rotational sequence, the last one would be at the 11 o'clock position.

Note

All of the cast members must be arranged contiguously, and in proper order, in the Cast window in order for the scripts to work.

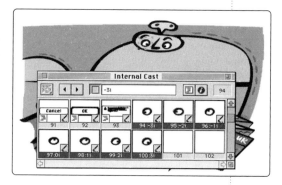

3. Once the objects are created and stored in the global gFollowList, they are animated using an if...then...else statement in the on idle handler.

```
on idle
    if not(the visible of sprite gBigMapChan) then
     rotateAllFO gFollowList
  else
      checkMapRolz
  end if
end
```

4. Whenever the full-screen map is not displayed, the rotateAllFO command will update all objects supplied in the argument represented here by gFollowList. (We'll return to the inner workings of rotateAllFO later.)

5. Let's examine the new handler in the FollowObject Parent Script to determine exactly what occurs when a new object is created.

```
property pWatchObject,pMySprite,pMySteps,pMyMembers

on new me,mySprite,watchObject, zeroCast, hiCast
  set pWatchObject = watchObject
  set pMySprite = mySprite
  puppetSprite mySprite,1
  set zeroCast = the number of member zeroCast
  set steps  = (the number of member hiCast) - (zeroCast) + 1
  -- the following calculates the angle range for each image
  set pStepAngle = 360/steps
  set pMySteps = []
  set pMyMembers = []
  repeat with i = 1 to steps
    set castRef = zeroCast + (i-1)
    -- these 2 lists are used as lookup tables to match
    -- the angle with the proper cast member
    append pMySteps,((i*pStepAngle) - (pStepAngle/2))
    append pMyMembers,castRef
  end repeat
  append pMySteps,360
  append pMyMembers,zeroCast
  -- to use findPosNear, the list must be sorted
  sort pMySteps
  return me
end
```

The FollowObject Parent Script's new handler sets up distiguishing properties for each object: what the object will follow, which sprite it will use, and which cast member it will use to represent a specific angle between itself and the followed, or watched object.

6. First, the watched object is recorded and the new object's sprite channel is puppeted. The properties declared at the top of the parent script will persist for each object as long as that object exists, or until the value of a property is changed.

```
set pWatchObject = watchObject
set pMySprite = mySprite
puppetSprite mySprite,1
```

The new handler generates a lookup table to match cast members against specific angle ranges.

7. Next, we must calculate how large an angle each member will cover:

```
set zeroCast = the number of member zeroCast
set steps  = (the number of member hiCast) - (zeroCast) + 1
-- the following calculates the angle range for each image
set stepAngle = 360/steps
```

This calculation is simple; the number of cast members between zeroCast and hiCast is divided by 360—the number of degrees in a full circle. The resulting stepAngle is the angle allocated to each member. For example, if there are six members between zeroCast and hiCast, each member must cover a range of 60 degrees.

```
repeat with i = 1 to steps
   set castRef = zeroCast + (i-1)
   -- these 2 lists are used as lookup tables to match
   -- the angle with the proper cast member
   append pMySteps,((i*stepAngle) - (stepAngle/2))
   append pMyMembers,castRef
end repeat
append pMySteps,360
append pMyMembers,zeroCast
-- to use findPosNear, the list must be sorted
sort pMySteps
return me
```

8. Next, the repeat loop generates a lookup table that contains a list of the "border" angles—that is, the angles at which one member will be switched to the next member. The angles must be calculated while considering the angle at which each member is apparently pointing is at the center of its range of coverage. For example, the first piece of artwork (which points toward 12 o'clock position) will cover from 330 to 30 degrees, the second from 30 to 90, and so on. The following line of code sets up each border angle so that the apparent angle of the artwork is at the center of that member's range.

```
append pMySteps,((i*stepAngle) - (stepAngle/2))
```

9. Then, the corresponding member is placed into the same position in another list, pMyMembers:

```
append pMyMembers,castRef
```

10. The resulting lists, pMySteps and pMyMembers, look like this:

```
pMySteps = [30, 90, 150, 210, 270, 330]
pMyMembers = [111, 112, 113, 114, 115, 116]
```

11. The repeat loop will always leave a gap between the end of coverage for the last member in the sequence (in this case 330 degrees) and the end of the circle. Luckily, whatever the size of this missing angle, it always ends at 360 degrees and will always use the same member as the beginning of the sequence (since it is located to the left side of the first member's coverage area). The following Lingo closes the circle.

```
append pMySteps,360
append pMyMembers,zeroCast
```

12. After the lists are sorted (so they can be accessed using the findPosNear command), they look like this:

```
pMySteps = [30, 90, 150, 210, 270, 330, 360]
pMyMembers = [111, 112, 113, 114, 115, 116, 111]
```

Animating the Eyeballs

Earlier, we discussed the single line of code used to animate both eyeballs. Again, it is as follows.

```
rotateAllFO gFollowList
```

Here's the Lingo for the entire handler, which is found within the FollowObject Parent Script.

```
on rotateAllFO objectList
  repeat with k in objectList
    rotateFO k
  end repeat
  updateStage
end
```

1. The rotateFO handler is basically just a macro that passes a list of objects to another handler, rotateFO, to update each FollowObject individually. The RotateAllFO handler does not need to reside inside the FollowObject Parent Script (as it does not require access to any of the object properties); however, it is stored there for easy portability. The rotateFO handler is as follows:

```
on rotateFO me
  if integerP(pWatchObject) then
    set watchPoint = the loc of sprite (pWatchObject)
  else if pWatchObject = "mouse" then
    set watchPoint = point(the mouseH,the mouseV)
  else if listP(pWatchObject) then
    set watchPoint = pWatchObject
  else
    exit
  end if
  set nextCast = getAt(pMyMembers, findPosNear(pMySteps, ¬
    integer(getFollowAngle(pMySprite,watchPoint))))
  if the memberNum of sprite pMySprite <> nextCast then
    set the memberNum of sprite pMySprite = nextCast
end
```

2. The first part of the rotateFO handler determines the object to follow, which is pWatchObject, and where the followed object is currently located, which is watchPoint. Three types of data can be used for pWatchObject:

- A sprite, designated by an integer in the pWatchObject property.
- The location of the cursor, designated by the mouse keyword.
- A specific point in Euclidean (x,y) space expressed as point(x,y). This can be used to make a moving FollowObject track a fixed point. Note that Director does not have a pointP() function, but points will evaluate to lists (as will rect data types) when the listP() function is used.

3. Once pWatchObject is set, the next line calculates the angle between FollowObject (the eyeballs object) and watchPoint (the tracking point) in order to display the proper member for this angle. To accomplish this calculation, the getFollowAngle function (described below) is used. Next, the findPosNear command determines the closest match for the angle that is contained in pMySteps. Similar to the rules for "The Price Is Right" game, findPosNear seeks the closest match without going over the value.

4. The way the command works is illustrated in the following example:

If pMySteps = [30, 90, 150, 210, 270, 330, 360]
and theAngle = 80
then findPosNear(pMySteps,integer(getFollowAngle)
will return a value of 2, representing the second position in the list.

Therefore, if pMyMembers = [111, 112, 113, 114, 115, 116, 111]
then nextCast will equal 112.

5. When all members are calculated and set, rotateAllFO will issue an updateStage command if necessary before returning control to the on idle handler.

Finding the Angles

This section examines the geometry behind the `getFollowAngle` function. Geometry-phobic Director hackers take heart—the programmer of this movie figured out the process detailed below in two nights during intimate sessions with *Cliff's Notes for High School Geometry*.

1. The `getFollowAngle` function uses basic Euclidean geometry to derive the angle between any two points on the screen. The syntax is as follows:

```
getFollowAngle(watcherSprite,watchedPoint)
```

The `watcherSprite` follows the `watchedPoint`. In the case of the CSAA movie, each eyeball is a `watcherSprite` and the location of the mouse is the `watchedPoint` for both eyeballs.

2. The angle is calculated as though the center of `watcherSprite` is at the center of a circle and the `watchedPoint` is a point on the circle's circumference. Angles are measured in degrees, with the 0 degree axis directly above the `watchedPoint` (at the 12 o'clock position), counting up to 360 degrees in a clockwise direction.

3. Calculating the angle between the two points requires making a right triangle that uses a line between the `watcherSprite` and `watchedPoint` as it's hypotenuse. (The hypotenuse is the longest leg of a right triangle—the side opposite the right angle.) The `getFollowAngle` function follows a number of steps to draw this triangle, concluding by using the arc tangent (`atan`) function to determine the angle.

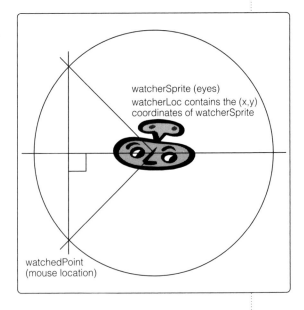

watcherSprite (eyes)
watcherLoc contains the (x,y)
coordinates of watcherSprite

watchedPoint
(mouse location)

```
on getFollowAngle watcherSprite,watchedPoint,rxPoint
  global oldWatchPoint,oldAngle
  if watchedPoint <> getAProp(oldWatchPoint,watcherSprite)
  then
    set watcherLoc = spriteCenter(watcherSprite)
    if not(rxPoint) then
      set rxPoint = getAt(watcherLoc,1)
    -- figure out the third side of an isocles
    -- triangle with the line between the points as one side
    -- a line of equal length at 12:00 as another side
    -- and a line between them as the third
    set hypLength = distance(watcherLoc,watchedPoint)
    set thirdSide =
      (makeIsoceles(hypLength,watcherLoc,watchedPoint)/2)
    -- now split it into 2 right triangles
    set chordLen = pythagoras(hypLength,thirdSide)
    setAProp oldWatchPoint, watcherSprite, watchedPoint
    if chordLen <> 0 then
      -- use arcTan for angle, double & convert to degrees
      set rVal = atan(thirdSide/chordLen)*(360/pi())
      if not(integer(rVal)) then
        if string(rVal) contains "-" then
          set rVal = 180
        end if
      else
        -- compensate for negative angularity
        if getAt(watchedPoint,1) < rXpoint then
          set rVal = 360 - rVal
      end if
    else
      set rVal = 180
    end if
    setAprop oldAngle, watcherSprite, rVal
  else
    set rVal = getAprop(oldAngle,watcherSprite)
  end if
  return rVal
end
```

4. The getFollowAngle function takes two mandatory arguments, watcherSprite and watchedPoint and an optional third argument, rxPoint.

The first argument, watcherSprite, is the eyeball sprite that is watching. The coordinates of watcherSprite are stored in a variable named watcherLoc for portability. The second argument, watchedPoint, is the point at which the watcherSprite is looking, in the form point(x,y). The third, optional argument is rxPoint, which is the x coordinate that getFollowAngle uses to calculate angles in relation to watcherLoc. If this parameter is omitted, the center of watcherSprite will be used as the watcherLoc. (This argument was primarily used for testing, but—if expanded to allow for x and y offsets—could create interesting rotational relationships between objects.)

Two globals are used by getFollowAngle to reduce unnecessary computation by storing the most recent state for each watcherSprite.

```
global oldWatchPoint,oldAngle
  if watchedPoint <> getAProp(oldWatchPoint,watcherSprite)
    then...
```

For example, when a calculation that involves sprite 9 is requested, getFollowAngle checks to determine whether the object's position remains unchanged since the last time the angle was calculated for sprite 9. If conditions have not changed, the last value stored in memory is returned, and floating-point calculations (which can be slow on computers without FPUs) are not executed.

5. Next, we use the spriteCenter(theSprite) function to return the center of the sprite.

```
set watcherLoc = spriteCenter(watcherSprite)
if not(rxPoint) then set rxPoint = getAt(watcherLoc,1)
```

The center of `watcherSprite` is used as the reference point for all calculations, unless the `rxPoint` argument specifies a different value to use for the horizontal coordinate.

```
on spriteCenter theSprite
  set rVal = point(the right of sprite theSprite -
    integer((the width of sprite theSprite)/2),
    (the bottom of sprite theSprite -
    integer((the height of sprite theSprite)/2)))
  return rVal
end
```

In most cases, the center of an object is used as the handle for rotation. While the center of an image is usually its `regPoint`, the `regPoint` is sometimes used for other purposes. The `spriteCenter(theSprite)` function allows the `getFollowAngle` script to be `regPoint`-independent, and also adds the capability to use bitmapped and shape members. (Shape members are positioned from their upper-left corner and their `regPoint` is not configurable.)

6. There is one last calculation to be performed before the right triangle can be drawn. Before constructing the triangle, whether the `watchedPoint` is to the left or to the right of the `watcherSprite` must be determined. This information is used later to index the angle to a range of zero to 360 degrees, rather than –180 to 180 degrees.

```
if getAt(watchedPoint,1) > rxPoint then
      set mult = 1
    else
      set mult = -1
. . .
```

7. The first step in drawing the triangle is calculating the length of the hypotenuse.

```
set hypLength = distance(watcherLoc,watchedPoint)
```

The distance function uses the equation d = (square root of x) to calculate the distance, in pixels, between any two points in the display space.

```
on distance point1,point2
  set xDiff = the locH of point2 - the locH of point1
  set yDiff = the locV of point2 - the locV of point1
  set dist = sqrt(power(xDiff,2) + power(yDiff,2))
  return dist
end
```

8.   Now that we have determined the length of the hypotenuse, an isoceles triangle is created by drawing a virtual line at the same length as the hypotenuse, along the zero degree axis directly above watchedPoint. Once the length of the third side of this triangle is calculated, the triangle can be split into two right triangles and the angle between watcherLoc and watchedPoint derived. The makeIsoceles function handles this part of the process.

```
set thirdSide =
(makeIsoceles(hypLength,watcherLoc,watchedPoint)/2)

on makeIsoceles hypLength,strtPt,closePoint
  set thirdPoint = point(the locH of strtPt, (the locV of strtPt -
hypLength))
  set thirdSide = distance(thirdPoint,closePoint)
  return thirdSide
end
```

The first line of makeIsoceles calculates the end point of a line in space which is directly above watchedPoint. This value then is placed into a variable named thirdPoint. Once this coordinate is determined, it's easy to use the distance function to get the length of the third side of the triangle.

9. A line drawn from the center of the unequal side of an isoceles triangle to the angle opposite this line creates two equal right triangles. When GetFollowAngle divides the result of makeIsoceles by two, the result is the length of two sides of the right triangle. Now we'll use a pythagorean theorem to calculate the length of the third side of the triangle. Pythagorean theorem states that in a right triangle, with c as the hypotenuse and a and b as the legs, $a^2 + b^2 = c^2$.

```
set chordLen = pythagoras(hypLength,thirdSide)
```

10. Since we know the length of the hypotenuse and one leg of the triangle, the pythagorean function uses the elements of the equation to solve the last leg length value.

```
on pythagoras radLen, sideLen
  set rvSquare = power(radLen,2) - power(sideLen,2)
  return integer(sqrt(rvSquare))
end
```

11. Now that we have determined the lengths of the sides of the triangle, we can solve for the angle.

If chordLen evaluates to 0, getFollowAngle will return a "divide by zero" Lingo error. In this situation, the angle can be only one of two values: 0.0000 or 180.0000 degrees. At this point, we can determine the correct angle by evaluating whether the vertical position of watchedPoint is above or below the vertical position for watcherLoc. However, if chordLen evaluates to 0 (although this situation is fairly rare), then the last angle value is returned for that sprite, rather than add more computational overhead.

The getFollowAngle function stores data for each sprite specified by watcherSprite.

12. The following line calculates the angle based on the arc tangent, which is referred to in Lingo as atan(). The arc tangent is multiplied by 360/pi to double the angle (remember, we split the triangle in half to make right triangles) and to convert from radians to degrees.

```
set rVal = atan(thirdSide/chordLen)*(360/pi())
```

Director's geometric functions calculate using radians as their base unit. One radian equals 60 degrees. The following functions can be used to convert from radians to degrees and vice versa.

```
on radians degrees
   set rVal = degrees*(pi()/180)
   return rVal
end

on degrees radians
   set rVal = (radians*180)/pi()
   return rVal
end
```

13. At this point, we have a number between –180 and 180 which represents the angle between watcherLoc and watchedPoint. The angles to the left of watcherLoc will range from 0 (at 12 o'clock position) to –180 (at 6 o'clock position). It's easier, however, to translate these numbers into specific cast members—if they are indexed along a straight 0 to 360 continuum, counting clockwise.

```
if getAt(watchedPoint,1) < rXpoint then set rVal = 360 - rVal
```

This segment of code tests for a negative angle and calculates a positive angle if necessary. This results in a reading somewhere between 0 and 360 degrees, suitable for the FollowObject functions detailed above.

14. These calculations, combined with Director's object-oriented scripting and repurposed artwork, provide developers with the capability to create many different `FollowObject(s)` which use different assets and angle granularity, while expending little effort. These functions could be used to make a screensaver, a dial-based interface, or anything that requires true object rotation. To use these functions in your projects, just copy the `FollowObject` and `Geometry` script cast members into your own movie.

The CSAA site tour movie combines Score-based and Lingo-based animation techniques to create and simulate motion and to provide feedback to users. The site tour was originally created using Shockwave for Director 4. In order to update information in surrounding frames, a combination of Shockwave, CGI and JavaScript were used to target the frames. The movie was later updated to take advantage of the built-in frame targeting capabilities of Shockwave for Director 5. Both versions of the csaaDrive.dcr movie are included on the *Shocking the Web* CD-ROM.

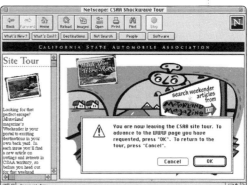

CASE STUDY

interactive
shockwave
entertainment

```
┌─────────────────────────── Netscape: DXM ───────────────────────────┐
│ ⇦o    o⇨    🏠     🔄      🖼       ⇨       🖨      🔍      ◯         │   N
│ Back Forward Home  Reload  Images  Open   Print   Find    Stop       │
│ What's New? | What's Cool? | Handbook | Net Search | Net Directory | Software │
├──────────────────────────────────────────────────────────────────────┤
│                                                                        │
│              D  X  M                                                    │
│                                                                        │
│         N E W   M E D I A   D E S I G N   A N D   P R O D U C T I O N   │
│                                                                        │
│                      Beat Man                                          │
│                     SUPER COMIC                                        │
│                                                                        │
├──────────────────────────────────────────────────────────────────────┤
│  Document: Done.                                                       │
└──────────────────────────────────────────────────────────────────────┘
```

http://www.dxm.com

DXM Productions worked with a popular artist in Tokyo, Japan, whose name is Mie Ishii, to create an online, interactive version of Mie's Beatman comic strip. Together, DXM and Mie developed an efficient process for creating multi-layered, hand-drawn artwork that would then be converted to digital Shockwave animations. The Shockwave animations can be published serially on the Web as new strips are developed.

The Web facilitates international collaboration by eliminating many of the expenses associated with international communication and transportation, and by allowing all parties to view work-in-progress instantaneously.

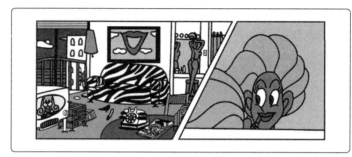

Beatman Animated Comic
Converting artwork for Web publication

In creating the Shockwave version of Beatman, it was important for DXM to recreate the artwork as faithfully as possible. A cartoonist's style is very much like a signature—there are strokes, loops, and spatial relationships that are unique to each artist, and are difficult at best to emulate. In addition, popular cartoon characters like those found in Beatman have established visual reputations. Fans of the comic strip are very aware of any digression in style. Recreation of the comic was a challenging task, not only for DXM, but for the capabilities of tracing and painting software available today.

This case study illustrates the process used to convert hand-drawn cartoon artwork to digital representations for publication on the Web using scanning, image editing, and tracing software. It also addresses the preparation of the artwork for animation in Director.

MOVIE SPECS

Original File Size:
LaCite.dir: 128K
gogoroom.dir: 92K

Audio:
LaCite.dir: none
gogoroom.dir: none

Afterburned file size:
LaCiteanim.dcr: 60K
gogoroom.dcr: 46K

Net Lingo Used:
preloadNetThing,
goToNetPage

Stage Size:
592w x 250h

LINGO
SCRIPTING
LEVEL
easy

The Drawing Process

An important preliminary step in the production process was for the artist, Mie, to adapt the print version of the comic for the animated Shockwave version. He conceptualized the animated parts of each panel and then split the artwork into two parts: background and movement artwork. The movement artwork would be composited over the background like animation cels. As in traditional animation, all of the artwork was drawn on punched animator's paper, and registered using a peg bar (available at any animation supply company).

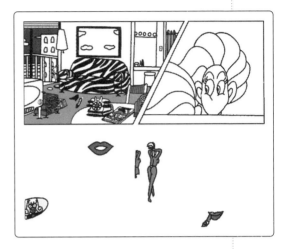

Digitizing Traditional Artwork

1. To maintain registration during scanning, the animator's peg bar was mounted to a flatbed scanner. Each drawing was held in place using the peg bar, and was registered automatically to the other drawings when scanned into Photoshop. (Although you can scan directly into Streamline, fewer touch-up tools are available in this application.)

2. Using ScanWizard II, the scanner software for a Microtek scanner, the same cropping boundaries were maintained over a series of scans. This ensured the same dimensions for each animation "cel."

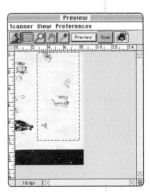

Note

To achieve a good trace for scans, Streamline recommends scanning artwork at 300 dpi or higher. The higher the dpi, the better the trace of the artwork.

Vector Conversion

An early decision was made to convert the drawings to vector graphics soon after they were scanned. Adobe Streamline, an art tracing program, was used to accomplish this. A vector version of all the drawings had many advantages over bitmaps for animation. Lines and curves could be adjusted infinitely, resizing could be accomplished without degradation to the image, and images would compress well for faster downloading over the Web.

1. All scans were saved as PICT files and imported into Streamline for tracing and vector conversion.

2. The heart of Streamline is the Conversion Setup dialog box. The following settings were used: Methods=Centerline; Accuracy, Line Thinning=2; Tolerance=2; and Lines=Curved lines only. Some experimentation with different permutations of these settings was required to obtain the best results. Setting the Method to Centerline is important because it forces the trace to be a unified line weight of your choice. Combining Outline and Centerline is possible, but this combination produced a line more calligraphic in style and differed from the artist's style.

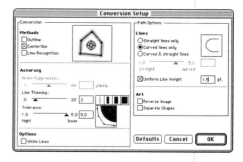

3. It is possible to batch convert a whole folder of artwork using Streamline. After determining the appropriate settings, the Settings option was selected from the Streamline menu, and a dialog box containing the last conversion settings appeared. The settings were named, and the Batch Select option was chosen. Files to be converted were selected, processed, and saved in EPS format within a specified folder.

4. After saving, the artwork was immediately opened in Adobe Illustrator to tweak some of the points and curves. Depending on the quality of the trace, a lot of work may be required at this point.

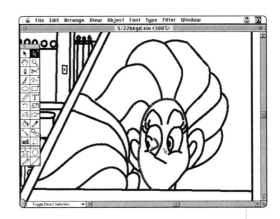

Coloring Layers in Photoshop

Mie's cartoon artwork contains large enclosed areas, so coloring it appeared to be a natural for the Paint Bucket tool. This was not necessarily the best choice. Filling areas with the Paint Bucket tool paints into the anti-aliased pixels that collectively are responsible for the softening of jagged, square pixels in a bitmapped image, and thereby causes line thickness to erode. One way to avoid erosion is to paint in layers while in Photoshop. The lines exist on one layer, and the colored areas exist on a separate layer beneath the lines. This is similar to the cel animation process, where a transparent acetate cel shows the image on one side, and is painted on the other. This method prevents overpainting into the line. Since the artwork was saved in EPS format, it could be rasterized into Photoshop as transparent layers, with all of the background regions dropped out. This mimics the acetate quality of an animation cel, and provides the transparency needed to paint in layers.

Another advantage of using vector graphics is that you can select the size of your artwork before you rasterize it in Photoshop. Before opening an EPS file in Photoshop, a dialog box prompts for dimensions and pixel depth. This enables you to resize an image before it is rasterized. (Remember, each time a rasterized image is resized, image quality can degrade.)

1. The first rasterized layer was named "line art." Regions in this layer were selected using the Magic Wand tool. When a selection is made, it applies to all layers until deselected, so it was important to make sure that this was the top-most layer.

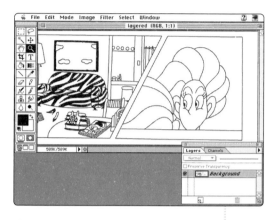

2. Next, a new layer was created and named "colors." This layer was placed beneath the line art layer. With the selection in the line art layer still active, the Expand option was chosen from the Selection menu to increase the selection by 1 pixel. Next, a color was chosen from the Color Look Up Table (CLUT) for the browser-compatible palette using the Eyedropper tool, and the selection in the coloring layer was filled using the Paint Bucket.

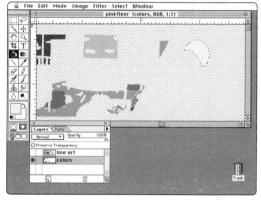

The browser-compatible palette is especially important to use for flat, non-dithered artwork such as cartoons. If the Web browser encounters a color it doesn't recognize, it will dither or remap an image (sometimes swapping undesirable colors).

The anti-aliasing option was turned off for the Paint Bucket tool while painting in the coloring layer. This is important because each region needs to be completely filled with a solid color, without anti-aliased pixels. (If left on, the fills may have included some anti-aliased pixels at the edges, which may have dropped out when compositing the images in Director.)

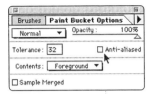

An added advantage of using a coloring layer that remains separate from the line art is the ability to experiment with different fills and color schemes. It is easy to select a color region in the coloring layer using the Magic Wand tool, and then replace it with another color. When both layers are viewed together, with line art on top, the results are very impressive and well worth the extra work. By coloring on a separate layer, line thickness is maintained and none of the aliasing is eroded.

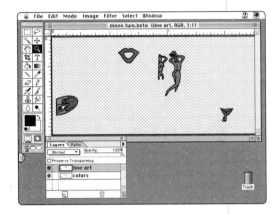

Registering Artwork for Director

When an image is imported into Director, the 100% white areas of the canvas are ignored, and Director will recalculate a new registration point (based on an image's immediate boundaries). To avoid this, it was necessary to create a frame around all of the artwork. Director recognized the frame as the image boundaries, and maintained a common registration point for all images. To draw a registration frame around each image, the following steps were used:

1. In the line art layer, Select, All was chosen to create a selection that encompassed the entire Photoshop window.

2. A three-pixel stroke was created around the selected area (by choosing Edit, Stroke), using solid black as a color.

3. Later, in Director, the Paint Bucket tool was used to eliminate the registration lines.

Merging Layers Without Flattening

Photoshop requires that you flatten an image before you index it. It was necessary to keep all of the images in layers (in case of any later changes), so a merged version was pasted into a new file.

1. With both layers visible, press the Option key as you select Merge from the Layers palette menu. This merges all visible layers into a new layer without the need for flattening the image.

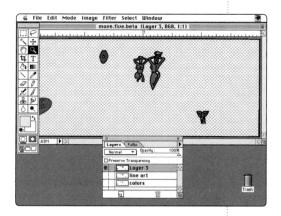

2. The new, merged layer was selected (by choosing Select, All), copied, and pasted into a new file named Background01.

Transferring Images to Director

It is important to consider how well your artwork will composite in Director's sprite channels before importing it. In Director, when using an ink effect such as Background Transparent or Transparent, the default background color is white. Any pixel other than the background color appears in the image. If an image has been composited previously against a background using anti-aliasing, the edges are blended to hide the jagged pixels around the outside of the image. If the image is subsequently placed over a different background, it will cause a "halo" effect to appear on the edges of your cast members.

Anti-aliasing the edges of an image to its intended background is a solution. Allowing a small clip of the background on the edges of a cast member allows for a clean composite. The following process was used to composite the various layers of the first comic strip panel before transfer to the Director Cast window:

1. The movement artwork file was opened in Photoshop. Instead of flattening the line art and colors layers for all of the movement artwork, the Option key/Merge Layers technique was used again to create a new layer containing the merged movement art-work. The new layer was then copied to the Clipboard and pasted directly into the Background01 Photoshop file as a new layer.

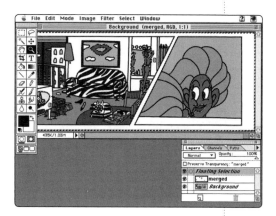

Because this layer was pasted into the file as a merged layer—and not flattened—it retained its transparency, which was desirable. When you paste a transparent layer from the Clipboard, the image is pasted as a floating selection. This selection was saved (by choosing Selection, Save Selection) as a separate channel that can be used later.

2. Up to this point, the file was in RGB mode in order to work in layers. The next step was to flatten the image by indexing it to the browser-compatible palette. After flattening the image, the saved selection was loaded (by choosing Selection, Load).

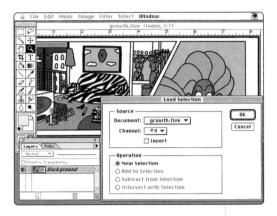

3. Next, the Expand option was chosen from the Selection menu to increase the selection by 1 pixel. The entire selection was then copied to the Clipboard, and pasted directly into Director's internal Cast window. This process was then repeated for the other images.

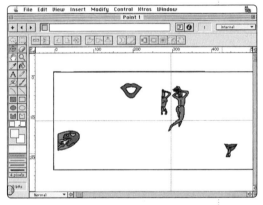

Expanding the selection and then copying the image after it was flattened created a cast member that retained parts of the composited background. When placed on the Stage in Director, the image integrated seamlessly over the appropriate background.

Note

Before copying to the Clipboard or exporting any graphics from Photoshop, make sure that they are saved at 72 dpi resolution. Otherwise, Director will resize your images when they are pasted into the Cast window.

Shocking Beatman

Reducing file size is always a key concern for Shockwave movie development.

1. Since only a portion of an entire
cast member usually animates, the
selection tool was used in the Paint
window to crop any non-animating
areas of each cast member.

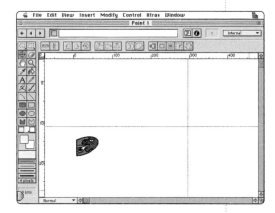

All cast members retained the same
registration point due to the registration frame that was added in
Photoshop. Once an image is imported
into Director, its registration point
remains the same unless it is changed
using the registration tool in the Paint window. Large areas of cast members were
cropped without affecting the registration point.

2. Next, cast members were dragged into the Score window. (The images
retained their original registration points, thereby eliminating the need to tweak
locations on Stage using the arrow keys.)

3. Lingo scripts were added to create buttons within each panel of the comic
strip. Animation loops serve as cues for "hotspots" and propel the user forward
through the linear story.

4. Because the Beatman comic advances from panel to panel in a linear fashion,
it was easy to take advantage of the `preloadNetThing` Lingo command to preload the next panel while a user interacts with the current one. By saving each
panel as a separate Shockwave movie and stringing together multiple movies
using the goToNetMovie command, individual movie sizes remained small, and
the amount of time required to preload each panel was kept to a minimum.

CASE STUDY

creating
animated
presentations

Chapter 16

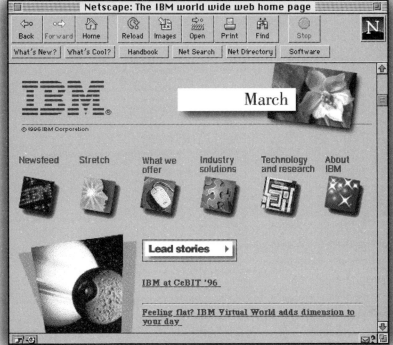

www.ibm.com

The 1995 IBM Annual Report Web site features a variety of
modules and applications that convey key corporate messages
and strategy. DXM Productions worked with Elemental Design
of Atlanta, Georgia, a division of Executive Arts, Inc., to create
Shockwave movies from five hand-drawn pencil animation
sequences created by artist, Bill Plympton. Working with
Plympton was a thrill for everyone at DXM, and optimizing his
animated shorts for the Web was a welcome challenge.

The Plympton Animations
Creating Simple Animations

The Shockwave authoring process for the Plympton animations was a simple one, requiring a minimal amount of Lingo scripting. The final Plympton files are primarily linear animations, but Shockwave for Director provides a level of audio and animation synchronization that is not available using animated GIFs or other Web animation techniques.

Shockwave movies need not be complex nor technologically-driven to be effective. The Plympton animations take a simple approach: basic, linear animations that convey a marketing message while entertaining Web site visitors. The emphasis is on the artwork and the entertaining message—not the technology used to create or convey the message.

Removing Redundancy

As a seasoned animator, Bill Plympton draws new artwork for each frame of an animation. Digital in-betweens and copy-and-paste techniques are not available to an animator who chooses to use pencil and paper.

1. Plympton's artwork was scanned and transferred to digital representations. Each animation frame was saved as a separate file.

2. The individual files were then resized and indexed to the browser-compatible palette before importing into Director.

3. Each animation frame was then imported into Director as an individual cast member. It became apparent that many art elements were duplicated from frame to frame—but with slight variation.

For example, in the frames shown, the clock drawn on the background wall is slightly different from frame to frame, and was redrawn from frame to frame in the original version. While the slight shifts in movement give the animation its hand-drawn quality, these slight differences appeared as prime targets for reducing file size.

4. In some cases, it was possible to edit the original artwork in order to maintain the slight motion shifts from frame to frame, which are characteristic of the artist's style, while eliminating redundant elements. A single bitmapped cast member was used for a constant element, but its position on the Stage was jiggled slightly from one frame to the next.

Note

If possible, an artist or animator should draw animated elements on multiple layers. This makes it easier to separate elements while working in Director. Sequences may be reused in other parts of a Director movie if they are not composited to a specific background. See Chapter 15, "DXM Productions Case Study," for related information.

5. Another example of eliminating redundancy from frame to frame can be seen in the security.dir movie. The image of the small criminal that tries to break into the computer was removed from the original background and from all subsequent animation frames. The small image was then pasted into a new cast member and placed in a higher Score channel (on top of the background). This reduced the size of the background graphic and substituted a single art element for multiple art elements throughout the animation.

"Storyboard" Animation

Bill Plympton's artwork is not ideally suited to benefit from image compression algorithms. Large areas of flat color compress well. On the other hand, the pencil drawings created by Plympton have a very delicate, low-contrast style. There are many fine lines, details, and various levels of color.

In order to balance quality with file size, Shockwave animations were built using the fewest number of frames possible. This approach is similar to selecting key frames in a film or video to define an action. In effect, a storyboard of the action is used to tell the story. The reliable.dir animation uses only five key frames, which are shown below, to establish the scene and to convey a message. Sound effects are used to add depth and credibility to the visuals. Transitions and tempo changes are used to convey time lapse.

Consider using standard film and video techniques as Shockwave shortcuts. Here are just a few examples: reverse angle "camera" shots can be used to establish and change a point of view; fades can be used to segue from one scene to another; and silence can be used to build suspense.

If you are interested in Bill Plympton's work, visit his Web site at:
http://www.awn.com/plympton or http://found.cs.nyu.edu/plympton

CASE STUDY
using algorithmic animation

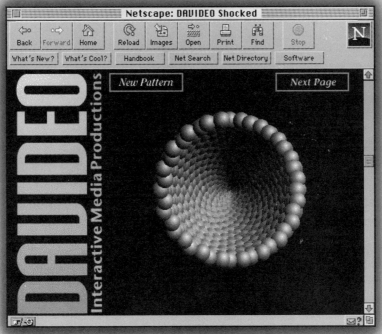

Chapter 17

http://www.davideo.com

David K. Anderson is the principal of Davideo, a San-Francisco-based multimedia production company. Davideo uses Macromedia Director as its primary production tool.

With the release of Shockwave, the company's productions are now available to a worldwide audience and potential clients can sample them almost instantaneously. Anderson is a frequent contributor to the *Macromedia User Journal*. The Analog Clock Puzzle movie discussed here first appeared in that periodical.

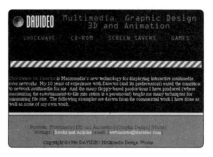

The Analog Clock Puzzle Movie
Drag and Drop Technique

The first example presented here is The Analog Clock Puzzle Movie, which was created by Davideo to exemplify a few Director techniques that can be used throughout many Shockwave movies. The second example is an ersatz QuickTime VR (QTVR) player that uses Lingo to simulate a real QTVR player. Although the simulator became superfluous with the release of Apple's QTVR plug-in, the Lingo technique it employs is useful for the display of any scrolling, looped images (such as a cartoon background).

When creating Shockwave movies (or any Director movies), certain design challenges recur regularly. One example is the simple task of dragging an item across the Stage and dropping it in a different location. Another example (especially in the creation of Director-based games) is a robust shuffling algorithm that can be used to randomize elements of a game. Using a puzzle created in Director, we will explore the methods necessary to perform both of these tasks. For your own investigation, this movie also contains a method to create a working analog clock using Director.

Moving a sprite by dragging it to another location on the Stage is one of the simplest interactions you can perform in Director. By selecting the sprite in the Score window and clicking the Movable check box, the sprite instantly becomes drag and drop-able, even without a puppetSprite declaration. However, what if we want the sprite to "snap-to" an invisible grid? Or have a drop shadow accompany the sprite wherever it is dragged? Or have the sprite and the drop shadow converge at a single location when released, as objects in the real world do? In order to accomplish these effects, the sprite must be puppeted and its actions controlled by Lingo.

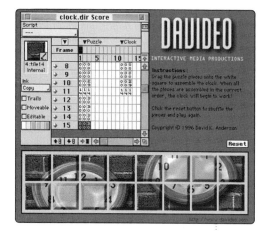

The Analog Clock Puzzle movie employs these techniques in the creation of a simple puzzle game. The goal of the game is to assemble a series of tiles to create the picture of a clock (albeit a clock without hands). If the pieces are placed correctly, the hands appear and a working simulation of an analog clock begins. Although square tiles were created, the pieces could be just as easily irregularly shaped (as in a jigsaw puzzle). In this example, the findPosNear command is used to create a snapping grid for the puzzle and to set the hour hand of the clock.

1. Let's start by examining the movie script for the puzzle. First, global variables and constants are initialized, the desired sprite channels are puppeted, and system conditions are set:

```
global cBoundSprite, cGridSprite, cGridL, cGridT, cGridSpace
global cHalfGridSpace, cGridHList, cGridVList, gTileTrackList
global gTileLocList, cShadowSprite, cFloatSprite
global gTileObjList, cTileOffset

on initPuzzle
  setPuzzleConstants
  setPuzzleGlobals
  puppetSprite cShadowSprite, 1
  puppetSprite cFloatSprite, 1
  set the randomSeed = the ticks
  puppetTempo 120
end
```

2. The initPuzzle handler calls the setPuzzleConstants handler to set the global constants:

```
on setPuzzleConstants
  -- Bounding rectangle sprite; a member of type #shape.
  set cBoundSprite = 1
  -- Rectangle (type #shape ) that encompasses entire grid.
  set cGridSprite = 2
  -- Number of sprite channels before the first tile piece:
  set cTileOffset = 8
  -- Constants used to determine grid coordinates:
  set cGridL = the left of sprite cGridSprite
  set cGridT = the top of sprite cGridSprite
  -- Used to determine snap-to coordinates:
  set cGridSpace = 50    -- tile sprite size
  set cHalfGridSpace = cGridSpace/2
  set cShadowSprite = 47 -- Blended shadow sprite channel.
  set cFloatSprite = 48  -- Drag and drop sprite channel.
  -- Width of stage.
  set cRightEdge = the stageRight - the stageLeft
  -- Height of stage.
  set cBottomEdge = the stageBottom - the stageTop
end
```

3. One important aspect of the `setPuzzleConstants` handler is that the grid is determined by `cBoundSprite` and `cGridSprite`. This means that elements can be repositioned in the Score without reprogramming the game. For example, if you decide to place the clock in the center of the screen rather than on the side, you can simply Shift-select both of the shape sprites in the Score and move them to the center. The virtual grid (created in Lingo) automatically adjusts to the new screen location. The following graphic illustrates the concept of the virtual grid.

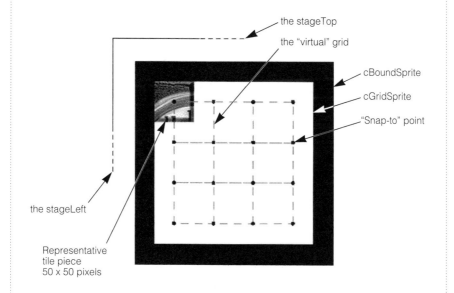

the stageTop

the "virtual" grid

cBoundSprite

cGridSprite

"Snap-to" point

the stageLeft

Representative
tile piece
50 x 50 pixels

4. The virtual grid and the snap-to points do not exist as sprites—only as Lingo constructs. These constructs are built in the next handler, setPuzzleGlobals:

```
on setPuzzleGlobals
  -- Initialize two lists used to determine snap-to grid.
  set cGridHList =[:] -- The horizontal list.
  set cGridVList =[:] -- The vertical list.
  -- The reg point of the bitmap is half the width.
  set firstPointH = cGridL + cHalfGridSpace
  set firstPointV = cGridT + cHalfGridSpace
  -- Add the first value to both grids.
  addProp cGridHList,firstPointH,firstPointH
  addProp cGridVList,firstPointV,firstPointV

  repeat with x = 1 to 3
    set HLoc = ( firstPointH + (x * cGridSpace) )
    addProp( cGridHList, HLoc, HLoc )
    set VLoc = ( firstPointV + (x * cGridSpace) )
    addProp( cGridVList, VLoc, VLoc)
  end repeat

  -- The lists must be sorted in order to use findPosNear().
  sort cGridHList
  sort cGridVList

  -- The tracking list is used to track tile positions
  -- and check for a winner.
  set gTileTrackList = ["11":"", "12":"", "13":"", "14":"", ¬
"21":"", "22":"", "23":"", "24":"", "31":"", "32":"", ¬
"33":"","34":"", "41":"", "42":"", "43":"", "44":""]

  -- Create a shuffled look-up table to scramble order
  -- of the tile sprites.
  set gTileLocList = []
  repeat with i = 1 to 16
    append gTileLocList, the loc of sprite (i+ cTileOffset)
  end repeat
```

```
  set shuffleList = ListShuffler(16)

  -- Instantiate the tile objects.
  set gTileObjList = []
  repeat with i = 1 to 16
    set whichSprite = (i+ cTileOffset)
    puppetSprite whichSprite, 1
    set whichMem = the name of member ¬
(the memberNum of sprite whichSprite)
    add(gTileObjList, new(script "Tile Parent Script", ¬
whichSprite, whichMem))
    set whichNum = getAt(shuffleList, i)
    set the loc of sprite whichSprite = ¬
getAt(gTileLocList, whichNum)
  end repeat

end
```

5. First, the setPuzzleGlobals handler determines the horizontal and vertical points that the tile sprites will snap to when released by the user. The lists of points, cGridHList and cgridVList, are scanned later by the findPosNear command in order to return the appropriate snap-to point. Next, the list that tracks the tile sprites, gTileTrackList, is initialized. This list is the virtual grid introduced earlier. The properties in this list correspond to a concatenation of the horizontal and vertical positions for the tile grid. The grid reads right to left, and then top to bottom, beginning with "11" (horizontal position 1, vertical position 1), and ends with "44". After each move of a tile sprite, this list is updated to store the position of the moved sprite and to determine whether the tile sprites are in the correct winning position.

6. The next set of commands in the `setPuzzleGlobals` handler stores the Stage positions of the tile sprites in `gTileLocList` for later use, and then calls the shuffling function mentioned earlier. Let's scan down the Movie script to find this function:

```
-- Generic shuffling function.
on ListShuffler howMany
  set shuffleList = []
  -- Initializes values in numeric order.
  repeat with x = 1 to howMany
    addAt shuffleList, x, x
  end repeat

  -- Here's where the shuffling occurs.
  repeat with x = 1 to howMany
    set randVar = random(howMany)
    set TempVar = getAt(shuffleList, x)
    set a = getAt(shuffleList, randVar)
    setAt shuffleList, x, a
    setAt shuffleList, randVar, TempVar
  end repeat
  return shuffleList
end
```

This shuffling function, as written in the script above, can be used without alteration in almost any situation that calls for a shuffled list of numbers. The function takes a single integer (x) as an argument and returns a list with the integers 1 through x randomly shuffled. The function is speedy—it shuffles 1 through 10,000 in under one second on a PowerMac 8500. Typically, the returned list is used as a look-up index in order to randomize other data.

The function's operation is simple. First, the ListShuffler handler initializes a list (shuffleList) which is used internally. Next, it takes the howMany argument and adds to shuffleList a series of integers beginning with 1 to howMany in correct order. Next, the handler enters a repeat loop with howMany iterations. During each trip through the loop, it sets a temporary variable, randVar, to a random number between 1 and howMany. It then gets the xth value in shuffleList and assigns it to another temporary variable, TempVar. Next, randVar is used to pull a random number out of shuffleList and the number is assigned to a third temporary variable, a. Finally, the xth value in shuffleList is set to the value of a and the value of the list at position randVar is set to TempVar, effectively swapping the original values in shuffleList. It continues this way until the last position in the list has been through the loop. At the end of the function, shuffleList is returned and can be assigned to a new list that can then be used as an index to look up numbers in a non-shuffled list.

7. Let's return now to the gSetGlobals handler to finish setting up the puzzle. After creating the shuffled index, the empty gTileObjList list is created. This list is filled with the offspring of the Tile Parent Script, which will be examined next. This task, along with a few other tasks related to the tile sprites, is performed within a repeat loop.

8. The repeat loop acts on each of the 16 tile sprites in turn. Using the cTileOffset variable set earlier, each sprite is puppeted, its sprite number recorded in whichSprite, and the name of its associated member recorded in another temporary variable, whichMem. In turn, a new tile object is created from the Tile Parent Script and added to gTileObjList. Finally, a random number drawn from the shuffled index created earlier is used to look up a location from those stored in the gTileLocList list. Consequently, what is shuffled is only the locations of the sprites, not their associated members. This is appropriate because in this game (as in real estate), location is everything!

9. After the initial global variables are set, the tile objects are stored in the `gTileObjList` list and are controlled by a parent script. Each object is created by the `new` handler of the Tile Parent Script. Let's begin by examining the `new` handler. After the necessary global declarations, we find the following:

```
property pMySprite, pMyMemNum

on new me, mySprite, myMem
  set pMySprite = mySprite
  set pMyMemNum = the number of cast myMem
  return me
end
```

Each tile object is instantiated with two property variables—`pMySprite` and `pMyMemNum`. In other words, each object knows its sprite number and its member number. These values do not change during the movie. In fact, the reason a parent script is used in this movie is because each tile has precisely the same behavior and differs from one another only in sprite number, member number, and location. A parent script is the most efficient method (and the easiest way, once you grasp the concept) to impart this behavior to the tiles.

10. We'll return to the parent script in a moment, but first let's examine on `moveTile`, the common handler which is assigned to all of the tile sprites in the Score. This handler is found in the main Movie script:

```
on moveTile
  set whichSprite = the clickon
  set whichTileObj = whichSprite - cTileOffset
  dragTile ( getAt(gTileObjList, whichTileObj) )
  checkForWin
end
```

This handler performs two functions: it identifies the active sprite and passes that information to the Tile Parent Script; it then checks for the winning tile formation. The only other necessary Score script in this frame is the standard `go to the frame` command found in the frame script. In the `moveTile` handler, the `clickon` function indicates which sprite was last clicked. In order to translate this into useful information, the `cTileOffset` variable stored earlier must be subtracted. The result, `whichTileObj`, is the number that is used to look up the appropriate object from the `gTileObjList`. The `dragTile` handler is then performed on this object.

11. Let's return now to the Tile Parent Script to see what this handler does to the current sprite.

Back at the Tile Parent Script, the `dragTile` handler controls the behavior of the sprite while the mouse button is down and directs the sprite to another handler when the mouse button is released:

```
on dragTile me
  -- get offset of mouse from center of tile
  -- to avoid an initial jump

  set mH = the mouseH
  set mV = the mouseV

  set HSTART = the locH of sprite pMySprite
  set VSTART = the locV of sprite pMySprite

  set spriteWidth = the width of sprite pMySprite
  set spriteHeight = the height of sprite pMySprite

  if HSTART - mH > 0 then
    set H_offset = min(spriteWidth, HSTART - mH)
  else
    set H_offset = max(-spriteWidth, HSTART - mH)
  end if
  if VSTART - mV > 0 then
    set V_offset = min(spriteHeight, VSTART - mV)
  else
    set V_offset = max(-spriteHeight, VSTART - mV)
  end if

  set the memberNum of sprite cFloatSprite = pMyMemNum
  set the loc of sprite cFloatSprite = the loc of ¬
sprite pMySprite
  set the loc of sprite pMySprite = point(-1000, -1000)
```

```
  repeat while the stilldown
    set the locH of sprite cFloatSprite = ¬
the mouseH + H_offset
    set the locV of sprite cFloatSprite = ¬
the mouseV + V_offset
    set the locH of sprite cShadowSprite = ¬
the mouseH + H_offset + 16
    set the locV of sprite cShadowSprite = ¬
the mouseV + V_offset + 16
    updateStage
  end repeat

  placeTile me

end
```

12. The lengthy `dragTile` handler above is designed primarily to move a tile over the playing surface in a realistic manner. The key to this realism is that any sprite that is selected and moved will appear above all the other sprites on the Stage and cast a shadow over them. The entire first half of the handler, however, is dedicated to ensuring that the sprite is dragged from the point at which it is first clicked.

It would be simple enough to place the sprite at the mouse location while the mouse is down. However, it is unlikely that the point on the sprite that the user clicks will be the regPoint (or registration point) of the member for that sprite. Consequently, the sprite will "jump" to align the regPoint of the member with the mouse location. Keep in mind that the larger the member, and the farther the distance from the regPoint the user clicks, the greater and more noticeable the jump. To prevent this behavior, the dragTile handler uses the horizontal and vertical positions of the mouse and the sprite, the height and width of the sprite, and the quadrant of the sprite's member (in relation to its regPoint) in which the user has clicked to determine a pair of offset values: H_Offset and V_Offset. It uses these two offset values in the second half of the handler to accurately position a sprite as it is dragged across the Stage.

13.   It is important to note that the sprite to be dragged is not the sprite that the user clicked (although the user will think it is). Rather, the "dragged" sprite is cFloatSprite (which was earlier assigned to channel 48, the highest channel in the Score). If the user were to drag the original sprite, it would appear to be sliding under one or more of the other sprites on Stage. Instead, the memberNum of cFloatSprite is set to be the same as the clicked sprite, and then the position of cFloatSprite (which is normally positioned off-stage) and the position of the clicked sprite are transposed. When the user drags the tile to the desired position, the tile will seem to ride above the other tiles. To enhance the effect, a second sprite, cShadowSprite (assigned to sprite channel 47) is added during dragging. This sprite is a solid black bitmap with the same dimensions as the tile members. Additionally, its ink is set to Blend with a blend value of 50 percent. As sprites are dragged, cShadowSprite (which also has been hidden off-stage) is set to the same location as cFloatSprite, plus 16 pixels down and to the right.

14. While the mouse is down the `dragTile` handler continually updates the position of `cFloatSprite` and `cShadowSprite`. It is most important that `updatestage` is called during every iteration of the repeat loop. Without this command, the sprites do not appear to be dragged, and suddenly "pop" into place when the mouse button is released. This brings us to the final command called from the `dragTile` handler:

```
on placeTile me
  if sprite cFloatSprite within cBoundSprite then
    set whichHPos = findPosNear(cGridHList, (the locH of ¬
sprite cFloatSprite - cHalfGridSpace))
    set whichVPos = findPosNear(cGridVList, (the locV of ¬
sprite cFloatSprite - cHalfGridSpace))
    set whichH = getAt(cGridHList, whichHPos)
    set whichV = getAt(cGridVList, whichVPos)
    slideIntoPlace(me, whichH, whichV)
    set checkProp = string(whichVPos) & string(whichHPos)
    setAt( gTileTrackList, (pMySprite - cTileOffset), ¬
checkProp )
    updateStage
    set the loc of sprite cFloatSprite = point(-1000, -1000)
    set the loc of sprite cShadowSprite = point(-1000, -1000)

  else

    setAt( gTileTrackList, (pMySprite - cTileOffset), "" )

    if the locH of sprite cFloatSprite > cRightEdge - 8 then
      set whichH = cRightEdge
    else
      if the locH of sprite cFloatSprite <  -8 then
        set whichH = 0
      else
        set whichH = the locH of sprite cFloatSprite + 8
      end if
    end if
```

```
        if the locV of sprite cFloatSprite > cBottomEdge - 8 then
          set whichV = cBottomEdge
        else
          if the locV of sprite cFloatSprite <  -8 then
            set whichV = 0
          else
            set whichV = the locV of sprite cFloatSprite + 8
          end if
        end if

        slideIntoPlace(me, whichH, whichV)
      end if
      puppetSound "Drop"
      updateStage
    end
```

15. The `placeTile` handler shown above is invoked immediately upon the release of the mouse button. It first checks whether the released sprite is within the area of the bounding sprite. If it is, the handler then takes the current horizontal and vertical position of `cFloatSprite` and uses the command `findPosNear` to identify which of the invisible snap-to points (as stored from the grid lists) is nearest to the sprite. As the `regPoint` for the tiles is located in the center, half the width and height of the member is subtracted from the initial horizontal and vertical positions of `cFloatSprite`. Each list search returns the position in each list of the item with the closest value. These positions are then used to look up the horizontal and vertical coordinates that the sprite will snap to. These coordinates are then passed to another handler, `slideIntoPlace`, as target values. If the tile is released outside the area of the bounding sprite, then the sprite is dropped to a location 8 pixels down and 8 pixels to the right of the release location (unless the sprite is released offstage, in which case the target point is set at the edge of the Stage).

16. Here is the handler that causes the tile to drop into place:

```
on slideIntoPlace me, targetH, targetV
  -- Horizontal distance to the target:
  set deltaH = targetH - the locH of sprite cFloatSprite
  -- Vertical distance to the target:
  set deltaV = targetV - the locV of sprite cFloatSprite
  -- Horizontal and vertical distances for the shadow:
  set deltaHS =(targetH - the locH of sprite cShadowSprite)
  set deltaVS =(targetV - the locV of sprite cShadowSprite)

  -- Move the tile and shadow 1/10th of the way to target
  -- with each iteration.
  repeat with i = 1 to 10
    set comp = 10 - i
    set the locH of sprite cFloatSprite = ¬
targetH - (comp * deltaH / 10)
    set the locV of sprite cFloatSprite = ¬
targetV - (comp * deltaV / 10)
    set the locH of sprite cShadowSprite = ¬
targetH - (comp * deltaHS / 10)
    set the locV of sprite cShadowSprite = ¬
targetV - (comp * deltaVS / 10)
    updateStage
  end repeat

  set the loc of sprite pMySprite = ¬
the loc of sprite cFloatSprite
  updateStage
end
```

The slideIntoPlace handler takes the target location provided by placeTile and moves the tile to its new resting location (whether on the grid or off). The effect is enhanced by moving the shadow sprite to the same location from the opposite direction. This gives the appearance of the tile dropping onto the surface.

17. Once the user drops the sprite onto the grid, the only action that remains is to store the results of the move and check for a winner. Returning to the `placeTile` handler, the horizontal and vertical positions are concatenated into a single string (`"11"`, `"12"` and so forth) and stored in the property list `gTileTrackList` at the position associated with the moved sprite. A null string (`""`) is assigned if the tile is dropped outside of the bounding sprite.

18. The `placeTile` handler then calls the `checkForWin` handler, located in the main Movie Script. This handler parses the `gTileTrackList` list and adds 1 to a cumulative sum if a tile is in the correct position. If the sum equals 16 at the end of the move, then the tiles are in the correct location and the game is over.

Note

This clock can be considered a "dumb" clock because all its hand movements are pre-drawn cast members. Other clocks created using Director are "smart" in that the hands are line sprites of type #shape which are positioned via a trigonometric formula. This approach is memory-efficient, but does not allow for graphic variations.

In summary, drag-and-drop, the shuffling function, and the `findPosNear` command are three of the most used techniques in Davideo's Lingo repertoire.

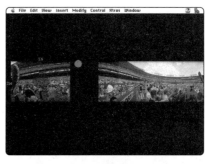

The Pan and Scan Movie
Simulating QuickTime VR

The Pan and Scan movie outlines a method using Lingo to create an endlessly looping panorama that functions like QuickTime VR from Apple Computer. The method is relatively simple and can be used for any type of looping image—that is, an image in which the left and right (or top and bottom) edges merge seamlessly.

MOVIE SPECS

Movie Name:
panscan.dir

Original File Size:
286K

Audio: none

Afterburned
File Size: 159K

Net Lingo Used:
none

Stage Size:
256w x 150h

**LINGO
SCRIPTING
LEVEL**
challenging

In this example, a panoramic photograph is used. The desired effect is a seamless pan as the user clicks, holds, and drags the cursor to the left or right within the Shockwave movie.

Most of the work for this example is accomplished using a single Lingo handler. However, the images must be placed initially in the Score for this technique to work. The following graphic illustrates how the images should be placed on the Stage and shows some of the attributes that are used in the handler.

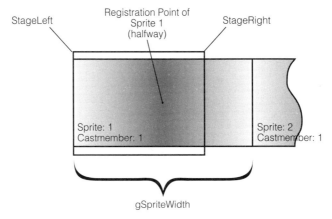

The graphic to be displayed is a panoramic image that has been imported as a cast member. The member is placed on Stage (as shown above) as sprite 1 and sprite 2. As you can see, the Stage is slightly taller than the sprites, and the sprites are wider than the Stage. Also, note that sprites 1 and 2 both use the same cast member, the panorama.

If the user drags the cursor to the right, the image should move to the left and reveal more of the image from off-screen. Conversely, when the user drags left, the image should move to the right. To achieve this effect, two sprites (1 and 2) that use the same cast member are used. Sprite 2 is used to "fill in" wherever sprite 1 leaves a gap (on either the right or left) on the Stage.

1. Let's examine the Lingo, beginning with the on startMovie handler in the Movie script:

```
global gSpriteWidth, gHalfWay

on startMovie
  set gSpriteWidth= the width of sprite 1
  set gHalfWay = gSpriteWidth/2
  puppetSprite 1, TRUE
  puppetSprite 2, TRUE
  set the locH of sprite 2 = ¬
(the locH of sprite 1) + gSpriteWidth
end
```

This handler prepares for the animation to follow. First, a global variable, gSpriteWidth, is set to the width of sprite 1. As sprite 2 is identical to sprite 1, gSpriteWidth also could be set to the width of sprite 2 without ill effects. Next, a global variable gHalfWay is set equal to half of gSpriteWidth. This variable is needed because the registration point for both sprites is at the center of cast member 1. The value is used when the sprites are positioned on Stage. Next, both sprites are puppeted in order to place them under Lingo control and to ensure that sprite 2 is lined up to the right of sprite 1 by setting its horizontal location to the locH of sprite 1 plus the width of sprite 1.

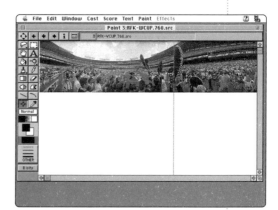

2. Here is the workhorse handler that makes the effect seamless.

```
global gSpriteWidth, gHalfWay

on mouseDown
  set myH = the mouseH
  repeat while the stillDown
    set mouseOffsetH = the mouseH - myH

    if mouseOffsetH > 0 then
      set mouseOffsetH = sqrt(mouseOffsetH)
    else
      set mouseOffsetH = 0 - sqrt(abs(mouseOffsetH))
    end if

    if the right of sprite 1 < mouseOffsetH then
      set the locH of sprite 1 = gHalfWay - mouseOffsetH
      set the locH of sprite 2 = (the locH of sprite 1) ¬
+ gSpriteWidth
    else
      if the left of sprite 1 > mouseOffsetH then
        set the locH of sprite 1 = ¬
gHalfWay - gSpriteWidth - mouseOffsetH
        set the locH of sprite 2 = ¬
(the locH of sprite 1) + gSpriteWidth
      else
        set the locH of sprite 1 = ¬
(the locH of sprite 1) - mouseOffsetH
        set the locH of sprite 2 = ¬
(the locH of sprite 2) - mouseOffsetH
      end if
    end if

    updateStage
  end repeat
end
```

3. This on mouseDown handler is located in a sprite script attached to sprites 1 and 2. The following section examines the code line by line.

The first action stores a temporary variable, myH, which traps the horizontal location of the mouse when the mouse button is first pressed.

```
set myH = the mouseH
```

The myH variable contains a unique value for each mouseDown occurrence (except, of course, when the user clicks in the same horizontal location repeatedly).

4. Next, the handler enters a repeat loop that remains in effect until the user releases the mouse button.

The first action item in the loop is to set a local variable, mouseOffsetH, that stores the current horizontal location of the mouse minus the original mouseDown location. This variable is updated on each pass through the loop.

```
set mouseOffsetH = the mouseH - myH
```

5. Next, the first if...then...else decision statement in the handler occurs:

```
if mouseOffsetH > 0 then
  set mouseOffsetH = sqrt(mouseOffsetH)
else
  set mouseOffsetH = 0 - sqrt(abs(mouseOffsetH))
end if
```

At this point, Lingo determines whether the user has moved the cursor to the right of the original mouseDown point or to the left (and implicitly, by non-action, whether the mouse has been moved horizontally at all). If mouseOffsetH is greater than zero, the mouse has moved to the right; if it is less than zero, then it has moved to the left. In either case, mouseOffsetH is reset to the square root of its value—that is, the value of the distance between the current horizontal mouse location and the original location. We will return momentarily to the reason for using the square root of this distance. For now, let's continue through the handler to see how this value is used.

6. Next, another `if...then...else` statement occurs; this one contains yet another `if...then...else` decision statement :

```
if the right of sprite 1 < mouseOffsetH then
   set the locH of sprite 1 = gHalfWay - mouseOffsetH
   set the locH of sprite 2 = ¬
(the locH of sprite 1) + gSpriteWidth
   else
      if the left of sprite 1 > mouseOffsetH then
        set the locH of sprite 1 = ¬
gHalfWay - gSpriteWidth - mouseOffsetH
        set the locH of sprite 2 = ¬
(the locH of sprite 1) + gSpriteWidth
      else
        set the locH of sprite 1 = ¬
(the locH of sprite 1) - mouseOffsetH
        set the locH of sprite 2 = ¬
(the locH of sprite 2) - mouseOffsetH
      end if
   end if
```

The first `if...then...else` detects whether the right of sprite 1 is less than mouseOffsetH—that is, whether the right edge of the sprite is less than the mouseOffsetH number of pixels from the left edge of the Stage (the left edge of the Stage equals zero value). The next `if...then...else` statement detects whether the left of sprite 1 is more than mouseOffsetH pixels from the left edge of the Stage. For now, let's assume that neither of these scenarios is true. In this case, the left of sprite 1 is off-screen to the left, and the right of sprite 1 is off-screen to the right. The Stage is filled with sprite 1. Sprite 2 is off-stage as shown.

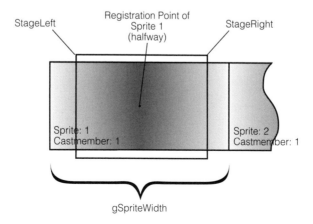

In this case, we want to take the current location of sprite 1 and move it mouseOffsetH pixels in one direction or the other (depending on whether the mouse is now left or right of the original horizontal location).

7. Let's return now to the first if...then...else statement in which the value of mouseOffsetH was changed to its square root. Why was this done? The handler could have been written so that the image only moved a set amount, 5 pixels for example, with each screen update. However, QTVR doesn't work that way and QTVR is the model that this movie is attempting to emulate. In QTVR, the farther the mouse is moved from the initial mouseDown point, the faster the panorama spins. This creates a more natural effect and gives the user a great deal of control over how far and how fast they pan the scene. This movie attempts to give Shockwave viewers the same control. Hence, the square root of the distance from the current mouseOffsetH to the original mouseDown point is used. The net effect is, like QTVR, the farther the mouse is moved, the faster the image pans.

The second question that may come to mind is: Why must we determine whether the user is panning to the right or to the left in order to use this feature? The answer lies in mathematics. The square root of a negative number is a mathematical construct known as an imaginary number. Lingo doesn't understand imaginary numbers and returns an error if an attempt is made to calculate one. Therefore, the offset amount must be converted to a positive number using the absolute value abs() function before calculating the square root. However, we still want to pan the scene in the negative direction, so we must subtract the result of our square root calculation from zero. This explanation is the reason for the first if...then...else statement.

8. Now that the value of mouseOffsetH has been set to achieve a natural feel, the next two lines of the sprite script handler take the current locations of sprites 1 and 2 and move them mouseOffsetH pixels. If mouseOffsetH is negative, the move is in the positive direction, or to the right. If it is positive, the move is to the left.

```
set the locH of sprite 1 = (the locH of sprite 1) - ¬
    LLmouseOffsetH
set the locH of sprite 2 = (the locH of sprite 2) - ¬
    mouseOffsetH
```

9. The situation becomes more interesting if one edge of sprite 1 is within the boundaries of the Stage.

If sprite 1 were pushed entirely off the screen to the left, sprite 2 could cover until its right edge was within the boundaries of the screen, at which point the background color of the Stage would be drawn beyond the edge. This would ruin the illusion of a seamless QTVR-like panorama. The second if...then...else statement in the handler is designed to prevent this unpleasant situation—one part determines if the right edge of sprite 1 is within the Stage boundaries and the other part determines if the left edge is within the Stage boundaries. You always want sprite 1 somewhere on the Stage. Jumping back to the beginning of the statement, we find the following Lingo:

```
if the right of sprite 1 < mouseOffsetH then
    set the locH of sprite 1 = gHalfWay - mouseOffsetH
    set the locH of sprite 2 = (the locH of sprite 1) + ¬
gSpriteWidth
```

This portion of the statement covers the scenario in which the right edge of sprite 1 is within the Stage boundaries and within mouseOffsetH pixels of the left edge of the Stage. In such a situation, we want to move the horizontal position of sprite 1 back to half its width (which we stored previously as the global variable gHalfWay) minus mouseOffsetH pixels. Since sprite 2 always abuts to the right side of sprite 1, in the next line we simply move it to the horizontal location of sprite 1, plus the width of sprite 1. This restores sprites 1 and 2 to the position shown in the figure above, minus the mouseOffsetH distance. We subtract this distance in order to make the image pan smoothly as the user holds the mouse down.

10. A scenario where the left edge of sprite 1 is in danger of moving off the right of the screen is covered by the second part of the if...then...else statement:

```
if the left of sprite 1 > mouseOffsetH then
  set the locH of sprite 1 = gHalfWay - gSpriteWidth - ¬
mouseOffsetH
  set the locH of sprite 2 = (the locH of sprite 1) + ¬
gSpriteWidth
```

In this case, if the left edge of sprite 1 is farther from the left of the Stage than mouseOffsetH pixels, it is once again moved to the gHalfWay position, but this time minus the width of sprite 1 and minus mouseOffsetH pixels. This moves the right edge of sprite 1 over to the left edge of the Stage plus mouseOffsetH pixels (mouseOffsetH in this instance would be a negative number so subtracting it would move sprite 1 positively, or to the right). This action would meet the requirement of keeping sprite 1 on the Stage. As before, sprite 2 is updated by moving it flush right of sprite 1.

The second if...then...else statement covers all three possible positions for sprites 1 and 2. Once the requisite repositioning of the sprites has occurred, the Stage is updated and continues to be updated while the user holds the mouse button down.

11. The net effect for the viewer is a QTVR-like panorama with a seamless 360° looping scan of the scene. In this example movie, the perspective is not interpolated on the fly as with QTVR and we cannot zoom into and out of the scene, but it does offer a simple alternative. The Pan and Scan movie does have the added capability of permitting additional sprites to overlay the scene, and it can take advantage of any interactivity provided by Lingo. With the addition of custom cursors, the QTVR knockoff is ready for the Web.

In order to work effectively within the constraints associated with building low-bandwidth Shockwave movies, efficient use of Lingo is required. A file that is under 100K can contain only a limited amount of visual and audio content. Lingo scripts should be designed to enhance a user's experience with this content. Techniques such as drag and drop, shuffling, and pan and scan can be implemented to provide a high degree of interaction between the user and the Shockwave content.

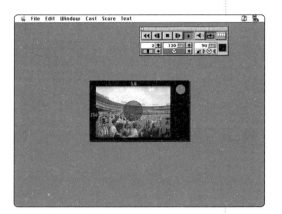

Part 3:
Shocking Developments

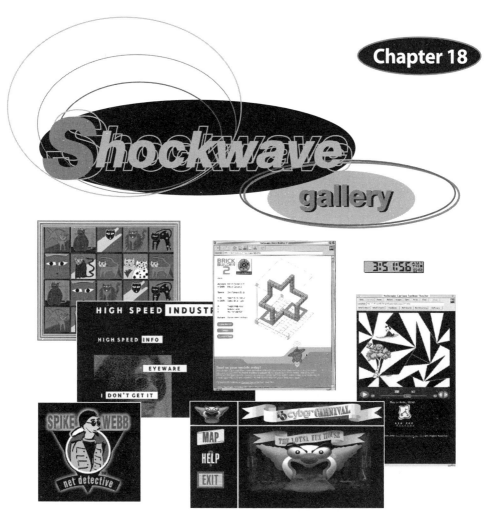

Shocking Developments
Gallery of Developer Samples

This section contains a list of Shockwave application categories, along with some specific examples of existing and potential uses for Shockwave within each category. The remainder of the chapter showcases several developer examples that are included to provide inspiration and to demonstrate real-world techniques. The majority of contributing developers have generously provided unprotected source files for your reference on the *Shocking the Web* CD-ROM. Feel free to learn from these examples, but please do not appropriate the files for your own use and/or publication. The companion Web site, www.shockingtheweb.com, will be updated regularly as new, creative, ground-breaking examples continue to increase.

Shockwave Applications

Within a very short amount of time, Shockwave has swept the Web—with shocked sites now numbering in the thousands. A variety of innovative applications have been created in the areas of multimedia entertainment, education, and business. The following is a list of Shockwave application categories, along with some specific examples of existing and potential uses for Shockwave movies within these categories. Web sites which we feel best represent each category are listed, and bookmarks to these sites (and others) are included on the *Shocking the Web* CD-ROM.

www.inter.co.jp

Advertising

- Interactive ad banners
- Promotional games
- Smart logos; logos with navigation links
- Sponsorship of Shockwave content
- Multimedia-enhanced data capture
- Multimedia commercials; interactive or linear
- Multimedia infomercials
- Downloadable content

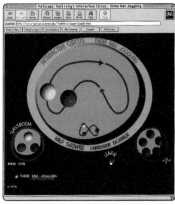

www-personal.umich.edu/~toddlevy/juggle/juggle_information.html

Education & Training

- Distance learning
- Job training
- Employee orientation
- Online seminars

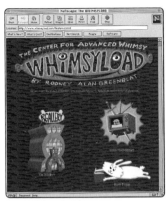

www.whimsyload.com

Entertainment

- Original web content for all genres
- Original web content for all demographics
- Repurposed content
- Serial comics, stories, soaps
- Radio shows (live and archived)
- Talk shows and interviews
- E-zines

www.acmefruit.com

Intranet Applications

- Training
- Sales and Marketing
- Human Resources
- Public Relations
- Executive speeches and presentations
- Financial charts and data
- Discussions and meetings
- Company News

www.iuma.com

Marketing Communications

- Online product launches and presentations
- Multimedia collateral; product data, brochures
- Demo versions, previews, and simulations
- Virtual roadshows and reviewer's guides
- Multimedia-enhanced press releases
- Interactive press kits
- Targeted promotions
- Interactive sweepstakes
- Game competitions with giveaways

www.poprocket.com/shockwave/home.html

Online Games

- Single and multi-player games
- Online galleries, arcades
- Pay per play; micro-cash transactions
- CD-ROM previews; play before you pay
- Game of the Day/Week/Month/Year

www.hyperstand.com
courtesy of HyperMedia Communications, Inc.

Online Publishing

- Electronic newspapers and magazines
- Reference works
- Real-time data retrieval and display
- Archives, resources
- Multimedia interfaces for complex data

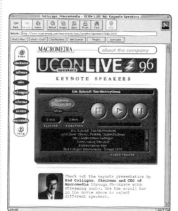

www.macromedia.com

Presentations

- Speaker support
- Sales presentations
- Announcements
- Business presentations
- Lectures
- Internet and/or intranet presentations

www.ionmusic.com

Unique Applications

- Web art
- Web cameras
- Remote device control
- Utilities; calculators, calendars, clocks

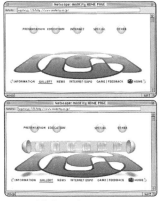

www.midicity.co.jp

Web Site Enhancements

- User interface; buttons, sliders, navigation
- Eye candy; shockbytes, logos, animations
- Audio; soundbytes, feedback, tours, prompts
- Guided tours; interactive site maps
- Interactive forms; enhanced data collection

When new technologies are introduced, innovative developers are quick to identify and develop new applications. Shockwave technology presents multimedia developers with a great opportunity to broaden existing services, to provide multimedia content to an extremely wide audience, and to promote, sell, and distribute products. The following example movies demonstrate innovative use of Shockwave technology. Each example includes developer introduction and contact information, Shockwave movie data, and a brief Shockwave project description.

The Nasu-Otoko (Eggplant Man) Movie
Toppan & Moak Co., Ltd.

This Shockwave movie, entitled "Where has the Eggplant Man gone?," is a small game created by Toru Ueno for his personal Web page. To play the game, it is important to watch carefully as Eggplant Man ("Nasu-Otoko" in Japanese) moves quickly to the right and left. Then, faced with three eggplants that have been shuffled, the player must select the one which is Eggplant Man. The more points you score, the faster Eggplant Man moves.

According to Toru Ueno, the original movie was made with very simple Lingo scripts and very simple Score animation. While there are no Net Lingo commands used now, the

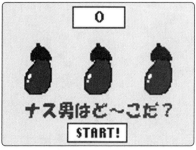

MOVIE SPECS

Original File Size: 62K

Audio: 21.6K

Afterburned File Size: 25K

Net Lingo Used: none

Stage Size: 160w x 120h

LINGO SCRIPTING LEVEL — easy

next version of the game will be updated to add links to other Web pages. These links will be accessible based on a player's score.

A Few Words from the Company

Toru Ueno's philosophy on Shockwave needs no explanation: "Let's love small movies such as this one for worldwide low-bandwidth users!"

Toru Ueno
Toppan & Moak Co., Ltd.
Sori-Machi Building 7F
1-3-5 taitou, taitou-ku
Tokyo, Japan 110
Tel: 813-3837-2681
Fax: 813-3837-2683
URL: http://www.bekkoame.or.jp/~uenknown
Email: uenknown@lib.bekkoame.or.jp

The Shockwave on Shockwave Movie
Fastel Multimedia

MOVIE SPECS

Original File Size:
531K

Audio: 123.5K

Afterburned
File Size: 255K

Net Lingo Used:
none

Stage Size:
448w x 336h

LINGO
SCRIPTING
LEVEL

intermediate

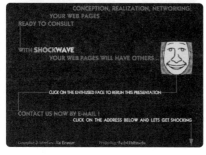

The Shockwave on Shockwave movie was designed by Kai Brunner and programmed by Pascal Rossini of Fastel Multimedia. The primary goal in creating this movie was to demonstrate the heightened impact of a publicity message through interactivity and animation on the Web.

Creating the movie involved four steps: planning construction, establishing specifications, converting to Shockwave, and verifying it on the Web. To reduce file size, they restricted the number of colors used in the graphics and used two-dimensional graphics with flat color areas. The sound file size was reduced by using only onomatopoeias. The movie was then converted and compressed using Afterburner, and placed on Fastel's Web server.

A Few Words from the Company

Founded in 1988, Fastel Multimedia has positioned itself as a pioneer in making the most recent communications technologies available to the public. Fastel specializes in the authoring of interactive multimedia applications, and is currently focused on developing for the Web.

Fastel Multimedia
CP 716
1215 Genève, Switzerland
Tel: +19 41 22 788 22 11
Fax: +19 41 22 788 03 93
URL: http://www.fastel.com
Email: rossini@fastel.com

Big Top's Cartoon Theatre Movie
Big Top Productions, L.P.

The Big Top Productions Web site publishes a daily cartoon created using Big Top's Cartoon Toolbox Starring Felix the Cat software. This easy-to-use animation program enables users to create their own professional-looking cartoons by choosing animations, sound, backgrounds, and special effects. After the cartoon has been assembled, it can be exported to a standalone file containing only the content used in that cartoon.

The animation and sound content of the exported cartoon is then copied into a low-bandwidth, optimized version of the Cartoon Toolbox interface. The resulting Director movie is a cartoon player that permits a user to play, stop, and step through the cartoon frame by frame. The size of the cartoon is reduced further using SoundEdit 16 to downsample sounds to an 8-bit, 11kHz format.

Finding compelling cartoons with minimal content is a challenge. Big Top has been effective in getting the most "bang for the bandwidth" by choosing cartoons that re-use content. The team at Big Top Productions believes that "after all, as in any media, the final measure of success is the quality of the story told."

About Big Top's Cartoon Theater

The original product, Big Top's Cartoon Toolbox Starring Felix the Cat, contains over 40MB of animations, backgrounds, props, and sounds. Before being processed by Afterburner, each individual cartoon is created by saving a Director movie with only the content used in that cartoon. Therefore, the size of each Shockwave cartoon movie varies, depending on the particular sounds and animations included in the particular story. The source files for the cartoons published on Big Top's Web site to date range from 408K to 1.9MB, and the compressed .dcr files range from 153K to 816K.

A Few Words from the Company

Big Top Productions makes tools: thinking tools, writing tools, relaxing tools, music tools, and creative tools. Big Top believes that "the promise of multimedia lies in providing people of any age and gender with tools to exercise, explore, and expand their creativity."

Big Top strives to make products that involve the player to the fullest extent, to allow the user to direct the action and decide the next step. As Big Top sees it, "interactivity is the power of multimedia."

Big Top produces only non-violent and gender-inclusive products. Big Top does not create titles with wars, battles, marauders, or murders. Nor do they build games that pander to negative female stereotypes.

Finally, whether it's one of Big Top's children's educational products, Cartoon Toolboxes or music driven titles, it's first and foremost goal is fun.

Big Top Productions, L.P.
548 Fourth Street
San Francisco, CA 94107
Tel: (415) 978-5363
Fax: (415) 978-5353
URL: http://www.bigtop.com
Email: bigtop@bigtop.com

The U.S. Capital Quiz Movie
Digital Dreams Talk Media

This Shockwave movie demonstrates the use of ShockTalk,™ a Speech Xtra for spoken user interactions. The U.S. Capital Quiz demo movie prompts for the names of various state capitals in the United States of America. You actually speak your answer to each question.

The original U.S. Capital Quiz Director movie was 2.7MB. It was designed for a traditional 640 x 480 stage and contained artwork and audio samples for the 50 states. To create the Shockwave demo version, the stage was rearranged to incorporate elements that were absolutely necessary, reducing the movie size to 1.6MB and the stage size to 176 x 274. Artwork and audio were then eliminated for all but ten states (40 x 40K/state=1,600K).

MOVIE SPECS

Original File Size:
512K

Audio: 240K

Afterburned
File Size: 264K

Net Lingo Used:
none

Stage Size:
176w x 274h

LINGO
SCRIPTING
LEVEL
challenging

Next, disabled Lingo commands were removed from the movie script. The only Lingo function previously used in the Director file was the path-name, in order to locate the ShockTalk Xtra. The Lingo function was not required for the Shockwave version because Shockwave only looks for Xtras in the Support folder.

The movie then was converted and compressed with the Afterburner Xtra, and placed on the Digital Dreams Web server. (In addition, Digital Dreams requested that their ISP add support for the Director MIME type.)

About ShockTalk

ShockTalk is a Macromedia Director Xtra that allows Webmasters to create speakable Web sites, as well as Shockwave movies that incorporate spoken user interactions.

Webmasters can add support for ShockTalk simply by embedding a small (12K) Shockwave movie in their Web pages. The Shockwave movie automatically scans each Web page for hyperlinks. To visit a link, you say "link to" followed by the name of the link.

ShockTalk requires the following hardware and software:
- Apple Quadra AV or Power Macintosh
- Netscape Navigator 2.0 or later by Netscape Communications Corp.
- Shockwave for Macintosh by Macromedia, Inc.
- ShockTalk by Digital Dreams
- PlainTalk Speech Recognition by Apple Computer, Inc.

A Few Words from the Company

Digital Dreams was founded by Timothy J.C. Morgan and Dana De Puy Morgan in 1993 to promote the use of speech technologies. Digital Dreams has licensed its Speech Plug-In technology for the Macintosh CD-ROM version of Star Trek™ Omnipedia™ by Simon & Schuster Interactive. The U.S. Capital Quiz was designed by Studio Software and programmed by Tim Morgan of Digital Dreams.

Digital Dreams Talk Media
4308 Harbord Drive
Oakland, CA 94618
Tel: (510) 547-6929
Fax: (510) 547-6799
URL: http://www.surftalk.com
FTP: ftp://emf.net/users/dreams
Email: dreams@surftalk.com

The Velma Apparelizer Movie
Headbone Interactive

Headbone created the Apparelizers as downloadable, freeware games for kids and to promote some of the characters in their CD-ROM titles. Originally designed by Roman Laney and programmed by Camille Nims, the Apparelizer was later made into a Shockwave movie by Kent Peterson. They wanted to see how difficult it would be to create something small, fun, and feasible online.

There were a few problems along the way. Shrinking the graphics seemed like a good idea, but due to the nature of the game it was not a viable solution. The clothes are designed to fit on Velma's body exactly and shrinking the graphics had the effect of a bad laundry cycle. Rather than shrink the art, a few elements were changed and moved closer together on a smaller stage. Then the background itself was minimized.

When the movie was tested, a few bugs were found. A cursor visibility problem was fixed by setting the cursor to the arrow (–1), then blank (200), and then back to the arrow again. The first frame of the movie was then duplicated because some initialization code didn't "catch" when residing in the first frame. Finally, the custom palette was adjusted to appear correctly within the Web browser.

A Few Words from the Company

Headbone Interactive was founded by Susan Lammers in 1993 to produce the next generation of children's software. According to Headbone, the company's CD-ROM titles and Internet programming are distinguished by witty stories, arresting graphics, extended playtime, and a pioneering "active learning" approach to interactivity.

Headbone Interactive
1520 Bellevue Avenue
Seattle, WA 98122
Tel: (206) 323-0073
To Order: 1-800-267-4709
Fax: (206) 323-0188
URL: http://headbone.com
Email: info@headbone.com

MOVIE SPECS

Original File Size: 176K

Audio: none

Afterburned File Size: 48K

Net Lingo Used: none

Stage Size: 544w x 357h

LINGO SCRIPTING LEVEL intermediate

The High Speed Industrial Movie
SP3D Digital Production Company

MOVIE SPECS

Original File Size:
448K

Audio: 114K

Afterburned
File Size: 224K

Net Lingo Used:
none

Stage Size:
324w x 512h

LINGO
SCRIPTING
LEVEL
intermediate

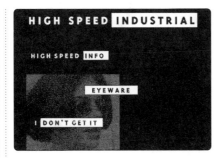

Since 1993, there's been a cool group of UV-protected people walking around wearing High Speed Industrial Sunglasses. They've been stared at, stopped, and asked out on dates. Through this reactive revolution, HSI, the sunglass manufacturer, learned that they couldn't market their products like Puppy Chow.

They came to SP3D in the fall of 1995, wanting a campaign to match their product's "personality"—high speed and high-impact. HSI felt that multimedia was often a tedious interaction of point and click, and they wanted something fast and furious, with a little darkness. Composing effective music became a key component in reaching this goal. HSI's existing library images were given new life, saving time and money. The digital promotion was originally created for floppy disk distribution to be included with store orders, domestically and abroad. Since space optimization was a major concern for the floppy disk, maintaining low bandwidth for the Web presentation was easy with Shockwave.

A Few Words from the Company

SP3D Digital Production Company produces high-impact digital presentations, 3D graphics and animation, ear-shattering original music, and advice. SP3D assumes "intelligence on the part of our audience."

SP3D Digital Production Company
601 Van Ness
San Francisco, CA 94102
Tel: (415) 546-3776, (415) 923-9653, or (415) 826-7535
Fax: (415) 826-9482
URL: http://www.sp3d.com
Email: humans@sp3d.com

The Ruby Quest Movie
Ingenius

Ruby Quest was originally designed for Ingenius' cable-delivered kids' new product, *What On Earth*, as a 640 by 480 pixels, 450K movie. Its purpose was to teach vocabulary and word-association through trial-and-error gameplay. It was converted to a Shockwave movie after decreasing the stage size to fit inside the Netscape browser; converting the MIDI music to short, internal sound files; and downsizing the graphics to make the file as small as possible.

The game has two opening screens. The first lets you choose your character. There is a desert landscape and a sign warns that the "Dangerous Cavern" is nearby. The second screen places you outside the cavern, where you translate some strange runes into English. These runes give you the information you need to cross the cavern.

Upon entering the cavern, players need to jump on 33 pillars to cross the cavern where the "priceless Ruby" awaits them. Words appear over the pillars as players decide which pillar to jump on. By associating these words with the information obtained from the runes, players can make it safely across the cavern.

The information and words are accessed from an external text file on the server and change occasionally, thus enabling new challenges daily.

A Few Words from the Company

Ingenius is all about kids' multimedia entertainment. At home, Ingenius products entertain while educating, and at schools they educate while entertaining.

Ingenius
4 Inverness Court East
Englewood, CO 80112
Tel: (303) 705-8877, (303) 705-8800
Fax: (303) 705-8899
URL: http://www.ingenius.com
Email: info@ingenius.com

The Cyber Carnival Movies
Media Connection of New York

MOVIE SPECS

THE FUNHOUSE
Original File Size:
571K

Audio: 120K

Afterburned Size:
385K

Net Lingo Used:
GetNetText
GoToNetMovie

Stage Size:
400w x 300h

LINGO
SCRIPTING
LEVEL
intermediate

MOVIE SPECS

DUCK-HUNT
Original File Size:
180K

Audio: 30K

Afterburned Size:
115K

Net Lingo Used:
GetNetText

Stage Size:
400w x 200h

LINGO
SCRIPTING
LEVEL
intermediate

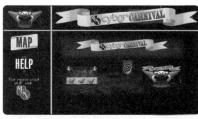

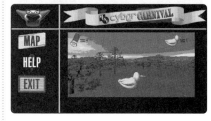

The Cyber Carnival was developed by Media Connection of New York (MCNY). The Cyber Carnival was the brainchild of Peter Anders and was developed in conjuction with Dave Furfero and Gabe Evans. They created it as a prototype for the next wave of Web development.

MCNY believes that content-oriented sites will be the "television shows" of the Web in the not-so-distant future, and that Web users will find true entertainment on the Web. This means the production quality of Web sites must improve in order to capture viewers' attention. The Cyber Carnival is a compilation of Shockwave movies within a frame-based HTML page. The movies exemplify intermediate Lingo scripting and Director techniques.

The Cyber Carnival is comprised of three different game modules. The Duck-Hunt is a simple shooting game, the Funhouse is a Myst-type mini-adventure game, and the Rollercoaster is essentially an .AVI digital video that was sequenced in Director and then converted to a Shockwave file. Each module represents a different level of interaction, from reflex-oriented shooting to passive viewing. The Carnival helped provide a benchmark for file sizes from which MCNY can gauge future productions.

A Few Words from the Company

Media Connection of New York (MCNY) is a Manhattan-based, premiere developer of Web sites and Web content. The team at MCNY has several years' experience in the industry, and believes that the company has a true vision of the future. Stay tuned for more content-oriented sites, as well as a full-featured network, from MCNY.

Media Connection of New York
443 Park Avenue South, 3rd Floor
New York, NY 10016
Tel: (212) 686-3845
Fax: (212) 686-3856
URL: http://www.mcny.com/Carnival/carnival.htm
Email: info@mcny.com

The Menu Widget & Menu Bar Movies
Ink & Image, Inc.

Ink & Image, Inc. affectionately calls their Shockwave movie the "menu widget." It was originally created for the company's home page. Jim Kelton, the graphic designer, wanted something eye-catching and fun to use. Mark Woodman did the Lingo programming to refine Jim's initial work and added the Shockwave Net Lingo. He also produced the company's Web site, and set a 60K file-size limit for any Shockwave piece that would be included within the site. Despite the power Shockwave can provide, he felt it was important to be considerate of download time for users. The final version of the menu widget was developed after several refinements.

MOVIE SPECS

Original File Sizes
Widget: 153K
Menu Bar: 62K

Audio:
Widget: 46.6K
Menu Bar: 3K

Afterburned Size:
Widget: 54K
Menu Bar: 20K

Net Lingo Used:
GoToNetPage

Stage Size:
Widget: 480w x 240h
Bar: 496w x 80h

LINGO
SCRIPTING
LEVEL
intermediate

The compressed .dcr file uses sounds, animation, and rollovers to make it come alive. The graphics were created in Adobe Illustrator, rendered in Specular Infini-D, and modified in Adobe Photoshop before being imported into Director. This was the first Shockwave menu to be put on the Ink & Image home page.

Ink & Image believes the strategic use of rollovers is what puts Shockwave applications ahead of the pack on the Web. Adding a click sound and a highlight box over a hot spot lets the user know precisely what is active on a menu. A display window that further explains each button's function is easy to program, takes little file space, and is very user-friendly.

Additionally, they created a convenient Shockwave menu bar to replace the old-hat imagemaps. The repeating menu bar is found at the bottom of every page of the site. "Load once, use often" became the mantra as Mark and Jim sought to get maximum use of Shockwave elements. The movie was programmed using `gotoNetPage` commands that take users to other areas of the Web site.

The compressed .dcr file is 20K and uses sound and rollovers to emulate a "CD-ROM-style" menu bar. Some imagemaps can be extremely frustrating—hot spots are impossible to find until they are clicked. This menu bar uses a "tink" sound and a highlight box to quickly and easily identify hot spots.

Ink & Image recommends that new Shockwave producers use Lingo to its fullest. "While looking good is important, make Shockwave movies as interactive as possible. Interactivity is commonplace in the CD-ROM world, but the Web surfer has become accustomed to a very passive environment. Shockwave interactivity invites exploration."

A Few Words from the Company

Ink & Image, Inc. is a multimedia production group located in the heart of Illinois. The company provides superior creative and technical services including Web site creation, interactive authoring, presentation graphics, and digital video production.

Ink & Image, Inc.
207 Main St., Suite 200
Peoria, IL 61602
Tel: (309) 671-0206
Fax: (309) 671-0208
URL: http://www.inkimage.com
Email: service@inkimage.com

The Quizzer Movies
Maricopa Center for Learning & Instruction

This movie, created by Alan Levine, is a shell that derives its functionality from text files that reside on the Web server at the Maricopa Center for Learning & Instruction (MCLI). The content can be recreated and updated easily, and any number of quizzes are possible.

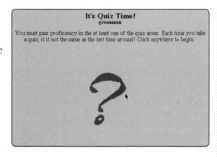

There also can be any number of questions, and each quiz can have a different "passing" score. Each question has four answer choices and corresponding feedback. Every time a user enters the quiz, questions are asked in a different order; every time a question is assembled, the answers are presented in a different order. This way, the quizzes never look the same.

The Quizzer starts with a 1.3K front-end Shockwave movie—a bouncing question mark. When the question mark is clicked, it uses the `gotoNetPage` command to load the main movie. A text file containing the names of the available quizzes is read via `getNetText`, and the text is put into a field. Clicking a line initiates `getNetText` which retrieves data for the selected quiz. Lingo parent scripts create the quiz items.

In conjunction with the `getNetText` command, The Quizzer movie checks `netDone()` over a series of looping frames and not in a repeat loop (the latter hogs CPU cycles from the Web browser). Animation or visual cues indicate a net operation by ink swapping, forecolor changing, and animating a variably-sized question mark bitmap along a sinusoidal path. The Quizzer also utilizes a small loader movie so the user is not left staring at blank space while waiting for the main movie to appear.

According to Alan Levine, a trick he learned from the ShockeR listserv is to import a blank text file into Director for the fontmap. This can shave several kilobytes from the final .dcr file.

MOVIE SPECS

Original File Sizes
Front-end: 3.5K
The Quizzer: 50K

Audio: none

Afterburned Sizes
Front-end: 1.3K
The Quizzer: 11.4K

Net Lingo Used:
GoToNetPage
GetNetText
GoToNetMovie
NetTextResult()
NetDone()

Stage Size:
448w x 240h

LINGO
SCRIPTING
LEVEL
challenging

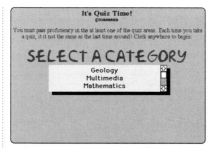

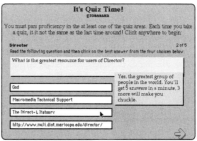

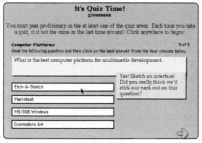

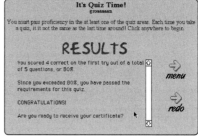

A Few Words from the Company

The Maricopa Center for Learning and Instruction (MCLI), located at the Maricopa Community Colleges, is considered a national model for motivating, infusing, and promoting innovation and change in the community college environment. Maricopa is the second largest community college system in the United States.

Maricopa Center for Learning & Instruction
Maricopa Community Colleges
2411 West 14th Street
Tempe, AZ 85281-6941
Tel: (602) 731-8297
Fax: (602) 731-8282
URL: http://www.mcli.dist.maricopa.edu
The Quizzer can be found at http://www.mcli.dist.maricopa.edu/alan/nojava/quiz
Email: levine@maricopa.edu

Spike Webb: Memorex Movies
ISYS Idea Systems, Inc.

Spike Webb is a detective/science-fiction adventure series. The story is based on Spike Webb—a quasi-AI program with an attitude. Together with three cohorts, Spike works hard to protect the Internet and everything in it from greed and corruption. Adventures span a six-week period with a new chapter published every week. The format integrates original artwork with hypertext.

With the advent of Shockwave, ISYS Idea Systems has been able to extend the reach and appeal of their digital super-hero. Each week, the previous week's plot line is recapped in a mini-movie. Minimizing file size,

of course, is the biggest challenge. ISYS starts with a 300w x 300h stage size. Images created for the weekly hypertext episodes are reduced and indexed to make them as small as possible. Director's built-in text is used because it requires only a small amount of memory. With creative sound design and Sound Forge software, ISYS manipulates clips to create compelling sound effects and music loops.

A Few Words from the Company

ISYS is a digital and graphic design company. The company's strength is its ability to translate the client's message into effective electronic media. The objective is to keep movies under 300K. Tune in weekly to follow Spike and his crew! Spike Webb is created by Cathy Dew, Sally Dew, Thom Smith, and Terry Brandt.

ISYS Idea Systems, Inc.
6025 Valley View Road
Oakland, CA 94611
Tel: (510) 339-6265
Fax: (510) 339-3858
URL: http://www.ideasystems.com
Email: isys@ideasystems.com

MOVIE SPECS

Original File Sizes
Chapter 1: 496K
Chapter 2: 608K

Audio:
Chapter 1: 118.5K
Chapter 2: 166.7K

Afterburned Size:
Chapter 1: 158K
Chapter 2: 232K

Net Lingo Used:
none

Stage Size:
300w x 300h

LINGO
SCRIPTING
LEVEL
easy

Catsentration
Studio Software

MOVIE SPECS

Original File Sizes
316K

Audio: 53.4K

Afterburned Size:
188K

Net Lingo Used:
none

Stage Size:
352w x 270h

LINGO
SCRIPTING
LEVEL

challenging

Catsentration is based on the classic game of Concentration. The player's goal is to match the pairs of images hidden behind tiles. When all pairs are found, the viewer is rewarded with a fun animation.

Catsentration was created originally as one of the games on Studio Software's CD-ROM game sampler. For the shocked version, the overall byte size of the game was reduced by removing the opening music, cutting some of the animation, scaling down the size of the art by 20 percent, and reducing the sounds from 22.050 kHz/8-bit to 11.025 kHz/8-bit.

A Few Words from the Company

Studio Software offers complete multimedia production to clients in the entertainment, advertising, and publishing industries. The company creates multimedia in all formats including CD-ROM, floppy disk, and Web sites. Catsentration credits are as follows: Leslie Safarik, Design; Laurence Tietz, Programming; Chris Sands, Art implementation; and Hillary Safarik, Webmaster.

Studio Software
2140 East 7th Place, Suite A2S
Los Angeles, CA 90021
Tel: (213) 614-1126
Fax: (213) 614-0868
URL: http://www.studiosoftware.com
Email: studio@ncinter.net

Jesse's Gravity Well Movie
Vanguard Media Corporation

Jesse Erlbaum's primary goal in creating the Gravity Well was to use all the Lingo techniques he knew to see how fast he could make Director run. He already knew (from benchmark tests conducted for the *Politically Correct Bedtime Stories* CD-ROM, on which he was a programmer) that Lingo was considerably faster than Score animation, and that Director moved fastest when running in a repeat loop. He also knew that conditionals were a CPU hog, so he built the movie without them, using instead Boolean math and recursion to derive a result. One example of this approach can be seen in the way the sprites in the animation are looped using the mod operator to perform the clock arithmetic.

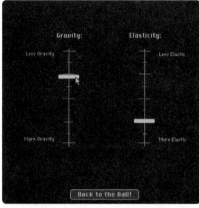

MOVIE SPECS

Original File Size:
85K

Audio: none

Afterburned Size:
24.8K

Net Lingo Used:
none

Stage Size:
400w x 400h

LINGO
SCRIPTING
LEVEL
challenging

As you may already suspect, one interesting side-effect of this speed optimization was that it actually interfered with Netscape Navigator's interface. Using Director, many events are locked out while the playback head is in a repeat loop. When a repeat loop occurs in a Shockwave movie, the browser's navigational buttons do not respond. Unfortunately, the only way to correct this is to exit the repeat loop. As an alternative to "locking up" the browser, an on idle handler is recommended in place of a repeat loop. In the particular case of the Gravity Well, speed optimization was chosen as a priority over interface. It is important that Shockwave developers consider this trade-off up front when designing their movies.

While building the Gravity Well movie, Jesse discovered the math that created the "orbital" motion quite by accident while trying to assemble a formula that would simulate gravity. The formula works by recursion—constantly updating the vertical and horizontal speed (delta) of the object—accelerating it towards the position of the mouse. At the same time, the "inertia" of the object is created by averaging the changing delta over time. The relationship between these values can best be understood by simply hacking around with them, and observing the changing characteristics of the motion in the movie provided on the CD-ROM.

A Few Words from the Company

Vanguard Media is a leading east coast interactive media developer and publisher. The company focuses on entertainment software for the home market. Vanguard has developed CD-ROM and online consumer products for Time Warner Interactive, Mindscape, Macmillan Digital USA, and Random House. Vanguard publishes the CD-ROM series and Web site for the Anime HyperGuide.™

Vanguard Media Corporation
132 West 21st Street, 4th Floor
New York, NY 10011
Tel: (212) 242-5317
Fax: (212) 929-9496
URL: http://www.vm.com
FirstClass BBS: (212) 242 7685
Email: info@vm.com

The shockClock Movie
Zoetek

Zoetek's shockClock is a digital clock featuring a clock, an alarm, a timer, a stopwatch, and an international time zone map, designed and programmed by Eric Iverson.

shockClock stays under 20K by limiting the bit-depth of its graphical cast members—none have a bit-depth greater than two. Since it is meant to emulate a monochromatic LCD display, this does not detract from the overall function or design. An exception is the individual time zones that change color when selected. Originally the color changing was accomplished by creating two cast members for each time zone: one with a light gray background, and one with a dark gray background. These were then swapped when the user clicked on the display. This resulted in needless duplication, thus increasing the applet size.

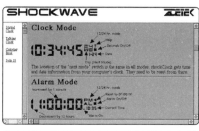

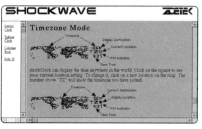

MOVIE SPECS

Original File Size: 80K

Audio: none

Afterburned Size: 17K

Net Lingo Used: GoToNetPage

Stage Size: 224w x 39h

LINGO SCRIPTING LEVEL — intermediate

To fix this, a black rectangle was placed under the time zone sprites, and the dark gray cast members were removed. Color changes were recreated using ink effects, where the blend of the selected sprite is set to 50, allowing the underlying black to partially show through. When the sprite is deselected, the blend value resets to 100, causing it to revert to its original light gray color. This technique reduced the size of the applet by nearly 25 percent.

A Few Words from the Company

Founded by Eric Iverson in 1993 in response to interest in his graduate work on applying Artificial Life programming to computer music composition, Zoetek has expanded into graphic design, video production, and multimedia development. Zoetek is based in Minneapolis, Minnesota.

Zoetek
1257 Forest Ridge Trail, #4
Eagan, MN 55123
Tel: (612) 686-6648
Fax: (612) 686-6657
URL: http://zoetek.com/entrance
Email: zoetek@zoetek.com

The IdleTest Movie
@dver@ctive, Inc.

MOVIE SPECS

Original File Size:
21.5K

Audio: none

Afterburned
File Size: 6K

Net Lingo Used:
none

Stage Size:
288w x 160h

LINGO
SCRIPTING
LEVEL
challenging

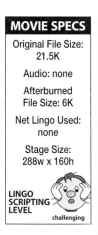

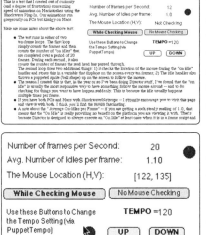

The IdleTest movie measures the speed of idle handler execution within Shockwave movies. It is useful for comparing the playback speed of a movie running on Macintosh versus Windows systems. The test runs in either of two ten-frame loops. The first loop simply counts the frames and then counts the number of "on idles" that are completed over a span of 20 frames. During each second, it also counts the number of frames the read head has passed through. The second loop accomplishes two additional actions: (1) it checks the location of the mouse during the `on idle` handler and stores this in a variable that displays on screen every ten frames; and (2) the `on idle` handler also displays a puppeted sprite (a ball shape) on screen to follow the cursor.

A Few Words from the Company

@dver@ctive specializes in two things: cramming good interactive multimedia onto a floppy disk, and cramming good interactive multimedia into small Shockwave files.

@dver@ctive, Inc.
Shock-Bauble Originators Extraordinaire
1802 S. Lakeshore Drive
Chapel Hill, NC 27514
Tel: (919) 932-6657
Fax: (919) 932-3722
URL: http://adveract.com
Email: sbullock@adveract.com (Steve Bullock)

The Brick Builder and Brick Builder 2 Movies
The Planet

Brick Builder (BB) is possibly the world's smallest 3D modeler, letting you build models with isometric sprite bricks. Brick Builder 2 (BB2) also lets you exchange models with others through an online gallery.

Brick Builder was created by Rasmus Keldorff of The Planet mainly as a test. He wanted to include some level of 3D in a Director movie because he found it to be the ultimate Lingo programming challenge, and he was fascinated by the beautiful isometric desktop icons being produced for the BeBox.

A further goal was to implement a creative exchange online other than chat rooms, believing that creative

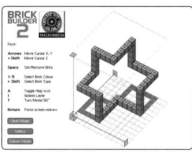

MOVIE SPECS

Original File Sizes
Brick Builder: 25K
Brick Builder 2: 73K

Audio: none

Afterburned Size:
Brick Builder: 7K
Brick Builder 2: 19K

Net Lingo Used in
Brick Builder 2:
GetNetText

Stage Size:
640w x 480h

LINGO
SCRIPTING
LEVEL
challenging

exchange provides extra inspiration and is an art form to be explored. Thus, Brick Builder 2 was created. BB2 offers new features such as more brick types, model rotation, and online model exchange.

The interesting aspect of Brick Builder is that it can be a toy or a tool— not an animation that takes minutes to download, watch, and then forget. BB can be incredibly small because most of its graphics are colored bitmaps, and it contains only one 8-bit image (the brick). It is fast to load and makes learning fun.

Initially, string manipulation was chosen over lists within lists, mainly for ease of scripting. However, after running speed tests, Rasmus found that the list method performed seven to 60 times faster than strings! Therefore using lists is recommended, although Rasmus finds it an illogical way of dealing with arrays.

For BB2, which has an online model gallery, the brick model data is compressed into an ASCII string (using only "safe" characters, 33-255) by looking for repeated data. The data is then moved to the clipboard (using the `CopyToClipBoard` command). Next, a mail window is opened using `GetNetText "mailto:" & "<net@address>"` and the user is prompted to Paste and then send the mail. The incoming models are then manually compiled into an uploaded model database. When the user wants to retrieve a model from the database, the movie uses the `GetNetText "http://net.address/file"` command again, parses the input, and writes it into a scrollable text field as a model list.

A few Shockwave tips from Rasmus Keldorff at The Planet:

1. Don't take for granted that all the features you use will work on multiple platforms. For instance, a Shockwave file running under Windows doesn't allow you to color 8-bit sprites. Thus, a check of the `machineType` was included in BB to switch Windows bricks to 1-bit sprites. However, the movie does have much faster sprite handling when running under Windows.

2. BB crashed some systems because it was launched in 16- or 32-bit mode, and it originally made the switch to 8-bit without prompting the user (something for which Netscape apparently was not prepared).

3. Currently, it's impossible to Paste into an editable text field in a Shockwave file.

A Few Words from the Company

The Planet is a small Danish multimedia studio formed in October, 1995, by Rasmus Keldorff, Mads Rydahl, Jacob Tekiela, and Søren Ebbesen (all formerly of MouseHouse, a successful Danish multimedia startup, and Space Invaders, which is now a government-funded multimedia project).

The Planet deals primarily with cutting-edge graphic design and multimedia development. They are graphic designers with experience in all the leading graphics and multimedia programs and have acted as subcontractors in several large multimedia projects including the award-winning CD-ROM *TRANSfigured* by Sony Music, and a forthcoming Lego product.

The Planet
Frederiks Allé 112b
DK-8000 Aarhus C
Denmark
Tel: +45 86 18 06 99
Fax: +45 86 18 06 39
URL: http://www.danadata.dk/planet
Email: rzrmouse@inet.uni-c.dk

Turntable Scratchpad
Turntable Media

Turntable Media's Scratchpad movie was created to experiment with the capabilities of Shockwave and to provide a fun interactive demo that expresses the company's hip-hop flavor. The movie was programmed by Peter Fierlinger, and uses the Turntable logo designed by Philip Fierlinger and Push. The programming involved some use of trigonometrics to find the angular velocity of the "finger-scratching" as the mouse cursor is moved forward or backward by the user. Beyond that, the programming is fairly simple.

The movie includes a backbeat loop that plays in the background, and sounds for the forward and backward scratches. A fine-tuning adjustment was necessary to stop the backbeat on Windows computers when either scratch sound is played, due to the latency of mixing sounds in Director running under Windows. Without this modification, there was an unacceptable delay between when the user moved the mouse to scratch the logo and when the actual scratch sample played. The audio samples were downsampled as much as possible while still providing acceptable audio fidelity.

To reduce the size of the Shockwave movie as much as possible, the logo images were indexed to a 4-bit palette that contained a subset of colors used in the final Director movie's 8-bit palette (in this case, the 8-bit system palette was used). These 4-bit images were then imported into Director at 8-bit. By importing them into Director at 8-bit rather than 4-bit, Afterburner still compressed the images based on their original bit depth, but the movie's playback performance was slightly improved. It helps to make sure that the movie color depth matches the system color depth, which is set to 8-bit for most systems. Performance can be affected adversely if individual cast members in a movie have different color depths than the system.

MOVIE SPECS

Original File Sizes
shocker13bert.dir
137K
shocker13ola.dir
157K

Audio:
shocker13bert.dir
35.1K
shocker13ola.dir
54.3K

Afterburned Size:
shocker13bert.dcr
68K
shocker13ola.dcr
82K

Net Lingo Used:
GoToNetMovie

Stage Size:
240w x 230h

LINGO
SCRIPTING
LEVEL

intermediate

An additional feature of the Scratchpad movie is the ability to load another movie that is essentially the same, but contains different audio samples. In addition to supporting new sound samples, future plans for the Scrathpad movie include allowing users to create their own samples and upload them to Turntable's site, and enabling users to download the samples, place them in the Shockwave Support folder, and never have to download them again. Turntable also plans to implement Shockwave Streaming Audio to further reduce file size while improving audio fidelity.

A Few Words from the Company

Turntable is a multimedia design and development firm that specializes in instant gratification. Owned and operated by brothers Peter and Philip Fierlinger, the company has several music-related products on the market, including "Don't Mosh in the Ramen Shop," an enhanced CD title that was created for the Beastie Boys. Turntable is a pioneer in merging the online and CD-ROM worlds through the use of Shockwave and the integration of Web sites and browsers with CD-ROM content.

Turntable Media
300 Brannan Street, Suite 502
San Francisco, CA 94107
Tel: (415) 284-0600
Fax: (415) 284-0685
URL: http://www.turntable.com
Email: kids@turntable.com

3-D Navigation Tool and Periodic Table Toy
Elemental Design

Elemental Design used Shockwave to create two distinct applications: a site navigation tool and a fun toy. Because the Elemental Design site showcases the firm's people and services, the technology used had to reflect the company's experience and abilities. The team at Elemental felt that text and imagemaps alone weren't enough to make people notice them.

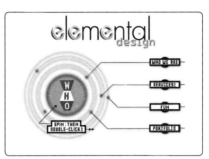

The navigational tool—a rotating graphic that provides click-and-drag links to each of the four main sections of the site—was created first using a 3-D rendering program, and then images were imported into Director for animation, scripting and Afterburner compression. To keep file size small, animation was created with the fewest number of frames that would maintain fluidity. Because the Netscape browser color cube features many different values of chromatic red, the navigational tool graphic was made red and white to reduce the amount of dithering when indexed; this allowed for more effective compression.

A clever 5K preloading movie was created to entertain users while the main Shockwave movie that contains the navigation menu downloads.

Elemental's second Shockwave movie reflects the company name, and uses the periodic table of the elements as the motif for a simple toy. By mixing an element shown on the left with the element "e" in the petri dish, the user is rewarded with an irreverent animation. Whenever possible, 1-bit animations were created and colorized on the Director Stage. By setting sprites to background transparent ink mode, layered 1-bit graphics were used to create images. All internal sound effects were downsampled to 11.025kHz.

A Few Words from the Company

Elemental Design is an interactive media and Web site development company devoted to communicating through leading-edge technologies.

Elemental Design
351 Riverside Avenue
Fremont, CA 94536
Tel: (510) 793-8079
URL: http://www.elementaldesign.com
Email: info@elementaldesign.com

MOVIE SPECS

Original File Sizes
main.dir:135K
fun.dir: 133K

Audio:
main.dir: 8.2K
fun.dir: 20.8K

Afterburned Size:
main.dcr: 60K
fun.dcr: 60K

Net Lingo Used:
GoToNetMovie,
GoToNetPage

Stage Size:
480w x 300h

LINGO
SCRIPTING
LEVEL
easy

Director Basics with a Shockwave Slant

If you are interested in developing Shockwave applications for the Internet, it is important that you first become a competent Director user. An exception to this rule is made for Power Applets, which are ready-made Shockwave and Java applets that enable end users to generate Shockwave movies without authoring in Director. Power Applets aim to provide simple interface templates for creating very specific applications easily, such as scrolling text and basic slide shows. However, it is our guess that most readers of this book will be interested in creating Power Applets as well as using them, in which case Director experience is required.

Director's greatest strength as an authoring tool lies in its support for cross-platform authoring and multi-platform playback. Director movies can be authored on Macintosh and Windows PCs. The file format is binary-compatible, which means that the same file can be opened and edited on both platforms. The same Director source file can then be distributed via floppy disk, CD-ROM, Enhanced CD, networked kiosks, the World Wide Web, consumer players, interactive television systems, and, potentially, any new distribution medium that comes along.

A very basic understanding of Director goes a long way, and your expertise with the software can scale according to your comfort level. From simple animations and slide shows to interactive consumer titles and networked applications, Director provides an environment that is flexible enough to accommodate multiple user levels. Very often, many members of a production team—including artists, animators, sound designers, and programmers—work within Director to accomplish their individual goals.

This section provides an overview of Director and emphasizes features of the software that are particularly relevant to Shockwave movie creation. The information is organized by the various interface components, which are centered around Director's theatrical metaphor.

The Stage

Director's Stage provides the back-drop for your text, graphics, digital video, and animation. The Stage can be resized by selecting Movie Properties from the Modify menu.

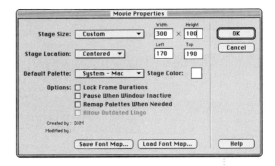

Stage size is especially relevant to Shockwave production because the height and width of the Stage (in pixels) is used to specify the display rectangle for a Shockwave file within the HTML <EMBED> tag.

Stage Size

During authoring, the Stage width must be set to a multiple of 16 on Macintosh systems. If an invalid number is entered, Director will automatically adjust the size down to the nearest multiple.

If you wish to use an exact Stage width that is not a multiple of 16 for your Shockwave movie, it is possible to set the Director Stage size to a multiple that is larger than necessary by leaving a blank area on the right of the Stage, then setting the <EMBED> tag to the smaller, desired size.

If you set your <EMBED> tag dimensions to less than the movie's Stage size, then your movie will be cropped from the bottom and/or the right within the display window.

If you set the <EMBED> tag dimensions greater than the movie's Stage size, then your movie will be placed upper left within the display window, with a blank border on the bottom and/or the right.

For the most reliable results, however, it is good practice to make sure that the values specified in the <EMBED> tag are equal to the movie's Stage dimensions.

Note

It's helpful to keep track of Stage sizes for your Shockwave movies by keeping the dimensions in a text file, or (on Macintosh systems) by typing the Stage size into the Info window's Comments box for each file. Once a movie is processed through Afterburner, you must open the source Director file in order to check the Stage size. If you store the dimensions outside of the source file, you can paste them into HTML pages quickly.

Stage Color

If an HTML page has a solid background color (specified using the tag <BODY BGCOLOR = #??????>), the Stage color can be set to the same background color so that a Shockwave movie is seamlessly embedded. To further create a seamless effect, the background color of the empty "Macromedia logo" rectangle that appears while a Shockwave movie is downloading also can also be set to match the Web page background color (and the Stage color). This can be accomplished by setting the BGCOLOR parameter within the <EMBED> tag.

The following HTML code sets the Web page background to black, and then sets the downloading rectangle to black (assuming that the Shockwave movie to be embedded also has a black Stage):

```
<HTML>
<TITLE> Black Page with Shockwave</TITLE>
<BODY BGCOLOR = #000000> )
<EMBED SRC= "movie.dcr" WIDTH=300 HEIGHT=120 BGCOLOR= #000000>
</HTML>
```

Casts

A Cast stores a Director movie's elements, which are referred to as members. These members can be graphics, audio, text, animation, palettes, transitions, digital video, Director movies, and Lingo scripts. Members can be created in Director or they can be imported, and each Cast can store up to 32,000 members. The same Director movie can reference multiple external Casts—that is, members from one Cast can be swapped on the fly with members from another Cast while a movie is running.

For Shockwave, this raises the notion of multiple Shockwave movies on the Web sharing Cast (.cst) files that have been installed by a user into their local Support folder. This addresses the developer's need to store media-rich elements locally (on hard disk, or CD-ROM, for example), as opposed to requiring large downloads from the Web.

Linked media (such as digital video and audio files) can be downloaded by users from the Web to a local Shockwave Support folder. These downloaded files can then be called by an active Shockwave movie that contains links to these members.

The Score

The Score window is the composite controller for your Director authoring. It provides a visual representation of everything that occurs within a movie. The Score is made up of rows (channels) and columns (frames), and features a playback head that represents activity over time.

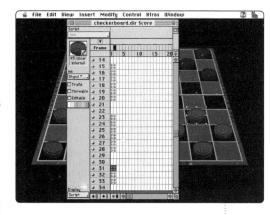

When a member is placed on Stage, the instance of that member is represented in the Score and is then referred to as a sprite. The Score contains 48 sprite channels, a Tempo channel, a Transition channel, a Palette channel, two sound channels, and a Script channel.

Sprite Channels

The 48 sprite channels hold visual information that is layered on the Stage. Channel One is the bottom sprite layer, or the one that is farthermost in the background; channel 48 is the topmost sprite layer.

The Score window also provides control over ink effects, trails, moveability, editability (of field sprites), and visibility for any given sprite. These properties also can be controlled via Lingo.

For Shockwave text, graphics, and animations, you can experiment by changing inks and layering them in different combinations. Note that certain inks perform slower than others because more complex calculations are required to render the ink effect. The Director 5 CD includes an Ink Effects Lab that shows how different inks can affect animation.

Be cautious when using the trails ink mode within Shockwave movies. If an HTML page containing a Shockwave movie is reloaded, trails will obviously disappear. Trails will also disappear if a window, dialog box, or other onscreen element appears in front of the movie's Stage.

Tempo Channel

The topmost Score channel is the Tempo channel, which controls the movie's playback speed.

Shockwave movies will adhere to the Tempo fps (frames per second) settings selected during authoring. However, we do not advise using any of the built-in `Wait` and `Wait For...` options in the Set Tempo dialog. When these options are selected for a given frame, the movie does not respond to user events and users are "locked out" until the specified action is completed.

In general, it is best to replace the `Wait` and `Wait For...` Tempo channel settings with simple Lingo scripts that are entered in the Script channel. For example, instead of selecting `Wait for Sound1 To Finish` in the Set Tempo dialog, use the following frame script:

```
on exitFrame
    if soundBusy (1) then go the frame
end
```

Transition Channel

Director provides 56 different types
of transitions to use between frames.
Many of the transitions can be cus-
tomized for chunk size and duration.
In addition, there are a number of third-
party Transitions Xtras available.

The same transition may appear
differently on Windows and Macintosh
computers. For example, pixel dissolves are chunkier when running under
Windows. Make sure to test your Shockwave movies on various client machines
to make sure that differences are acceptable. You can also test for the
machineType using Lingo and then puppet a transition accordingly.

During transitions, the movie does not respond to user events. In most Director
applications, transitions occur so rapidly that the user is unaware of the lack of
interactivity. However, in the Shockwave environment, the Web browser and
Shockwave movies share CPU cycles so that transition speeds may be unpredictable. It is best to set transitions to the shortest duration available and to use
them sparingly throughout your Shockwave productions.

Palette Channel

The Palette channel enables you to select and change the active palette in your Director movie. The transition from one palette to another can be an abrupt one or one that uses an interim fade to black or white.

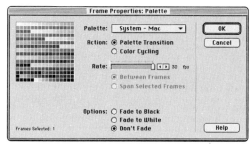

For Shockwave movies, you will need to consider the Web browser's default color palette when deciding which color palette to use during authoring. If your movie uses colors which are not included in the browser's palette, you have a few options.

The most straightforward approach is to remap all cast members to the browser's palette during authoring. The palettes .cst Xtra that ships with Director includes the Netscape and Microsoft Network palettes, among others. If you use this technique, there is no need to designate a custom palette in the Palette channel of your movie.

If you must embed your movie with a custom palette, you can set the PALETTE parameter within the <EMBED> tag to gain some degree of control over the movie's display. By setting the PALETTE parameter equal to foreground, your custom palette is forced upon the browser, which can sometimes yield odd visual effects. By setting the PALETTE parameter equal to background, the browser's palette controls the display. (The PALETTE parameter is not supported by Internet Explorer.)

The Set Palette dialog box also offers color-cycling options that can be used to create animation and special effects within your Shockwave movies without adding memory requirements.

Sound Channels

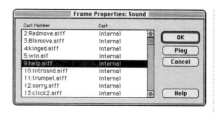

Two sound channels appear in Director's Score window. In addition to playing sounds placed in the Score, Director can support playback of sounds through Lingo scripting. (Up to eight sounds can be played simultaneously!) Sounds placed in the Score are tied to linear Score animation while sounds played via Lingo can be accessed randomly at any time.

For Shockwave development, you should take advantage of Shockwave Audio (SWA) compression for playing high-quality sounds within your Shockwave movies. SWA compression can be used for internal sounds that are embedded in the Director Cast, or for external sounds that are streamed from a Web server.

See Chapter 6, "Shockwave Media Creation," for information about using Shockwave Audio.

Script Channel

Lingo scripts entered into the Script channel are executed (by default) as the playback head leaves the frame containing the script, or on exitFrame in Lingo. Scripts entered into the Script channel also appear as members in the Cast window.

During Shockwave authoring, try to avoid entering scripts into the first frame of the

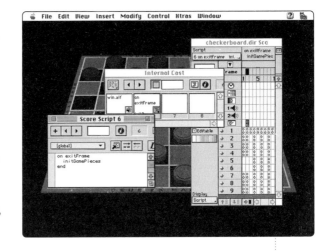

movie's Script channel. Director's legendary "first-frame weirdness" may cause these scripts to be bypassed when a movie starts playing.

Also during authoring, Director will loop a movie by default when it reaches the last frame of the movie. This will not occur in the runtime Shockwave version, so remember to enter a script in the Script channel for the last frame to loop a section of the movie, or to keep the playback head looping in the last frame.

Control Panel

The Control Panel windoid provides control buttons for rewinding, stepping through, stopping, and playing your movie. In addition, it includes buttons for adjusting the sound level, looping the movie, and playing only selected frames.

The Control Panel also provides information about the movie's current status. Frame number, selected tempo, and actual tempo appear within the windoid.

The Control Panel's loop button is selected by default. Movies do not automatically loop when they are converted to runtime players or Shockwave .dcr files.

Paint Window

Many of the features of Director's Paint window were designed and refined back in the days of developing for floppy disk distribution. Small file sizes were, and still are, critical for floppy development, as they are for the bandwidth-constrained world of the Internet. Many of the Paint window's features—ignored or passed over by CD-ROM developers in favor of imported graphics—can be very useful to the Shockwave developer.

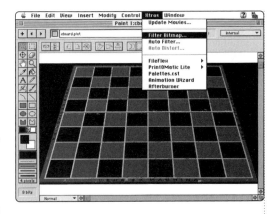

Artwork created in the Paint window is bitmapped, as opposed to vector shapes and lines created using the Tool palette. Standard paint tools are available, along with ink effects and patterns. Images can be flipped, rotated, traced and distorted. The colors and color depth of bitmapped images also can be changed in the Paint window.

The Onion-skin feature provides layering cababilities in the Paint window for creating animation, and makes it possible to view a bitmapped image against other reference cast members. Creating Shockwave movies often requires enhancing or animating existing Web graphics. The onion-skinning feature can be used to create animation roughs (or finished art) based on a still reference graphic.

Director also supports Photoshop and Premiere plug-in filters for bitmapped members.

Text

In Director versions prior to 5.0, the Text window was used generically to create and edit display type, Lingo scripts, and text fields. The distinction between different types of text is much clearer now that there are separate member types and windows for text, fields, and scripts.

Text Window

The Text window is used to enter, edit, and format text during authoring. Text can be edited in the text window or directly on Stage (by double-clicking on a text sprite on the Stage).

Text created in the Text window is, in the majority of cases, meant for the user to see. Director imports the rich text format (RTF) and supports anti-aliasing of non-bitmapped fonts.

When anti-aliasing is on (as it is by default), it basically means that text plays back at runtime as an 8-bit bitmap. For Shockwave development, the improved quality of anti-aliased text and the flexibility related to font selection must be weighed against an increase in file size.

Fields

Fields are used to create editable text, or text that can be modified while a movie plays. Create a field using the Field tool in the Tool palette or by choosing Control, then Field from the Insert menu.

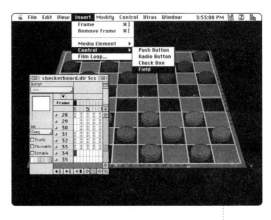

Text displayed in fields is controlled by operating system software and is subject to font mapping across platforms. In addition to requiring that fonts be installed on the user's system, another disadvantage is that fields animate slower than text cast members.

However, fields require less space than other types of text, and they are particularly important for storing, formatting, and manipulating strings using Lingo. Within Shockwave movies, fields can be used to display any text or data that is retrieved over the net.

Tool Palette

The Tool palette provides you with everything you need to create low-bandwidth shapes, lines, patterns, and buttons of various foreground and background colors. (This windoid also contains the Field tool mentioned in the previous section.)

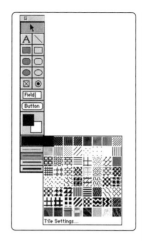

Shapes (referred to as QuickDraw objects in earlier versions of Director) are rendered to screen in real-time and use less memory than bitmaps. They can be resized, distorted, and colored using Lingo, without adding any overhead. One thing to keep in mind when designing Shockwave content, however, is that shapes animate more slowly than bitmaps.

Color Palettes

You can use the Color palettes window to create custom palettes and to view and edit existing ones. You can create a custom palette by copying and modifying an existing palette, or by importing an image that uses a custom palette in order to install the image's palette in the Cast.

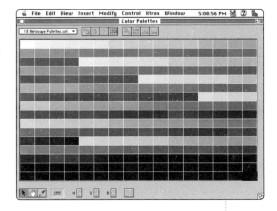

Because only one palette at a time can be active on a computer display, Shockwave development requires that you consider the color palettes used by Web browsers and those used by operating systems when designing your movies. Ideally, a Shockwave movie's palette should incorporate color values used by the target browser and any color values reserved by the target playback systems. (Some additional information related to Shockwave palettes is included above in the "Palette Channel" section.)

Lingo Scripts

Attempting to write a brief overview of Lingo, Director's scripting language, is like trying to summarize a dictionary.

The majority of Lingo elements available in Director are also available for Shockwave movie development. Aside from the handful of net-specific Lingo elements, scripting for Shockwave requires the same skill and efficiency as scripting for any other distribution platform using Director.

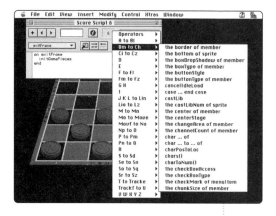

A few general areas that relate to authoring in Director for Internet playback are covered here, including types of Lingo scripts and where they are located, working with net Lingo extensions in Director, and Shockwave support for Xtras.

Script Locations

When you want Lingo scripts to execute determines *where* you place the scripts.

Score scripts are attached to individual cells or entered into the Script channel in the Score window.

Score scripts attached to individual sprites are
further defined as sprite scripts. Sprite scripts are
executed when a sprite is clicked. Director's default
sprite script is the on mouseUp handler.

Score scripts entered into the Script channel are referred to as frame scripts.
Frame scripts are executed as the playback head enters or exits a frame. The
default frame script is the on exitframe handler.

Individual cast members also can store scripts which are activated on a global
basis whenever the particular member is clicked. The default cast member script,
like the sprite script, is the on mouseUp handler.

Movie scripts are used to define
handlers that can be called at any time
throughout the duration of a movie.
The startMovie and stopMovie
handlers are placed in a Movie script.

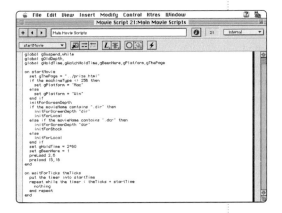

Net Lingo

Most of the net Lingo commands, such as `getNetText`, `goToNetPage`, and `goToNetMovie` start asynchronous operations—that is, a network request is initiated by a movie, and the result may not immediately be returned from the network. To deal with the asynchronous nature of Web operations, network Lingo commands can start an operation, check to see if it is completed, and then get the results of the operation. Conversely, commands issued in Director, or in a non-networked player environment, immediately return results.

After issuing an asynchronous command, such as `gotoNetMovie`, the current Shockwave movie continues to play until the new file or data is downloaded. Consider using this latent period for a simple, looping animation or a message that gives status information to the end user.

Lingo continues to evolve, and Director will eventually support net Lingo within the authoring environment. Until that time, error messages appear during authoring when net Lingo is used because Director does not recognize the Lingo sup-

ported by the Shockwave plug-in. In order to save time and avoid repeated error messages, it is convenient to use handlers that trap, or intercept, the net Lingo commands during offline authoring. We've included a movie containing sample "interceptor" scripts on the CD-ROM.

Xtras

The Director 5.0 release added support for Xtras, making Director's architecture more extensible. Shockwave supports Xtras, which are cross-platform code extensions that take the place of XObjects and DLLs used in earlier versions of Director. Net users can choose to download and install Xtras into a Shockwave Support folder to extend the functionality of particular Shockwave files.

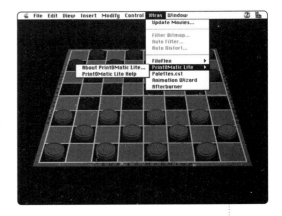

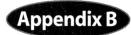

Internet Basics:
Getting Connected

Computers are networked via common protocols. IP (Internet Protocol) is the network-layer protocol that provides the ground rules for the transmission of data, and governs the distributed packets of data transmitted and reassembled across the network. The distribution and reassembly of data packets is a fundamental feature of Internet communication. A message transferred over the Internet can be broken into many small packets that can travel over various routes in order to reach their final destination. This provides a great deal of economy, and adds a type of backup system in the event of damaged packets or "roadblocks" on the data highway.

Note

This distributed network strategy has its roots in the military beginnings of the Internet. The original intention of the U.S. military in designing the Internet during the 1960s was to maintain a working communications system in the event that certain central locations were destroyed by enemy forces.

In addition to being a distributed network, the terms "asynchronous" and "synchronous" are often used in conjunction with Internet communication. Over dialup modem connections, data is transmitted in an asynchronous fashion—meaning that data is sent one bit at a time, with each character framed by a start and stop bit. In this way, the message is not dependent upon synchronized timing between the transmitter and receiver (which is the defining characteristic of synchronous transmission over a high speed T-3 line, for example).

Dialup connections at transmission speeds such as 14.4 and 28.8 kbps are analog and asynchronous. Switched/leased connections such as those at 64, 128, or 256 kbps are digital and synchronous. ISDN (Integrated Services Digital Network) is a switched digital network service that is offered, and heavily promoted, by telephone carriers. ISDN connections are digital and on-demand, and differ from both analog and switched/leased connections. The ability to access the Internet through the same coaxial cable that currently delivers cable TV to your home will be available in the near future. Cable modems, whether linked by hybrid fiber-coax, wireless cable, or satellite will provide high-speed digital connections. Fiber-optic networks are also competing on the high-speed, switched digital horizon.

This section does not address issues specific to intranets. Intranets are local area networks (LANs) usually interconnected via Ethernet with transmission speeds up to 10 mbps. The LAN, in turn, is usually connected through a high-speed line directly to the Internet backbone, or more commonly to an ISP (Internet Service Provider), which in turn links to a regional hub, and then to the backbone. Intranet configurations vary widely and would be difficult to cover in a general overview like this one. For this reason, the following information examines options available to developers for connecting to the World Wide Web.

Serving Your Web Site

Unless you have access to a direct Internet feed, you need to pay for Internet access through a commercial provider. Like universities or government institutions, a commercial provider pays for its part of the network. Commercial providers, in turn, sell Internet access to their machines or network to other providers or to end users.

In conjunction with establishing Internet access, you need to decide whether to run your own Web server or lease server space from an ISP or other third party. Running your own Web server provides you with control and flexibility, but requires a committment of resources. (Be aware that the server will require on-going planning, administration and maintenance.)

If you choose to run your own server and already have the server machine and server software, here are the general tasks to complete for getting your site up and running:

- Negotiate with an ISP to establish an Internet connection
- Get IP addresses (each network can have up to 254 IP addresses)
- Request and register domain name(s) with NIC (Network Information Center)
- Set up domain name service (DNS)
- Set up email service
- Get IP stacks and utilities
- Get navigational tools
- Set up Web and FTP servers

If you choose to serve your Web site from a server other than your own, shop around for an arrangement that best suits your needs. Keep in mind the amount of data you plan to publish on the site, the amount of anticipated traffic to your site, whether you will need public FTP space, security, electronic commerce capabilities, support for custom programming, support for your domain name, technical support, and available expansion options.

If your site resides on a remote server, you will probably need to transfer your Web site data to the server using an FTP client.

Connecting to the Web

There are a number of options available for connecting to the Web, whether you intend to browse sites or publish Shockwave movies. The options outlined below begin with the most simple and inexpensive, and move on to the more complex and costly. Keep in mind that speed, performance, and bandwidth are available at a price, and that these factors are more important to the Web developer than to most Web surfers.

Option 1
Indirect Connection Through A Shell Account
Shell accounts are available for logging into a host computer and running terminal emulation software. Shell accounts are useful and inexpensive for email and Telnet services, but they are typically Unix command-line based, and do not support Web browsers and other graphical Internet navigation tools. Establishing a shell account with an ISP is not a valid option for Shockwave development.

Option 2
Indirect Dialup Through Commercial Online Services
Commercial online services such as America Online (AOL) and CompuServe provide Web access to subscribers via their proprietary networks. While AOL provides users with server space to store personal Web pages, using a commercial service for Internet connectivity during Shockwave development is not recommended. While commercial services are convenient for end users because they eliminate many configuration headaches, developers will find that network performance via online services is unpredictable and generally slow. In addition, it is usually more expensive to access the Web via a commercial service than to establish a direct dialup account with an ISP.

Option 3

Direct Individual Dialup Connection

A direct individual connection is a dialup connection to the Internet over a leased line or via switched digital services through an ISP, or through a telephone company such as AT&T, to the Internet. With a direct Internet connection, your computer is an individual node or a simulated node on the Internet. Your ISP will assign you a numerical IP address and will issue you a DNS (Domain Name Server) address which designates your "domain" (for example, user@shockingtheweb.com or yourname@isp.com).

The most common type of Internet access is direct dialup via a modem. For this type of Web access, a PPP (point-to-point protocol) or SLIP (serial line internet protocol) direct connection is required. Access is established by dialup connection to a server that is connected to a network on the Internet. Your client computer and the server use PPP or SLIP to communicate, and data is transmitted using TCP/IP. SLIP is an early Internet protocol used to run IP over serial lines such as telephone circuits or RS-232 cables between two systems. PPP is the successor protocol to SLIP; it provides router-to-router and host-to-network connections over synchronous and asynchronous circuits and is recommended over SLIP for direct connections.

You will need the following for direct dialup Web access via a modem:
- Internet (PPP) account
- Hardware: a computer with minimum 16MB RAM (recommended for Shockwave viewing); and a modem (with a minimum speed of 28.8 kbps highly recommended)
- Software: a TCP/IP Protocol stack (for Macintosh, TCP/IP; for DOS/Windows, various options such as NetManage Chameleon or Win95's TCP/IP stack); PPP client software (for Macintosh, MacPPP or FreePPP; for DOS/Windows, Trumpet Winsock or Win95's Microsoft PPP); and Web browser software (Shockwave is currently supported by Netscape Navigator and Microsoft Internet Explorer)

Option 4

Direct Connection from Your Network to the Internet—Dialup or Dedicated

In this scenario, PPP is used to connect a router on your network to an ISP's router on the Internet. This usually means that you are establishing a commercial account with your ISP as opposed to an individual account.

Direct access via a higher-speed service that does not require modems is usually referred to as dedicated service. ISP prices for dedicated lines are substantially higher than dialup modem connection service, but you should ask your ISP about available high-speed options. The benefit of a dedicated line is that it can connect to your LAN to provide everyone in the company with LAN and Internet access, thereby eliminating the need for individual direct accounts and numerous modems. A dedicated connection also saves you a great deal of time during Shockwave development.

The following is a checklist of the items you'll need for a direct connection from your network to the Internet:

- An IP router. For a dial-up analog connection, a mimimum 28.8 kbps modem is required. For a switched/leased connection, you'll need a CSU/DSU (carrier service unit/digital service unit). For ISDN, you will need a terminal adapter and NT-1 hardware.
- A fast network computer for running Mail, DNS, Web, and FTP service (preferably dedicated)
- Optionally, a remote access server for direct individual access

It is possible to mix-and-match networking solutions. For example, an ISP may agree to provide you with a dedicated connection while agreeing to also serve and maintain your Mail, DNS, Web, and FTP services. Some providers on the other hand will serve and maintain your Web, DNS, and FTP services while you run your own mail server. You will be better prepared to negotiate if you determine the services you will need before approaching service providers.

Resources

For more information about getting connected, consult the following resources:

http://rs.internic.net

This URL provides links to InterNic domain name registration, IP address assignments, and database services and directories, including a searchable directory of directories.

http://www.w3.org

The World Wide Web Consortium's site, which contains links to Web-related resources, technology reports, and technical papers.

ftp://nic.merit.edu

The Merit Network Information Center's FTP site, which contains Internet-related guides and utilities.

JavaScript Reference
for Director Developers

JavaScript is a scripting language developed by Netscape for the purpose of providing computational capabilities within HTML documents. Some of the operations that JavaScript is useful for include:

- verifying form input
- displaying alert dialogs
- opening new browser windows, with specific attributes and content
- providing dynamic feedback, such as status bar updates in Web pages
- writing HTML on-the-fly in response to contextual variables, such as browser type
- testing for plug-ins and support for specific MIME types
- interacting with the user's Magic Cookie file
- manipulating browser functions

The JavaScript language is a fairly high level language; syntactically, it's much easier to use than C—but it is not as English-like as Lingo. JavaScript is also case sensitive. It supports most typical code structures, such as event handlers, conditional statements, repeat loops, and to some extent object-oriented programming. Naming conventions notwithstanding, JavaScript has very little to do with Java, save some common roots. Like Lingo, JavaScript is an interpreted language— compiling is not required to use them. JavaScripts are interpreted on-the-fly by the browser. Unfortunately, as of this writing, there are no real development environments available for JavaScript. The debugging process is rudimentary at best. You write JavaScripts with a text editor or HTML editor, and test them by opening them in the browser. Browsers that support JavaScript will provide some specific error messages when they encounter errors in scripts, but these messages can be inconsistent and their usefulness limited.

You probably will find JavaScript useful for reading client-side data and manipulating elements intrinsic to the Web browser. JavaScript also has some ability to detect rollovers and mouseDown events, and play flipbook animations. While these functions are interesting, the ability of JavaScript to alter the appearance of the browser window is very limited. Producers of dynamic Web pages most likely will find their needs better satisfied using Shockwave movies. Still, there are some JavaScript functions that cannot be duplicated by Shockwave movies, and JavaScript does not require plug-ins or controls. JavaScript support is built into both Netscape Navigator and Microsoft Internet Explorer.

JavaScript Code Structures

The following section summarizes the various code structures supported by the JavaScript language.

Script Placement and Simple Statements

JavaScript statements should be placed within the <SCRIPT> tag. The general format for including JavaScript statements within your HTML documents is as follows:

```
<SCRIPT language=JavaScript>
[statements]
</SCRIPT>
```

You also can include a <NOSCRIPT> tag to provide content for Web surfers who have disabled JavaScript, or are using a browser that does not support JavaScript.

```
<SCRIPT language=JavaScript>
[statements]
</SCRIPT>
<NOSCRIPT>
All kinds of groovy things would be happening right now if your
browser supported JavaScript<br>
</NOSCRIPT>
```

Scripts can be placed in either the head or the body of an HTML document. JavaScript handlers, referred to as functions, generally should be placed inside the head of the document to ensure that they are loaded into memory and available for use before the page is displayed (and before they can be called by any statements in the body of the script). JavaScript statements can be placed anywhere in the body of the script and will execute in the order in which they appear in the HTML code. For more information on writing JavaScript functions, see the "Methods and Functions" section below.

JavaScript allows you to place the contents of external files inside <SCRIPT> tags. This is very useful for code encapsulation: if you have a JavaScript function that is used by multiple HTML pages, you can store the function in a text file and have the relevant HTML documents load the file. To change the function, you need to edit only the text file that contains the contents of the script—not every HTML page that uses it. You can include an external file in your JavaScript functions by adding a SRC parameter to the <SCRIPT> tag. For example:

```
<SCRIPT SRC="mimeCheckScript.js">
</SCRIPT>
```

The SRC parameter can specify a relative or absolute path to the JavaScript text file. Referenced JavaScript files must have the .js suffix. If you reference a file in the <SCRIPT> tag, any subsequent statements before the </SCRIPT> end tag will be ignored. Still, you cannot omit the </SCRIPT> end tag.

JavaScript also can tie function execution to specific events, such as completion of page loading, or a mouseDown event in a form element. For more information, see the "JavaScript Event Handlers" section below.

JavaScript also supports standard HTML comments. Commented code segments begin with <!-- and end with -->.

Here is a sample HTML document with JavaScript in the head and body. We will use the JavaScript function writeln(string), which writes text into your HTML document and then follows this text with a carriage return.

```
<HTML><HEAD>
<TITLE>Simple JavaScript Page</TITLE>
<SCRIPT SRC="myJSfunctions.js"></SCRIPT></HEAD>
<BODY>
<IMG src=logo.GIF><BR>
<SCRIPT language=JavaScript>
document.writeln('The path to this document is ' +
document.location );
document.writeln('and your browser is ' + navigator.userAgent +
'<br>');
<!-- Ignore
all this stuff -->
</SCRIPT>
The above text was written by JavaScript.
</BODY></HTML>
```

When this HTML page is opened in the browser window, the following text is printed after the logo.GIF image as a result of the JavaScript code:

```
The full path to this document is
http://www.dxm.com/shocknet/jtest.html and your browser is
Mozilla/3.0 (Macintosh; I; PPC)
The above text was written by JavaScript
```

Note that we did not utilize any of the functions in myJSfunctions.txt. Also, the data returned by navigator.userAgent is specific to the browser that is used during authoring.

All of the JavaScript statements above end with semicolons. The semicolons are not necessary unless you place multiple JavaScript statements inside an event handler, or at the start of a repeat loop. However, it is good form to use semicolons to indicate the end of JavaScript statements. You cannot use semicolons at the end of the first line of a conditional (if) statement or repeat loop.

Another odd feature of JavaScript is the way that it deals with string literals when they are passed as arguments.

```
document.writeln('The path to this document is ' +
document.location );
```

Notice that the quoted text in the method arguments are enclosed with single quotes—as opposed to the more common double quotes. Whenever you supply a text argument to a JavaScript method or function using a literal—as opposed to a variable name—you must enclose the text in single quotes. Using the more intuitive double quotes will result in a script error. The use of string literals for variable assignments, however, maintains the standard double quote convention, so the following code could replace the body script in the simple JavaScript Page example above.

```
var pathIntro="The path to this document is "
var browserIntro="and your browser is "
document.writeln(pathIntro + document.location);
document.writeln(browserIntro + navigator.userAgent + '<br>');
```

Variables

JavaScript variables share the loose typing characteristics of Lingo variables; that is, you do not have to tell JavaScript whether the contents of a variable are integers or strings, for example—JavaScript can figure it out. You can use any names for JavaScript variables, provided they meet the following criteria:

- The first character of a variable name must be a letter (upper or lower case), or an underscore (_).

- Subsequent characters may also contain integers.

- Variables cannot use the same names as JavaScript commands, or any built-in JavaScript variables or constants.

JavaScript variables must be declared before they can be used. Attempting to evaluate an undeclared value will result in a script error. Declaring a variable with an initial value of null is the closest a JavaScript variable ever gets to the <void> value in Lingo.

Setting global variables is simple. For example:

```
x = 1
username = "eric"
tryme = null
```

Once set, these variables are available to all JavaScript statements and functions within a particular HTML document.

Local variables require the use of the var keyword. For example:

```
var mycounter = 100
```

The mycounter variable is available only to the function in which it is declared.

JavaScript uses "+" for concatenation, which is equivalent to the ampersand (&) in Lingo. There is no equivalent to && in JavaScript. If you want to add spaces between concatenated strings, leave whitespace within a string's quotation marks. For example, the statement sometext = "you" + " and me" will evaluate to "you and me".

There are several special characters that can be used within JavaScript strings. You may use these characters in variables and literals (which are text values passed directly to handlers without being stored in a variable).

\b = Backspace
\f = Form feed
\n = New line character
\r = Carriage return
\t = Tab (indicates a carriage return)
\" = Inserts a quotation mark inside a string

Expressions

An expression is any statement that evaluates to a single value. These statements may include string and integer literals, variables, and Booleans, and may evaluate to a string, integer, or Boolean.

Some example statements include:

```
8 + 2
true
false
"I like " + "ponies"
```

An expression may be used to set the value of a variable, as in the following:

```
dogyears = 7 * 5
simpleflag = false
```

JavaScript also supports conditional expression, a sort of one-line conditional statement used to set the value of a variable based on a Boolean condition. Here is the syntax for a conditional expression:

```
myVariable = (condition) ? var1 : var2
```

If (condition) evaluates to true, myVariable will be set to the value of var1; otherwise it will be set to the value of var2.

Arrays/Objects

JavaScript arrays (also known as objects) are used both as data storage mechanisms and as the foundation for methods, which are JavaScript's version of parent-child scripting. Even if you have no need to create these relatively complex data structures, you will need to learn arrays, because all of the browser-related data gathering and manipulation functions are ensconced in these objects.

Retrieving Data From JavaScripts Objects

As data containers, JavaScript objects are very similar to property lists in Lingo. To retrieve data from an object, use the following syntax.

```
objectName.propertyName
```

So, the following line in JavaScript:

```
var basket = fruitObject.apples
```

is equivalent to the following Lingo statement (where basket is not declared as a global variable):

```
set basket = GetAProp(fruitObject,#apples)
```

The syntax for setting property values in JavaScript objects is also straightforward. For example:

```
fruitObject.apples = ["macintosh"]
fruitObject.quantity = [67]
```

Methods and Functions

In some cases, what appears to be a property of an object is actually a method, or a function that can be executed on that object. Methods are directly analagous to handlers that are inside parent scripts in Lingo. Generally speaking, elements of the browser window are manipulated using methods.

The following snippet of JavaScript code will open a new browser window named "contents," set the dimensions and options for the window, and load the HTML document toc.html into the new window.

```
window.open("toc.html","contents",menubar=yes,width=400,
height=252");
```

In JavaScript, there is no distinction between handlers and functions. All subroutines are called using the standard function syntax myFunction(arguments). Any subroutine may return a value to the calling script, since it is a function. A simple function is shown below. Notice that the statements inside the function are enclosed by curly brackets, and the line ends with a semicolon.

```
function docInfo()
    {
    var returnVal = ('The path to this document is ' +
document.location);
    return returnVal
    }
```

The following JavaScript placed in the body of the HTML document will call the function:

```
document.write(docInfo())
```

JavaScript functions are typically placed within the <HEAD> tag of an HTML document, and commands triggering these functions are typically placed inside the body of a document. While it's not absolutely necessary to place JavaScript functions in documents, this convention ensures that all of your functions are loaded before they are called by the document.

Conditional Statements

The basic JavaScript syntax for conditional statements is as follows.

```
if(condition) {
   statement;
   statement;
   }
```

Condition can be any JavaScript statement that evaluates to TRUE or FALSE. Statement can be any JavaScript statement, including nested conditionals and repeat loops.

JavaScript conditions also can use the else keyword to designate a series of statements to execute if condition returns FALSE. For example:

```
if(condition) {
   statement;
   statement;
   }
else {
   statement;
   }
```

The conditional statement structure in JavaScript is an "either/or" structure, and does not allow for else if statements. You usually can substitute nested or multiple conditionals for Lingo-style else if statements.

The following JavaScript function can be used to determine if the user's browser supports Shockwave movies:

```
<SCRIPT language=JavaScript>
function shockwave()
   {
   var shockSupport = (navigator.mimeTypes["application/x-director"])
   if (shockSupport) {
     var returnVal = true
     }
   else {
     var returnVal = false
     }
   return returnVal;
   }
</SCRIPT>
```

Repeat Loops

JavaScript supports a number of loop structures. For loops are functionally identical to repeat with i = loops in Lingo.

```
for ([initial expression] ; [condition] ; [increment] ) {
   statement;
   statement;
   ...
}
```

The [initial expression] statement is used to initialize a counter variable for loop control. The repeat loop ceases execution when [condition] is no longer TRUE, or when a break statement is encountered. Break is equivalent to exit repeat in Lingo. The [increment] statement determines how the control variable changes with each iteration of the loop. The most common incrementors are ++, which adds a value of 1 to the control variable with each iteration, and --, which subtracts a value of 1 with each iteration.

```
for (var j=2; j <= shockParamArray.length; j++) {
   paramExists = (eval(shockParamArray[j]) !=null) ? true : false;
      if (paramExists == true) {
         tagText += '<PARAM NAME=\"' + shockParamArray[j] + '\"';
         tagText += 'VALUE= \"' + eval(shockParamArray[j]) + '\"';
      }
   }
}
```

The previous for loop is used as part of a routine (described below) that writes tags for Shockwave movies based on browser type, and substitutes other media if Shockwave support is not present. The values for the Shockwave tag are stored in the shockParamArray array. The variable j is used to scan this shockParamArray, starting from the second slot in the array. The variable is incremented positively by j with each iteration, and subsequent statements execute when j is greater than the length property of the array. The length property indicates how many slots are used in an array. Using Lingo in Director, you could write a similar loop as follows:

```
repeat with j = 3 to count(shockParamArray)
  [statements]
end repeat
```

Another loop structure supported by JavaScript is the while loop. While loops execute as long as a condition is TRUE. Here is an example of the while loop syntax:

```
x=0;
while (x < 10) {
   x++;
}
```

Break and continue statements are useful for controlling repeat loops. The break statement halts loop execution and skips to the next statement after the end of the loop. The continue statement only halts execution of the current iteration of the loop, and returns to the evaluated condition at the head of the loop.

By modifying the loop shown above with a break statement, the loop stops executing when x equals 5:

```
x=0;
while (x < 10) {
   if x == 5 {
     break
     }
   x++;
}
```

With a few changes and the addition of a `continue` statement, the loop displays an alert dialog on each iteration, except when x equals 5:

```
x=0;
while (x < 10) {
   if x == 5 {
     continue
     }
   alert('The count is ' + 5);
   x++;
}
```

Lastly, the `for...in` statement is also used with JavaScript loops. This statement is especially useful for processing all of the data in an object or array.

```
for (variable in object) {
   statement;
   }
```

The `for...in` structure is very similar to the `repeat with variable in list` structure in Lingo—except for one important detail: the value that JavaScript places in the variable is an index to the data in the object, and not the data itself. You need to use standard object manipulation syntax to get to the actual data. For example, the following JavaScript loop puts all data from `shockParamArray` into a string variable:

```
tagText = ""
for (var i in shockParamArray){
   tagText += shockParamArray[i] + ':';
   }
```

Event Handlers

JavaScript supports a number of event handlers that can be used to trigger functions. These event handlers are very similar to Lingo's event handlers, such as `startMovie`, `stopMovie`, `mouseUp`, and so forth.

Event handlers are invoked by placing the name of the event handler—along with JavaScript code to execute—inside the tag of an HTML element. For example, the `onMouseOver` event is analogous to the `rollover()` function in Lingo. By default, passing the cursor over an `HREF` anchor displays the path to the anchor in the status bar in the lower left corner of most browsers. You can use an `onMouseOver` handler to display a custom message instead. The following example code displays the value returned by a function called `docInfo()` in the status bar while the cursor is over an image named static.GIF.

```
<A HREF="foo.html"
onMouseOver="window.status=browserInfo();return true">
<IMG src="Images/static.GIF"></A>
```

You may place multiple JavaScript statements inside event handlers as long as they are separated by semicolons. Note that TRUE must be returned in the example above in order to force the status bar to update with the string you have provided.

Here is a list of JavaScript event handlers (along with short descriptions) and the Lingo equivalents, if applicable.

Event: `onAbort`
Description: The `onAbort` event can be used to define a set of JavaScript functions that execute if the user aborts the loading of an image by clicking on the browser's Stop button.
Relevant HTML Objects: `IMG`
Example: `<IMG src=fancy.gif height=400 width=600`
`onAbort="alert('Sorry, I know my images are too big')">`

Event: `onBlur`
Description: A blur event in a browser window or frameset occurs when a user shifts focus from the current window by clicking on a different window. In the form objects context, `onBlur` events occur when the user completes data entry into a form object, and uses the mouse or Tab key to focus on a different HTML form object.
Relevant HTML Objects: `Body, frameset, select, textarea, text`
Example: `<INPUT TYPE="text" VALUE="" NAME="voicePhone"`
`onBlur="checkTemplate(this.value ,'phone')">`
`<BODY onBlur="window.close()">`
A direct Lingo equivalent for the `onBlur` event does not exist. However, this event handler could be simulated using a combination of Lingo functions.

Event: `onChange`
Description: The change event is similar to the blur event, except that it is activated only if data in the form object that is losing focus has been changed.
Relevant HTML Objects: `select, textarea, text`
Example: `<INPUT TYPE="text" VALUE="" NAME="voicePhone"`
`onChange="checkTemplate(this.value ,'phone')">`

Event: `onClick`
Description: A click message is passed when the user clicks on a form object or a link.
Relevant HTML Objects: `link, button, checkbox, radio, link, reset, submit`
Examples: `<INPUT TYPE="button" VALUE="Verify" onClick="evaluate(this. form)">`
`<A HREF="joe.shtml" onClick="return confirm('I will cry if you leave my site.')">Joe's Pages</A>`

Event: `onError`
Description: The error event can be used to determine behavior if JavaScript runtime or syntax errors occur. The following example code suppresses all JavaScript error dialogs in the current window.
Relevant HTML Objects: `image, window`
Example: `<SCRIPT>window.onerror=null</SCRIPT>`

Event: onFocus

Description: An onFocus event in a body or frameset tag executes JavaScript commands when a window is clicked by the user, if another window has previously been the active window. In form objects, a focus event occurs when the focus shifts to a form field as a result of clicking on it or tabbing to it. Returning a value of FALSE to an onFocus event handler in a form object cancels the action normally associated with that particular mouse click.

Relevant HTML Objects: body, frameset, link, select, textarea, text

Example: `<input type=text name="daddy" value=yerdaddy size=25 onFocus="focusHandler(this.name,navigator.appVersion);">`
`<body onFocus="document.bgColor='white'" onBlur="document.bgColor='black'">`

Event: onLoad

Description: An onLoad event occurs when an image has been loaded. The image does not necessarily have to be displayed; onLoad may be used in conjunction with JavaScript's image display capabilities to control flipbook animations.

Relevant HTML Objects: Image

Example: `<IMG NAME="logo" SRC="newLogo.gif" ALIGN="top" onLoad="document.bgColor='white'">`

Event: onMouseOut

Description: The onMouseOut event is called when the cursor leaves the area over a link, or over a client-side imagemap.

Relevant HTML Objects: Area, link

Example: `<A HREF="foo.html" onMouseOut="window.status=browserInfo();return true">`
`<IMG src="Images/static.GIF"></A>`

Event: onMouseOver

Description: An onMouseOver event occurs when the cursor moves over a link or area object from outside that object. This behavior is similar to rollovers in Lingo. The onMouseOverevent handler will not function unless there is an HREF tied to the object.

Relevant HTML Objects: Area, link

Example: `<A HREF="foo.html" onMouseOver="window.status=browserInfo();return true">`
`<IMG src="Images/static.GIF"></A>`

Event: onReset

Description: The onReset event executes when the user presses the Reset button in a form. The onReset event is specified in the <FORM> tag. Returning a negative value to the onReset event prevents the form from resetting.

Relevant HTML Objects: Form

Example: <FORM method="GET" action="foo.cgi" onReset="return confirm('Are you sure you want to erase everything you just filled in?')">

Event: onSelect

Description: An onSelect event occurs when a user highlights a block of text in a text or textarea field.

Relevant HTML Objects: text, textarea

Example: <TEXTAREA name="diary" rows=20 cols=60 onSelect onSelect="doSelect(this.name)">
</TEXTAREA>

A direct Lingo equivalent for the onSelect event does not exist. However, this event handler can be simulated using mouseUp events.

Event: onSubmit

Description: Use the onSubmit event to process the data in a form. JavaScript may be used to evaluate whether the data in the form should be sent to the server. It also can be used to display messages to the user upon form submission. Returning a value of FALSE to the onSubmit event prevents form data from being passed to the server.

Relevant HTML Object: Form

Example: <FORM method="GET" action="formProc.cgi" onSubmit>

> **Note**
>
> *For a complete JavaScript reference, refer to Netscape's JavaScript Authoring Guide at http://home.netscape.com/eng/mozilla/3.0/handbook/javascript*

Using JavaScript to Write Proper Shockwave Tags

JavaScript has a built-in function that tests browser support for any MIME type. You also can use JavaScript to test for specific plug-in support, but testing for MIME type support is a safer option because multiple plug-ins are available for certain MIME types. In addition, there is a tendency among popular plug-ins to eventually find their way into the native architecture of Web browsers, so the plug-ins available today may not exist as plug-ins at a later date.

The following function returns a value of TRUE or FALSE, reflecting the browser's support for Shockwave for Director movies.

```
function shockwave()
   {
   var shockSupport = (navigator.mimeTypes["application/
x-director"]);
   if (shockSupport) {
     var returnVal = true
      }
   else {
     var returnVal = false
      }
   return returnVal;
   }
```

You can place this function in the <HEAD> tag of any HTML document. You then can use the returned value, combined with the document.write function, to substitute HTML content depending on the returned value.

The following example is a fairly complex JavaScript that gathers information about the user's browser and uses a single template to write the <EMBED> or <OBJECT> tag for a Shockwave movie. The files referenced in this example are all available on the *Shocking the Web* CD-ROM. You can use these files, with minimal JavaScript coding, by editing them to suit the needs of your Shockwave movies, and then using the <SCRIPT src=xxx> statement to reference the files in your HTML pages.

The ShockDataTemplate.js File

This file contains all of the data required to display your Shockwave movie within a Web page, along with placeholder slots for optional parameters supported by all browsers.

```
height=0
width=0
src="yourMovieName.dcr"
palette=null
textfocus=null
bgcolor=null
sw1=null
sw2=null
sw3= null
sw4= null
sw5= null
sw6= null
sw7= null
sw8= null
sw9= null
swURL= null
swText= null
swForeColor= null
swBackColor= null
swFrame= null
swColor= null
swName= null
swPassword= null
swBanner= null
swSound= null
swVolume= null
swPreloadTime= null
swAudio= null
swList=null

altSrc=null

properShockTag(altSrc);
```

For all of the parameters listed above, the left side of the equals sign contains the parameter name; the right side contains the value. At the very least, you must enter values for the first three parameters: height, width, and src. For more information on Shockwave <EMBED> and <OBJECT> tags, see Chapter 7, "Shockwave Authoring." All text values should be enclosed in quotation marks, and any unused values should be left null. The altSrc parameter is provided to define the HTML that will be displayed to browsers that do not support JavaScript. The last line of the file calls the function that actually writes the HTML tag.

Follow these steps to use the file:

1. Fill out all of the necessary parameters, along with any optional parameters your Shockwave movie will use, and the altSrc property.

2. Select Save As... to name the new file with the name of your Shockwave movie—but with the suffix .js instead of .dcr. For example, if your Shockwave movie is named myMovie.dcr, name the file myMovie.js.

3. Place the new file in the same directory where your HTML documents are stored.

The autoTagger.js File

This file contains the functions that JavaScript uses to write the tag for the Shockwave movie(s). Before using the autoTagger functions, review the JavaScript code contained in the file named autoTagger.js on the *Shocking the Web* CD-ROM.

Then, follow these steps to use the autoTagger JavaScript:

1. Place a copy of autoTagger.js in the same directory as your HTML documents.

2. Include a reference to the file in the <HEAD> tag of your HTML document using the following template syntax:

```
<HTML><HEAD><TITLE>My Shockwave Page</TITLE>
<SCRIPT src="./autoTagger.js"></SCRIPT>
</HEAD>
```

Referencing Your Shockwave Movies

Instead of writing <EMBED> or <OBJECT> tags for your Shockwave movies, include a reference to the JavaScript file that contains the information about each movie in your HTML document. Place the reference at the location in the document where you would like each movie to be displayed.

1. At the proper location within the <BODY> tag, include a reference to your modified JavaScript template file.

```
<BODY>
Here's some text<br>
<SCRIPT src=myMovie1.js></SCRIPT>
<br> That's the first Shockwave movie.<br>
<SCRIPT src=myMovie2.js></SCRIPT>
<br> And that's the second.<br>
```

2. You may also want to provide <NOSCRIPT> information for users who have browsers that do not support JavaScript, or for those users who have turned off JavaScript support.

Happy JavaScripting!

SHOCKING THE WEB CD-ROM Contents

The CD-ROM bundled with this book contains the tools you need to create Shockwave movies for the Web. It includes a variety of clip media that can be incorporated into your own Shockwave productions. Explore the tools and browse through example movies for each of the case studies and developer gallery entries. Open HTML files using your Web browser to connect to the accompanying Web site (shockingtheweb.com) or to visit Shockwave directories and developer sites. You will find the following items on the *Shocking the Web* CD-ROM.

About This CD
A directory of the folders and files on the CD-ROM.

BookSite Bookmarks
The HTML links to shockingtheweb.com.

Shocking Bookmarks
HTML links to Shockwave developer sites and Shockwave directory sites.

Movie Browser
A standalone viewer for all of the Shockwave movies on the CD.

Shockwave Tutorial Movies
Director movies that provide examples of Shockwave Lingo scripts. Movies include simple command demos, network Lingo tutorials, and example movies that are referenced throughout the book.

Case Studies
Source code Director movies for Chapters 10–17, with accompanying HTML and Shockwave movies.

Developer Gallery
HTML, Shockwave, and source Director movies from successful Shockwave developers.

Shockwave Software
Macromedia Shockwave plug-ins for Director, Authorware, FreeHand, xRes, and SoundEdit16. Afterburner Xtra for Director also is included.

Power Applets
Create your own Shockwave and Java applets in minutes with these Shockwave and Java Power Applets.

Software Demo versions
Macromedia Director, Authorware, SoundEdit16 (Macintosh), Xres, FreeHand, Fontographer, Extreme3D, and Backstage. Also includes Equilibrium DeBabelizer Lite.

Multimedia and Web Resources
EarshotSFX sound library sampler that features over 25MB of royalty-free sound effects; the Direct Loops demo, which includes 20 royalty-free music loops; the audiosyncrasy sound design demo; ViewPoint 3D model sampler; Adobe ImageClub Library sampler; CMCD digital photographs from PhotoDisc; g/matter, inc. multimedia product catalog, which includes 24 runtime Killer Transitions Xtras for Director; plus a variety of Web authoring utilities.

Index